FRANCE
Since the Revolution

FRANCE
Since the Revolution

AND OTHER ASPECTS OF
MODERN HISTORY

ALFRED COBBAN

BARNES & NOBLE
NEW YORK

THIS COLLECTION FIRST PUBLISHED IN THE UNITED STATES, 1970
BY BARNES & NOBLE, INC.
© 1970 BY MURIEL COBBAN

ISBN 389-01035-9

76-19191
1-29-75

PRINTED IN GREAT BRITAIN

CONTENTS

ACKNOWLEDGMENTS

I am indebted to the editors of the following journals for permission to reprint the papers which first appeared in their pages: the *English Historical Review* [4], *History* [11, 15], *Bulletin of the Institute of Historical Research* [3], *French Historical Studies* [1], *Political Science Quarterly* [13, 14], *Review of Politics* [10], *Law Quarterly Review* [2], *Political Quarterly* [5], *Canadian Journal of International Affairs* [7], *Cambridge Journal* [6, 9], the *Listener* [8, 12].

THE 'MIDDLE CLASS' IN FRANCE, 1815–48*

'THE sociologist who today writes about "class" in general and *in toto*', says T. H. Marshall, 'may soon find that he is shadow-boxing with a down pillow. Even his most vigorous mental strokes are liable to be smothered in the clinging embrace of this infuriating subject which so stubbornly resists all attempts to knock it into shape. At the present moment we shall gain more from a fresh examination of the parts than from the repeated contemplation of the whole.'[1]

I believe that this is true not only for the sociologist but also for the historian. A recent article on 'The Middle Class in Western Europe, 1815–1848'[2] by Lenore O'Boyle is a vigorous restatement of the opposite point of view. The article is essentially devoted to a defence of the proposition that the historian has still much to gain from the conception of a middle class, which includes all 'the middling ranks of society ... intermediate between the labouring class and the aristocratic landowners' (p. 827), treated as a single and united social category. This is as large a section of society as could ever have been called a 'class'; indeed it is more customary to refer to the 'middle classes'. For Miss O'Boyle, however, it is clearly a unity and a single class, and to make this more evident, contrary to what is perhaps the better practice,[3] she uses the terms 'middle class'

---

*This paper appeared in *French Historical Studies*, v, no. 1, Spring 1967.

[1] *New Society*, no. 192, June 2nd, 1966, 28.

[2] Lenore O'Boyle, 'The Middle Class in Western Europe, 1815–1848', *American Historical Review*, lxxi (1966), 826–45.

[3] See, for example, Adeline Daumard, *La Bourgeoisie parisienne de 1815 à 1848* (Paris, 1963), 64, where it is said that the terms *classe moyenne* and *bourgeoisie* 'traduisaient deux réalités différentes'.

and 'bourgeoisie' interchangeably. Her view is that the idea of the middle class is a necessary generalization for writing the history of long-term changes in Western Europe during the period 1750 to 1850. She chooses for detailed analysis the period from 1815 to 1848 in Western Europe, which, she believes, was marked by this middle-class, or bourgeois, ascendancy (p. 838).

Her restatement of the traditional view is so clear and uncompromising that it provides an admirable opportunity for an examination of the whole theory in the light of more recent social analysis and research. I lack the competence to follow Miss O'Boyle through all the countries of Western Europe from which she draws her material; and indeed I am not entirely happy about this method. It seems to me to involve a temptation to set up in one's mind a broad, general pattern, using here an example from one country to substantiate it and there an example from another, filling the gaps in the history of one nation's social development by referring to what happened in another, and in the end producing an abstract pattern that is vaguely reminiscent of the history of each country in general but specifically correct of none of them in particular. I do not feel that Miss O'Boyle has entirely escaped this danger. It will at least be a test to put together all that she says of one country, France, to see if it makes a coherent picture. This will also enable us to test the historical value of the idea of the middle class as a description of the ruling class of France in the period of the constitutional monarchy.

The first problem is, of course, to provide a definition of the middle class. When contemporaries used the term they meant all those who stood socially between a far smaller noblesse and a far larger populace. The historian has to provide a more positive description, and Miss O'Boyle does so. The French middle class in the early nineteenth century, according to her initial analysis, was divided into three components — businessmen, members of free professions, and state officials (p. 828). She also gives two subsequent and somewhat different definitions. The middle class is, secondly, described as 'a bourgeoisie composed of bankers, officials, merchants, landowners, and professional men' (p. 838). Thirdly, 'The picture of the French bourgeoisie is then of a small business group, a substantial contingent of professional men and state officials, and a large group of landowners' (p. 837). It will be seen that while professional men and officials keep their place in each definition, landowners are omitted in the first analysis (a note explains that this is intentional), enter into the second, and are a large group in the third. Businessmen appear in the first and third analyses but in the second are broken down into merchants and bankers. Now since the essence of the argument is that the middle class can be treated essentially *as a whole*, as a single, united class, it might be argued that the details of its composition could be ignored. But in the present state of historical interests this is impossible; and Miss O'Boyle does in fact attempt such an analysis repeatedly, though it presents her with a major problem. To discuss the composition of the middle class inevitably means breaking it down into its various component parts; to maintain its unity, they have to be put together again. I will discuss her treatment of these two issues in turn. In the first place we may examine the composition attributed to the middle class or bourgeoisie. The two elements of the middle class which seem to present most difficulty to Miss O'Boyle are the landowners and the businessmen. This may be because, in the past, there has been a tendency to take these categories at their face value and refrain from analysing them further. Miss O'Boyle creditably faces up to the difficulty. She refers to the landowners under two headings. There are 'the small and medium peasant proprietors'. These, she says, 'must surely be accounted middle class' (p. 837). Here the interchangeable employment of the terms middle class and bourgeoisie is useful. It would not have been quite so easy to have said that the peasant proprietors 'must surely be accounted part of the bourgeoisie'. However, this is of no great importance because the peasant proprietors are mentioned only to be dismissed as a passive element in French society. In terms of national politics and for the period from 1815 to 1848 this may be correct, though if we look at events on the level of local history a somewhat different picture appears.

The second group of landowners cannot be disposed of so easily. They are described as 'a *rentier* group who owned land but could scarcely have been classified as professional farmers' (p. 837). Adeline Daumard, on the other hand, whose knowledge of the social pattern of the Paris bourgeoisie in this period can scarcely be exceeded, writes of the *rentiers* that they 'par définition ne sont pas propriétaires'.[1] It is very puzzling. I have an uneasy but inescapable impression that Miss O'Boyle takes *rentiers* to be identical with *propriétaires non-exploitants*. At any rate, she nowhere refers to the *rentiers*, in the sense of owners of government stocks and shares, as an element in her middle class. She is evidently aware that there is some kind of problem here, saying, 'the *rentier* group constitutes a genuine difficulty for analysis' (p. 837). I do not want to make too much of this point, though there is always the possibility of confusion between French *rentes* and English 'rents'; but the result is really rather disastrous. Not only does Miss O'Boyle omit *rentiers* in any other sense than landed proprietors from her analysis, but she writes off the whole landowning sector of French society as well. She says, 'it does not appear necessary to treat the *rentier* group [i.e., presumably for her only landowners] as a fourth basic component of the middle class, at least not until further investigation demonstrates that the landowners did in fact have a psychology and interests differing significantly from those of business, the professions, and the officials' (p. 838). This is a remarkable statement, and it becomes no less remarkable if we look at it more closely.

Landowners, those who owned land without themselves working it, were, Miss O'Boyle has truly said, a large body in nineteenth-century France. To admit this is in itself a step forward. The tendency earlier was either to leave them out of

[1] Daumard, *La Bourgeoisie parisienne*, 486.

the social analysis or else to treat them as the relics of the 'feudal' class. But they still present a problem for orthodox social history. Miss O'Boyle's solution, while sometimes admitting that they were part of the middle class, is to deny that they were a 'basic component' of it. Her reason, as was said above, is that their psychology and interests were identical with those of some other group in the middle class, which therefore can be taken as the active element.

The argument now proceeds on the basis of an assumption which has been common in the writing of social history. This is the belief that at any given time there is one dominant social group which imposes its interests upon the rest. Society is considered in terms of a ruler-and-subject relationship rather than as a nexus of related or conflicting interests. It has indeed often seemed closer to the former than to the latter, and Miss O'Boyle obviously accepts the simpler pattern even though she only puts it in the form of a question. She asks if the component parts of the middle class were of equal importance or whether one of them dominated. Then, proceeding to take the answer to this question for granted, she asks: 'Through what means did one group succeed in determining the actions of the other two?' (p. 828). Now the three groups she recognizes as significant elements in the middle class are state officials, professional men, and businessmen. Even these three groups can be reduced effectively to two, for, as she says, there was naturally a predominance of professional men, especially lawyers, in government personnel, so these two groups are not easily separable (p. 831). Moreover, the professional men themselves, she argues, were in a state of clientage to those with economic power, that is to say, the rich. It is a common assumption that these were the businessmen, who thus become the heart of the middle class and the really effective power in the state.

Here Miss O'Boyle takes another essential step in her argument for granted. She asks how business exerted its influence, but not whether or how far it did. 'That it did exert influence', she writes, 'seems indisputable; there is no other explanation for the restructuring of Western European society in this period to suit the convenience of business interests' (p. 830). This is a rather vague generalization; but behind it seems to be the assumption upon which the whole thesis, so far as it relates to France, depends. That is the belief that the professional and official groups were clients of the businessmen and that in psychology and interests the landowners did not differ significantly from the businessmen. The last assumption is so difficult to reconcile with what we know of the social and economic history of the nineteenth century that some explanation of it seems called for. I believe it is to be found in a footnote which declares: 'Occupation is the decisive factor in classification ... Source of income is not considered crucial' (p. 828, n. 8). Although relegated to a note, this is an important part of the methodology of the article. I do not propose to consider whether it is justifiable in theory or not. I am concerned with the difficulty of applying it to French society in practice. For unfortunately some of those whom Miss O'Boyle would presumably include in her middle class or bourgeoisie, and in particular the *rentiers* and the landowners, in fact had *no* occupation. They were the heirs of that eighteenth-century bourgeoisie whose ambition, if they remained bourgeois, was at least to be *bourgeois vivant noblement*, what a favourable critic would describe as gentlemen, and an unfavourable one as parasites. We must not exaggerate the size of this sector. Mlle Daumard has wisely pointed out that among the wealthy Parisian bourgeoisie, apart from those who had retired, to have no occupation was rare; though she adds that the picture might be different if it included also the descendants of the noblesse of the *ancient régime* and of the Empire.[1] We need not take sides in this matter. The relevant consideration is that to disregard what may have been not a negligible section of French society simply because it had no occupation and lived on its income is to introduce a built-in element of distortion which, it seems to me, must be dangerous to any social analysis.

[1] Daumard, *La Bourgeoisie parisienne*, 172.

However, we now have this equation: The rule of the middle class equals the rule of the bourgeoisie, and the rule of the bourgeoisie equals the rule of the businessmen. It must be observed that the belief that businessmen did actually dominate French society between 1815 and 1848 is what one must frankly describe as no more than an assertion. Our confidence in it is not increased when we look at the notes and find that the only justification given is a reference to E. Beau de Loménie's *Les Responsabilités des dynasties bourgeoises*, where, we are told, there is strong evidence that France from the time of the Revolution was actually governed by a number of great business families (p. 832, n. 19). Making all allowance for the power of business, especially finance, in France as in other countries, I hope I may be excused for saying that this statement is nonsense and not one that a serious historian should appear to endorse by citing in a note, let alone rely on to support the weight of an argument.

Certainly, Miss O'Boyle makes a great point of the fact that she does not identify the whole personnel of the middle class with the businessmen (p. 837). The character of the French bourgeoisie, she writes, has puzzled historians because of this very lack of identification, which she sees reflected in the weakness of French industry and the predominance of landowners (p. 836). But there is only a puzzle if one has a preconceived pattern to which one is trying to make the facts conform. There can be no doubt that French industry, she admits, compared with English industry was at this time backward and progressing only very slowly. Instead of an attempt to explain this, however, we are referred back to the French Revolution. 'The fact remains', we are told, 'that the Revolution did bring about a new conception of property that cleared the way for capitalistic practices' (pp. 836-7). Capitalist practices, it seems to me, had been pretty well developed in France before 1789, and the reference to the Revolution seems to be introduced to get over the difficulty of reconciling the economic conservation of France with the supposed dominance of businessmen. The line of thought is something like this: Given the dominance of businessmen, French industry should not have been comparatively unprogressive, as it was. Yet the French Revolution, being a capitalist revolution, must have established the rule of the businessmen. Therefore, in principle French industry must have been progressing steadily, however contrary the evidence may be. All this, it seems to me, results from an unstated assumption that there was in France a united class of 'businessmen' with a common psychology and a specific aim of economic progress for their society. But the supposition that all businessmen are necessarily concerned with increasing productivity is an illusion. There have always been plenty of restrictive or even reactionary business interests. It must also be remarked that 'businessmen' as it is used by Miss O'Boyle is a very general term. On one occasion she specifies as components of it bankers and merchants (p. 838), and since she also talks of the steady growth of industry, she presumably includes industrialists. Now we know that financial (I assume that under the heading of bankers is meant the whole category of financiers), commercial, and industrial interests are far from being always and at all times the same. The triumph of some of them can be fatal to others. Before we can consider adequately the social and economic implications of a businessman's ascendancy, therefore, we need to know the kind of business interests involved. Unless we know this, to tell us that the psychology and interests of businessmen dominated the state is to tell us practically nothing.

Apart from this lack of precision there are other serious objections to the theory of the ascendancy of businessmen in French society. Miss O'Boyle believes that the combined official and professional group must have been the clients, and have served the interests, of the rich. We may think that this is probable and still not be convinced that the comparatively small, unprogressive, and less wealthy category of 'businessmen' could have been the precise rich whose interests they served, at a time when by far the greatest proportion of the wealth of

France was in the form of landed property. This was pointed out by Rémond, who wrote: 'Cette bourgeoisie orléaniste n'est en fait que très partiellement une bourgeoisie d'affaires.' 'La principale richesse est encore la terre.'[1] More recently Tudesq has established the dominance of landed wealth in Orleanist France statistically and beyond a shadow of doubt. 'Le notable, dans la France de 1840,' he writes, 'c'est d'abord le propriétaire; c'est à la propriété foncière, immobilière, que va d'abord la considération, c'est elle qui consacre l'enrichissement.'[2] He agrees that professional men and officials served the interests of the wealthy—indeed it is a common experience that those who pay the piper call the tune—but his conclusion, derived from a thorough survey, is the exact opposite of the view that the landowners were a passive factor about whom nothing need be said save that they echoed the ideas and interests of the businessmen.

On the contrary, he writes: 'Qu'il s'agisse de la direction politique ou de l'organisation administrative, c'était dans le groupe des propriétaires fonciers (auxquels se rattachaient hauts fonctionnaires et professions libérales) que se recrutaient les éléments dirigeants.' Even in strictly business affairs the influence of landed wealth was effective: 'L'étude de la direction économique nous a montré la prépondérance des maîtres de l'argent: banquiers et financiers, certes, mais aussi une fraction importante de la grande propriété' (p. 435).

There was a further source of influence which the landed proprietors possessed: land was the basis of political power. Miss O'Boyle tells us that 'an examination of the way in which France was governed confirms the picture of bourgeois ascendancy' (p. 838). She makes no examination herself and appears to ignore the one made some thirty years ago by Sherman Kent.[3] As he showed, the main qualification for membership of the small electorate, and the still smaller number of those

[1] René Rémond, *La Droite en France de 1815 à nos jours* (Paris, 1954), 78.

[2] André-Jean Tudesq, *Les Grands Notables en France (1840–1849): Étude historique d'une psychologie sociale* (2 vols. Paris, 1964), i, 429.

[3] Sherman Kent, *Electoral Procedure under Louis Philippe* (New Haven, 1937).

qualified to be elected, was provided by the tax on land.[1]

Similarly, she pays no attention to the recent study by David Pinkney on the Revolution of 1830,[2] when she makes the unqualified assertion: 'In France the Restoration saw a conflict between nobility and bourgeoisie for control of the offices of state that culminated in 1830 with the victory of the middle class' (p. 836). One reference is given in support of this view. It is to René Rémond's *La Droite en France*. But in fact her reference is to a passage where Rémond is describing not the defeat of the nobility but 'l'émigration à l'intérieur' of Legitimists after 1830.[3] I can only suppose that she assumes an identification of the conflict between Legitimists and Orleanists with that between a landed aristocracy and a bourgeoisie deriving its wealth and power from other sources than the land. This view is also put forward by Lhomme.[4] It identifies the Legitimists with the nobles and the Orleanists with the bourgeois and presupposes a fundamental opposition in the early nineteenth century between nobles and bourgeois as such. Neither the identification nor the opposition is supported by the evidence. Once again I cannot do better than quote the summary given by Tudesq. He writes: 'Les antagonismes idéologiques — l'opposition entre légitimistes et orléanistes, entre traditionalistes et libéraux — ne recouvrent qu'imparfaitement des rivalités sociales; les variétés régionales du légitimisme ... suffisent à montrer qu'il n'est pas possible de le réduire à l'idéologie de la seule aristocratie foncière, et la grande bourgeoisie capitaliste ne représente qu'une fraction du monde des notables partisans du régime de Juillet; les antagonismes économiques au sein du monde des notables traduisent des rivalités plus géographiques que sociales ... '[5]

[1] The French electorate numbered 201,000, or 1 in 170 of the population, compared with 1 in 20 after 1832 in Great Britain.

[2] David H. Pinkney, 'The Myth of the French Revolution of 1830', in *A Festschrift for Frederick B. Artz*, ed. David H. Pinkney and Theodore Ropp (Durham, N.C., 1964), 52–71.

[3] Rémond, *La Droite en France*, 57.

[4] Jean Lhomme, *La Grande Bourgeoisie au pouvoir, 1830–1890* (Paris, 1960), 36.

[5] Tudesq, *Les Grands Notables*, ii, 1232.

The more generally accepted interpretation of 1830 which Miss O'Boyle repeats is admittedly a well-established one, which began at the time. After 1830 the view was sedulously propagated by the victorious Orleanists that their rule was that of 'les classes moyennes', as opposed to both the 'classes populaires' and the 'classe aristocratique'. 'Cette interprétation,' writes Tudesq, 'dont Guizot avait été le plus brillant théoricien, était plus une pétition de principes qu'une traduction de la réalité' (I, 8). The idea of middle-class rule was a vague one, employed for polemical purposes by journalists and politicians.[1] It can no longer seriously be maintained, now that, basing himself on a formidable mass of new research, Tudesq has provided a more realistic picture. In his analysis the businessmen are still there, it is true, but how diminished in stature. The businessmen's regime disappears from sight beneath the weight of evidence. This was a time, says Tudesq, 'où l'ordre social repose sur la propriété, et l'on peut dire sur la propriété immobilière' (i, 98).

If it is asked how contemporaries could have been so mistaken as to describe the reign of Louis-Philippe as a bourgeois monarchy, the answer must be, in the first place, that, as has already been suggested, this was partly propaganda for the *juste milieu*. There is also a question of terminology. In the earlier part of the nineteenth century the social pattern of the *ancien régime* had still not been wholly outgrown. A landowner, whatever the size of his estates, if he did not belong to the noblesse, was described as a bourgeois. It was only subsequently that the term was associated essentially with industrial, mercantile or financial capitalists as opposed to the landowning class, which then came to be treated as a survival of the feudal order. Miss O'Boyle is far from unique in transferring the later usage of the term to the earlier period, but this is what, I suspect, leads her to interpret what was essentially a regime dominated by landed property as a businessman's government.

A second contributory cause may also be suggested for the

[1] Daumard, *La Bourgeoisie parisienne*, 217.

confusion of the ruling elite of the first half of the nineteenth century with the class of businessmen. It lies in the dominance of Paris over French life, and even more French history. The difference between a stable provincial society and a Parisian society that had been much more affected by the social and economic stresses of Revolution and Empire has perhaps not been adequately emphasized in histories of the period. In a comparison between a provincial town, Chartres, and Paris, it is pointed out that whereas in the capital everything induced the wealthier sections of the population to participate in economic activities, in Chartres a large proportion of personal wealth, even after the revolutionary upheaval, was held in unproductive forms.[1] Paris, on the other hand, during the first half of the nineteenth century, was becoming one of the principal economic centres of France,[2] and for this very reason must not be taken as typical. However, this does suggest that we should pay a little more specific attention to the special case of Paris, before leaving the problem of the rule of the businessmen. Fortunately, to guide us we have the magnificent thesis of Mlle Daumard, to which Miss O'Boyle makes only one rather perfunctory reference in a note. It will be some time before all the results of Mlle Daumard's work are fully digested and absorbed into the general picture of French nineteenth-century history. In the meantime her findings on the composition of the Parisian bourgeoisie are not without relevance to the present discussion. Undoubtedly a much higher proportion of businessmen is to be found in Paris than elsewhere. What is surprising is that even Paris proves to have less overwhelmingly a business bourgeoisie than we might have expected. Among the departmental electors of 1820, qualified on the basis of their tax assessments, 36·5 per cent belong to what Mlle Daumard describes as '*professions économiques*', as against 17·2 per cent for *fonctionnaires, officiers*, and liberal professions, and 46·2 per cent of *propriétaires* or without

[1] M. Vovelle and D. Roche, 'Bourgeois, rentiers, propriétaires: Éléments pour la définition d'une catégorie sociale à la fin du XVIIIe siècle', *Actes du quatre-vingt-quatrième Congrès national des Sociétés savantes, 1959* (Dijon, 1960), 419–52.

[2] Daumard, *La Bourgeoisie parisienne*, 416, 427.

profession (p. 149). Even more surprising, by 1842 the last category had risen to 49·9 per cent, while *professions économiques* had fallen to 29·4 per cent (p. 154). This trend is easily explicable by the fact that, as Mlle Daumard shows, the bourgeois of Paris habitually invested an important part of their wealth in real estate (p. 486). Where Miss O'Boyle wants us to believe that the landowner was a mere muted echo of the businessman, Mlle Daumard, with the advantage of her profound acquaintance with the documentation and statistical evidence, has no doubt that the opposite is true. 'Sous la monarchie censitaire,' she writes, 'le propriétaire foncier avait une prééminence politique et sociale trop accusée, des charges et des privilèges trop manifestes, pour qu'il soit licite de mêler biens immobiliers et valeurs mobilières, en fonction de leur destination' (p. 483). Again, 'presque tous les Parisiens riches donnaient une place prépondérante aux immeubles ruraux parmi leurs investissements immobiliers' (p. 499). What is even more striking, by the end of the July Monarchy, she says, 'de plus en plus les biens fonciers ruraux l'emportaient sur les immeubles urbains' (p. 501).

In spite of what was naturally a far greater representation of finance, trade and industry in Paris than in the provinces, therefore, the conclusions drawn from an exhaustive analysis of the social structure of the Paris bourgeoisie reinforce those resulting from Tudesq's work on the notables of all France. On foundations at least partially laid by the purchase of *biens nationaux* during the Revolution and by successful speculation during the Revolution and Empire, a new aristocracy had been created (pp. 300-301). 'Progressivement,' writes Mlle Daumard, 'une aristocratie nouvelle se constituait et s'affirmait face à l'aristocratie nobiliaire' (p. 316). As she also says, 'la notion d'aristocratie a pris désormais une acception plus bourgeoise' (p. 217); but it was still, even in Paris and to a greater extent than one might have expected, an aristocracy of landowners.

The important point is that the dominant class in France in

the first half of the nineteenth century was one of landed proprietors. It does not matter seriously whether we call it an aristocracy or a bourgeoisie, so long as this essential fact is grasped. As such, whatever its internal divisions, against those who had little or no property it would always be united. Some of its members also had income from investments in government stock or private business; some had a profession or office; some were financiers or merchants, some industrialists. Many may have combined more than one of these occupations or sources of income; but there can be no doubt that the largest number were landed proprietors and that the ownership of landed property was the highest common factor among them all. This united them in support of a common social policy whatever their other differences. Whether they were nobles, what Tudesq calls 'pseudo-nobles', or had no real or assumed claim to noblesse at all, they were held together by wealth and common values, and these were primarily the wealth and values of landowners. They had almost a monopoly of political life, which therefore became, as Miss O'Boyle says, largely a struggle over the spoils of office (p. 838). For the emergence of this ruling class of landed proprietors we can certainly look back to the Revolution. After the abolition of privileges, Georges Lefebvre wrote, nobles and *roturiers* joined in the same social class of *'propriétaires non-exploitants'*.[1] Miss O'Boyle objects to my description of this class as a 'landed aristocracy' (p. 837). It still seems to me the best description of a social group whose wealth, political power and social influence were based on land, and which claimed, and very largely succeeded in maintaining, a monopoly of political power. At the beginning of her article she expresses the belief that though the idea of the middle class, as she defines it, may be, not wrong, but unhelpful for the study of short-term changes, it is a useful generalization in discussing long-term ones (p. 827). I am not sure exactly why short-term changes require a different social terminology from long-term ones, but I hope what I have said will suggest to some readers

[1] Georges Lefebvre, *Études sur la Révolution française* (Paris, 1954), 238.

that, for the social history of France during the first half of the nineteenth century, the omnibus term 'middle class' is not merely unhelpful but can lead the student sadly into error and confusion.

2

THE NAPOLEONIC SYSTEM OF ADMINISTRATION IN FRANCE*

THE many problems involved in the rebuilding of the social and political structure of France will be dealt with in due course by the French nation itself. It cannot be pretended, however, that Great Britain has no interest in the establishment of a stable, democratic form of government in France. For this reason it may be justifiable for us to examine briefly one of the more important, yet less obvious, aspects of this question. The nature and significance of the central institutions of government are easy enough to appreciate: the purpose of this paper is to suggest that the form of local government is also a matter of major importance.

The centralized administrative system which has prevailed in France was the work of the Revolution and Napoleon. Centralization itself preceded the Revolution, which began with a spontaneous movement all over France for the establishment of local self-government. The National Assembly, alarmed at the prospect of the country falling under the control of thousands of little municipalities, but unwilling to perpetuate the *ancien régime* traditions of the provinces and *généralités*, attempted to canalize this movement by dividing France into *départements*. Successive revolutionary governments found it increasingly necessary to forestall possible opposition by depriving both *communes* and *départements* of the machinery of free self-expression. Finally, Napoleon eliminated the elective principle completely, and substituted for it the authority of nominated *préfets*, *sous-préfets* and *maires*.

*This paper appeared in the *Modern Law Review*, April 1946.

The machinery of administration thus created was too favourable to the powers of the state to be willingly sacrificed by any of the regimes that followed during the nineteenth century. In opposition, both republicans and monarchists might flirt with the idea of decentralization, in power they upheld the centralized system of government. The reason for this is plain. Fundamentally it was not the administrative merits of centralization that ensured its preservation, but its political advantages. The *préfet* was primarily the political agent of the government. Casimir-Périer exposed the basic principle of the system in his declaration that it was not the duty of the government to remain neutral in elections. The Ministry is convinced, he said, that its continuance in office is vital to the interests of the nation. All governments were of the same opinion, and the *préfet* was their chief instrument for putting it into practice. The situation was stated very clearly by a *sous-préfet* of Louis Philippe, appealing to a meeting to support the official candidate. 'My life, and that of my children,' he declared, 'are in your hands. If the Ministry's candidate is not elected I shall lose my post.' The revolution of 1848 did not change the situation fundamentally, for Ledru-Rollin's *commissaires* were bitterly criticized for their attempts to influence the elections, and under Louis Napoleon the *candidature officielle* became a recognized institution. The first circulars of the Ministry of the Interior under the Third Republic proclaimed the liberty of elections, but instructed the *préfets* and *sous-préfets* to guide the electors. The failure of the MacMahon-de Broglie attempt to stifle the Republic at birth in 1877, when seventy *préfets* and 226 *sous-préfets* were changed for the purpose of making the elections, undoubtedly dealt a severe blow to their political prestige, and after this the more blatant forms of administrative pressure were gradually dropped. But in 1911 M. Gaston Jèze could still describe the *préfet* as 'essentially an electoral agent', whose future depended on his success in influencing the elections. To succeed, he said, a *préfet* must have 'une grande souplesse, peu de scruples et de la poigne'. Like their predecessors, he

23

concluded, the *préfets* of the twentieth century were the great enemies of the public liberties.[1] More recent critics have found the chief evil in the political pressure exercised by senators and deputies over the *préfets*.[2] It is probably true that, especially after 1918, the political influence of the *préfets* suffered considerable diminution. The Tardieu attempt to make favourable elections by a wholesale change of *préfets* proved a failure. But the close relationship and interaction of politics and the centralized administration, however its mode of operation may have changed, remained a basic fact of the political structure of France.

During the Third Republic, however, there was one important breach with the tradition of centralization. This was the law of 1884 providing for the election of *maires*, which has been described as 'la loi essentielle et utile de la République, celle qui mieux que toute autre a assuré son triomphe et sa durée'.[3] Despite this concession, the republican parties were on the whole profoundly suspicious of the policy of decentralization. Gambetta is alleged to have replied, in 1879, to an advocate of federal ideas, 'Monsieur, si les idées que vous venez de m'exposer avaient la moindre chance d'être écoutées, vous ne sortirez pas libre de cette chambre, et vous seriez fusillé ce soir même.' Decentralization was particularly feared as likely to work to the advantage of clerical influence, and the unifying Jacobin tradition was still strong among the supporters of the Republic. 'C'est la centralisation,' declared one legal textbook, 'qui porte jusqu'aux extrémités du corps social cette action, partie du cœur et revenant au cœur, qui lui donne la vie. C'est la gloire, c'est la force et le salut de la France.'[4]

The monarchists put themselves forward as the advocates of decentralization, but how this was to be reconciled with their authoritarian principles was never satisfactorily explained, and when the Third Republic had fallen, the Vichy regime was hardly marked by an effective extension of local liberties. The

[1] G. Jèze, 'Du rôle des préfets en France', *Revue du droit publique* (1911), vol. 28.
[2] R. Maspétiol et P. Laroque, *La Tutelle administrative* (1930), 324.
[3] A. Thibaudet, *Les idées politiques de la France* (1932), 53.
[4] Trolley, *Cours de droit administratif*, i, 89.

regionalist movement, despite widespread support, achieved little or no legislative success. The *décret-lois* of the Poincaré Ministry of 1926 improved the functioning of the bureaucratic machine, but did not extend the powers of local government. It was still on the whole true, when the Third Republic came to its end, that, as Hauriou wrote in 1913, 'Notre édifice administratif a été organisé au lendemain de la Révolution en l'an VIII, par le premier consul, avec une centralisation tellement énergique q'après un siècle de durée et plusieurs poussées successives de décentralisation, il reste encore très fortement centralisé.'[1] The administrative history of France, from 1789 to 1939, can thus justifiably be regarded as a unity. Can we draw any conclusions from this history?

The first point to note is that a system which has lasted so long, and through so many vicissitudes of government, must be deeply rooted in the political habits of the nation. Nevertheless, after 1871 there was a slow extension of the rights of local self-government. Those whose task it is to refashion republican institutions in France will have the choice between continuing and developing this tendency, or relying on the traditional methods. What is the case for centralization? It rests on the furtherance of three main objects — economic improvement, administrative efficiency and political stability. The question we have to ask is whether centralization has in fact promoted these three aims in the past, and is likely to promote them in the future.

As the supervisor of the economic life of the *département*, the *préfet* was the heir of the *intendant*. The activity of such an official could achieve important results in an age when economic activities were mainly localized; but during the nineteenth century the regulation of economic life within the departmental framework steadily became more difficult, until it finally broke down during the First World War.[2] How far

---

[1] M. Hauriou, *Précis de Droit administratif* (8th ed., 1914), 63.
[2] Cf. H. Hauser, *L'organisation gouvernementale française pendant la guerre: le problème du régionalisme* (1924).

the economic tutelage of the state shall be extended in France is a matter for discussion, but there can be no doubt that in so far as it operates it will have to be on a national and regional basis. Economic life has clearly outgrown the departmental mould. It requires larger regional divisions, which for that very reason will not be so easily fitted into a bureaucratic system presided over by the Minister of the Interior.

From the point of view of administrative efficiency also the value of the prefectoral system has changed in the course of time. Centralized authority was exercised by hierarchical control, by the *tutelle administrative*, and by the judicial process of *recours pour excès de pouvoir*. The first of these, the specifically bureaucratic form of control, has all the characteristic defects of bureaucracy. Its effects have been described as fear of responsibility, favouritism, political interference in administration, and *'fonctionnairisme'*. It is fundamentally incompatible with any degree of effective local self-government. In fact, as soon as the first steps were taken towards decentralization it became necessary to rely chiefly on a new form of control. This was the *tutelle administrative*, which has been defined as 'l'ensemble des pouvoirs limités accordés par la loi à une autorité supérieure sur les agents décentralisés et sur leurs actes, dans un but de protection de l'intérêt général'.[1] This form of central control also has been severely criticized as more often a hindrance than an aid to local government.[2] 'La tutelle administrative en France,' wrote Jèze, 'il faut le dire hautement, a fait faillite. Les préfets l'ont faussée en se servant de leurs pouvoirs de tutelle pour tracasser leurs adversaires et pour favoriser leurs amis politiques.'[3] Its effectiveness gradually declined, and by 1926 it could even be claimed that it hardly existed except as a theory in textbooks of administrative law.[4] Finally, we have the *recours pour excès de pouvoir*. The disadvantage here is the

---

[1] Maspétiol et Laroque, *La Tutelle administrative*, 10.
[2] *E.g.*, H. Berthélemy, *Les réformes administratives et judiciaires de 1926* (1928), 34; M. Dendias, *Le gouvernement local* (1930), 113.
[3] Jèze, *Du rôle des préfets en France*, 280.
[4] H. Berthélemy, *Droit administratif* (1926), p. xxvii.

slowness, as well as the unsuitability, of judicial procedure for dealing with administrative problems. From the point of view of administrative efficiency, therefore, centralization in France seems to be justly open to much of the severe criticism that has been directed against it. It is necessary to ask if any of these methods of control is capable of improvement, or whether the solution may not be to leave more independence of action to decentralized, democratic authorities in all those fields in which direct national administration is not necessary.

The third claim that has been made on behalf of centralization is that it is needed for political stability. The history of France during the last century and a half hardly suggests that, if this were the object, it was successfully achieved, and we must ask whether the prefectoral system on the whole served to check or to promote the series of revolutionary changes of regime. It is clear that while a government remained in the saddle its powers were greatly increased by the existence of a centralized administration. But this source of strength was also a source of danger. Protected from the impact of public opinion by a bureaucracy which naturally tended to represent conditions in the most favourable light, Bourbon, Orleanist and Bonapartist regimes in turn lost the support of the country without realizing the fact. It was only necessary for a revolutionary movement to secure power in Paris for all resistance to collapse. Once the revolutionaries had obtained control of the Ministry of the Interior, the whole administration was paralysed. *Préfets* and *sous-préfets* were dismissed, sent in their resignations, or often, hopefully, their adherence. It is difficult to resist the conclusion that the centralized system of administration, while it stood in the way of timely adaptation, facilitated revolutionary changes of regime.

Our conclusion is, that in respect neither of economic and administrative efficiency, nor of political stability, can the claims of centralization be supported in France at the present day. It is possible, of course, that a more decentralized form of government might have other and worse defects. It might not work at all. But France had considerable experience in the functioning of local elective councils during the Third Republic. In the larger towns particularly, the *maire* and *conseil municipal* had considerable powers in practice and exercised them in some cases with conspicuous success. Decentralized administration of local affairs can, of course, merely spell corruption and in-efficency, but there is no reason for supposing that such results would necessarily accompany it in France. Above all, the decisive consideration is that local self-government has as obvious links with democracy as centralization has with authoritarian forms of government. Over a hundred years ago de Tocqueville wrote, 'C'est dans la commune que réside la force des peuples libres. Les institutions communales sont à la liberté ce que les écoles primaires sont à la science : elles la mettent à la portée du peuple; elles lui en font goûter l'usage paisible et l'habituent à s'en servir. Sans institutions com-munales, une nation peut se donner un gouvernement libre, mais elle n'a pas l'esprit de la liberté.' A century of further experience has not made de Tocqueville's verdict seem any the less true. Discussion there may be, and undoubtedly will be, over the size and nature of the areas of local government. The network of communes, varying in size from small villages to great cities like Lyons or Marseilles, is too well established to be capable of fundamental modification, and too successful to require it. The future of the *départements*, and the possibility of concessions to regionalist opinion, is a more open question, but it is too complex a problem to be discussed here. Our object has not been to discuss detailed reforms, but to indicate the im-portance of the subject, and to suggest that when a new constitution comes to be drawn up for France, if we wish to understand its spirit, and draw any conclusions as to its essential tendencies, we shall do well to look, not only at the forms of central government, but also at the scope allowed to democratic institutions of local government.

3

ADMINISTRATIVE PRESSURE IN THE
ELECTION OF THE FRENCH
CONSTITUENT ASSEMBLY, APRIL 1848*

IT is well known that one of the chief functions of the prefects
in nineteenth-century France was to manage elections in the
interests of the government. If their activities in this respect
have on the whole lacked detailed historical investigation, this
is doubtless due to their modesty, as well as to that of the
Ministers of the Interior from whom they derived their authority.

They were content that their political achievements should
speak for themselves, and one suspects that, rather than advertise the methods by which the desired result was brought
about, they preferred to leave them in obscurity, even to the
point of purging the official records. The absence of documents
relating to this topic is particularly notable for the period of the
Second Republic. It has been said, though as will be seen with
some exaggeration, that the political correspondence of the
commissaires and prefects with the Minister of the Interior during
this period has practically all disappeared; but a brief sketch of
the sources that have survived will indicate that the situation is
not quite so hopeless from the historian's point of view as this
statement might suggest.[1] In the first place we have the printed
circulars dispatched from the Ministry of the Interior to the

*This paper appeared in the *Bulletin of the Institute of Historical Research*, xxv
(1952).
[1] A valuable guide to the sources is provided in P. Caron, 'Les sources manuscrites parisiennes de l'histoire de la Révolution de 1848 et de la Deuxième
République', *Revue d'histoire moderne et contemporaine*, vi, 85–119.

départements.[1] These, in so far as they concern electoral matters, consist almost exclusively of technical instructions, with an occasional laudable injunction to maintain absolute freedom of voting. Written circulars are naturally of a more interesting nature, the reason being indicated by a note pinned to a draft of an electoral circular of March 22nd, 1848: 'Je pense que cette circulaire doit être autographiée et non pas imprimée, car il ne conviendrait guère d'y donner de la publicité.'[2] Perhaps for the same reason the collection of these circulars in the Archives Nationales is curiously scanty. For the whole of 1848 only three *'circulaires autographiées'* survive.[3] A collection of telegraphic dispatches concerns only administrative details of little significance.[4] The great series of cartons labelled *'Esprit public et élections'*,[5] from which so much material of importance for the history of France in the nineteenth century remains to be drawn, contain, at least so far as I have explored them, no more than an isolated document or two for each *département* on the elections in 1848, and only a little more for the years 1849–51. More valuable than these are three cartons which contain miscellaneous papers and letters of the Ministry of the Interior relating to elections between 1848 and 1853.[6] Among the materials deposited by the Ministry of Justice at the Archives Nationales there are six cartons which contain documents bearing on various aspects of the elections of 1848–50.[7] Finally, a great collection of administrative regulations survive,

[1] These, for the period of the Second Republic, are in the *Archives Nationales*, F 1ᵃ 45. Circulaires et instructions ministérielles, 1847–50; F 1ᵃ 46, ibid., 1851–2; F 1ᵃ 58. Circulaires. Elections 1793–1855. In subsequent notes A.N. means *Archives Nationales*, and A.D. *Archives Départementales*.

[2] A.N. F 1ᶜ II 58.

[3] A.N. F 1ᵃ* 2097. Circulaires autographiées du Ministère de l'Intérieur, 1848.

[4] A.N. F 1ᵃ 19. Dépêches télégraphiques, 1838–49.

[5] A.N. F 1ᶜ III. Esprit public et élections (classified by *départements*). Seignobos says that there is a complete gap for the period of the monarchy of July and the Republic of 1848. According to tradition, he adds, the massacre of the documents of the Ministry of the Interior occurred in 1863 and was committed not for political reasons but simply to create space. 'La Révolution de 1848', *Bulletin de la société d'histoire de la Révolution de 1848*, vol. iv, no. 23, pp. 303–4.

[6] A.N. F 1ᶜ II 56–8. Élections, 1848–53; F 1ᶜ II 97. Affaires électorales, 1848–55.

[7] A.N. BB³⁰ 319–23, 327.

but these contribute little to the subject under discussion.[1] Whatever the cause, the fact is that the central archives, though they contain useful material, are inadequate for a comprehensive study of the electoral pressure exercised by the administration at this period. The alternative, it might seem, would be to have recourse to the departmental archives. The number of these, and the very rough state of classification of the documents in many of them, make a complete survey of this field a long and difficult task. Moreover, the same influences have been at work here also. We may take it for granted that any document likely to throw light on our subject will have been headed *confidentielle* or *très confidentielle*. It is easy to see in some *Archives Départementales* that all such documents have been purged from the record. In some, indeed, the process has apparently been carried to the length of eliminating practically all political documents relating to the years 1848–52. In the archives of the Var, and in those of the Haut-Rhin, for example, one letter of a slight political interest survives in each case. However, some prefects were evidently less energetic in removing their traces than others; here and there can be found ministerial correspondence and circulars which help to fill the gaps in the collection at the Archives Nationales, and there are also valuable indications of local activities by the *commissaires* and prefects. I have supplemented a personal investigation of some twelve departmental archives, two or three of which yielded practically nothing, with material gleaned from departmental and local studies of the history of the Second Republic. The sparseness of relevant material in such studies is, however, further evidence of the extent to which it has disappeared from the archives.

A few biographies are of assistance, but on the whole rather in helping to clarify the policy of the government at Paris than in revealing the way in which that policy was put into effect in the *départements*. The press offers another source for investigation, but at the same time presents the difficulty that its allega-

---

[1] A.N. F 1ᵃ* 128¹⁻¹ᵃ. Amplifications des lois, ordonnances, etc., Ministère de l'Intérieur, Jan.–Sept., 1848.

tions of electoral manœuvres by the administration, though extensive and vigorous, are in the nature of things inspired by political passion and often incapable of being verified. It seemed doubtful, therefore, whether the time necessary for the exploration of a host of journals, both local and national, would be justified by the production of any evidence that could safely be used. I have been through one of the clerical journals, *L'Ami de la Religion,* and if time had permitted it would certainly have been desirable to have explored other periodicals, even though everything discovered would have had to be treated as the starting point of a separate investigation. However, leaving the press on one side, and allowing for the scrappy and haphazard nature of the remainder of the evidence, it has still seemed possible to gather sufficient material to enable a general picture of the influence exercised by the administration over the elections to be painted, though it will necessarily be composed by putting together a great many isolated facts drawn from diverse sources. For such a picture, moreover, it is not necessary to exhaust all the available material for the sake of proving the same point ten times over.

On the other hand it is not possible to write off the whole inquiry with the argument that administrative influence over the elections was so much an integral part of French politics in the nineteenth century that no specific examination of its operation during the Second Republic is required. Indeed, it might have seemed, in February 1848, that such electoral pressure was to be a thing of the past. The Revolution began, as revolutions are apt to begin, with a wave of idealism in which it was believed that the corrupt ways of the July monarchy were to be drowned for ever. Political corruption, it was thought, could not survive under a regime of universal suffrage, and the most astonishing feature of the Revolution had been the sudden and apparently unquestioning acceptance of this principle by the whole country. The man who was to put it into practice was the Minister of the Interior in the Provisional Government, Ledru-Rollin. His first circular, addressed to the *préfets* of Louis-Philippe, announced the establishment of the Republic and called on them to take the necessary measures for ensuring public tranquillity and the co-operation of the people with the new government. The prefects, however, could do little more than pronounce an administrative *morituri te salutamus*, and disappear. The perfection of administrative centralization, which the genius of Napoleon had created in France, achieved its finest hour in the passive, unresisting abdication of a whole regime once the voice of Paris had spoken. To take the place of the Orleanist prefects and *sous-préfets* Ledru-Rollin appointed revolutionary *commissaires*.[1] None of the prefects of Louis-Philippe, and only twelve *sous-préfets*, remained in office, and a good deal of confusion was caused by the appointment of so many new officials, often with ill-defined and overlapping functions. Calvados and the Yonne achieved the distinction of possessing four *commissaires* at the same time. The first list of *commissaires* was composed of conspicuously moderate men for the most part, but between March 17th and April 16th Ledru-Rollin made many changes, including the appointment of twenty-four *commissaires généraux*. The new appointments went to men of more advanced views. By the middle of April practically all the *départements* were under tried republicans, and some sixty-four of these belonged to the more democratic section of opinion that was represented by the *Réforme*.[2] Apart from ensuring the continuance of the normal administrative services, the chief task of the *commissaires* was to prepare for the elections, which were to be held as soon as possible to legitimate the Republic by popular vote.

In a decree of March 5th, Ledru-Rollin laid down regulations for putting universal suffrage into practice, and a series of circulars to the *commissaires* filled out the details. These regulations and circulars were all of a technical nature and free from any suggestion that the administration should attempt to

---

[1] The only general study is P. Haury, 'Les commissaires de Ledru-Rollin en 1848', *La Révolution française*, lvii, 438–74.
[2] Ibid., 461.

influence the results of the election. This did not mean that the Minister of the Interior accepted the idea of neutrality as between the Republic and its opponents. A circular of March 8th instructed the *commissaires*:

> En vous abstenant de toutes recherches contre les opinions et les actes politiques antérieurs, prenez comme règle que les fonctions politiques ... ne peuvent être confiées qu'à des républicains éprouvés ... Qu'ils nous donnent une Assemblée nationale capable de comprendre et d'achever l'œuvre du peuple ... le tout, bien entendu, sans qu'il soit porté la moindre atteinte à l'indépendance des votes et à liberté d'élection.[1]

This last promise was amplified in a proclamation drawn up on March 16th, by the Provisional Government, declaring: 'Le gouvernement provisoire, lui, n'imitera pas les gouvernements usurpateurs de la souveraineté du peuple, qui corrompaient les électeurs, et qui achetaient à prix immoral la conscience du pays.'[2]

There is no reason to question the sincerity of these sentiments, but at the same time the more democratic republicans could hardly avoid asking themselves whether France had in fact been converted overnight to democracy. When the voice of the people was heard, was it certain that it would be a democratic voice? Ledru-Rollin soon began to feel the desirability of taking precautions. Most of the men whom he had appointed to assist him at the Ministry of the Interior were moderate republicans, but among the minor appointments were some less reputable political adventurers, and his private secretary, Delvau, held advanced views and was doubtless not without influence on his policy.[3] In a circular of March 12th, Ledru-Rollin had already expressed himself in forcible terms. Though the actual drafting of the circulars was the work of the Secretary-General of the Ministry, Jules Favre, Ledru-Rollin's eloquence

---

[1] *Le Moniteur Universel*, March 8th, 1848.
[2] *Bulletin des lois*, Xᵉ série, i, no. 125, March 18th, 1848.
[3] Alvin R. Calman, *Ledru-Rollin and the Second French Republic* (1922), 64–8.

was perhaps responsible for the dramatic note with which this one opened:

> *Quels sont vos pouvoirs?* Ils sont illimités. Agent d'une autorité révolutionnaire, vous êtes révolutionnaire aussi ... Il ne faut pas vous faire illusion sur l'état du pays. Les sentiments républicains y doivent être vivement excités, et pour cela il faut confier toutes les fonctions publiques à des hommes sûrs et sympathiques ...
> Les élections sont votre grande œuvre ... L'éducation du pays n'est pas faite : c'est à vous de le guider. Provoquez sur tous les points de votre département la réunion des comités électoraux, examinez sévèrement les titres des candidats, arrêtez-vous à ceux-là seulement qui pourraient présenter le plus de garanties à l'opinion républicaine, le plus de chances de succès.[1]

This frank appeal to the *commissaires* to purge the administration for the purpose of securing republican elections aroused violent and natural indignation among those who did not in fact want the elections to be republican. The non-democratic journals burst into denunciations, of which one illustration may be given.[2] *L'Amie de la Religion* asked ironically: 'Est-ce le délégué temporaire d'un peuple souverain, ou le maître absolu d'un peuple esclave qui parle aujourd'hui dans le *Moniteur?*' 'Voilà,' it observed, 'comment des hommes qui avaient hier de si brillantes colères contre *l'abus des influences,* contre la *corruption électorale,* entendent aujourd'hui la liberté des élections.'[3] In spite of such opposition Ledru-Rollin repeated his injunctions in a circular of April 7th:

> Le gouvernement doit-il agir sur les élections, ou se borner

---

[1] *Le Moniteur Universal,* March 12th, 1848.
[2] Other examples may be found in L.-A. Garnier-Pagès, *Histoire de la Révolution de 1848,* 2nd ed. (1866), iii, 322–4.
[3] *L'Ami de la Religion, journal ecclésiastique, politique et littéraire,* 14 mars 1848, vol. 163, pp. 622–3.

à en surveiller la régularité? Je n'hésite pas à répondre que, sous peine d'abdiquer ou même de trahir, le gouvernement ne peut se réduire à enregistrer des procès-verbaux et à compter des voix; il doit éclairer la France et travailler ouvertement à déjouer les intrigues de la contre-révolution, si, par impossible, elle ose relever la tête.[1]

The task of enlightening the people had commenced with the distribution of the *Bulletins de la République*, written in the democratic interest by a group of Ledru-Rollin's friends. A circular of March 26th informed the *commissaires* that this journal, 'sous forme d'affiche', which had already been sent to the *maires* of their *départements*, emanated from the Ministry. It was described as 'une feuille politique qui ferait connaître, dans une langue accessible à toutes les intelligences, les véritables principes du Gouvernement républicain'.[2] Twenty-five bulletins were issued between March 13th and May 6th. Most of them were innocuous, but the sixteenth threatened that if the elections were not satisfactory Paris would take the defence of the Republic into its own hands by a new insurrection. This bulletin, which aroused violent criticism, was written by George Sand. By a chapter of accidents it escaped the notice of responsible officials, and it cannot be held to represent Ledru-Rollin's views in any sense.[3]

These *Bulletins* were not the only attempt to propagate democratic opinions. In the report by the Ducos commission on the finances of the Provisional Government, it was revealed that Ledru-Rollin had granted 123,000 francs from his secret funds for the purpose of sending delegates to the provinces to carry out democratic propaganda.[4] The original idea for this move

[1] *Le Moniteur Universel*, April 7th, 1848.
[2] A.N. F 1ᵃ* 2097.
[3] Calman, *Ledru-Rollin and the Second French Republic*, 144–5.
[4] 'Rapport fait par M. Théodore Ducos au nom de la commission chargée de l'examen du compte spécial de toutes les dépenses faites et ordonnancées par le Gouvernement provisoire, depuis le 24 février jusqu'au 11 mai 1848', *Le Moniteur Universel*, April 26th, 1849, pp. 1549–62. The further report, published in a supplement to *Le Moniteur*, June 26th, 1851, adds nothing that is relevant to the subject under discussion.

came from the *Club des clubs*, presided over by Barbès. To obtain wider support for their views, Barbès and his friends had organized a number of democratic societies into a federation which in turn appointed a commission, including among its members Ledru-Rollin's secretary, Delvau, to organize democratic propaganda. Some 400–450 delegates were chosen from the clubs of Paris to go to the provinces, and the Minister of the Interior was approached for funds to finance their journeys. He obtained the sanction of the other members of the government for spending a considerable sum of money on sending five or six delegates to each *département*, though apparently without revealing the connection of the *Club des clubs* with the plan. The object, according to the evidence of the former members of the Provisional Government to the Ducos commission, was to propagate republican ideas and facilitate the application of universal suffrage. Ledru-Rollin's explanation that in the interests of public tranquillity he was anxious to get a large number of workers away from Paris, and he thought the money granted was being spent for this purpose, is a patent invention.

There seems no reason to disbelieve the president of the commission of the *Club des clubs*, Longepied, who frankly declared: 'Le ministre savait que les délégués étaient envoyés pour préparer les citoyens à faire de bonnes élections.'[1] It seems more likely that by alarming the provinces with their extreme views they did a fair amount of damage to the republican cause. An even less happy idea was the sending of non-commissioned officers as delegates to the regiments, for the purpose, again to quote Longepied, of indicating to the soldiers 'les chefs suspects dont l'influence était redoutée pour les élections'. This move

---

[1] His evidence is borne out by a letter of June 22nd, 1848, from the Under-Secretary of State to the Minister of the Interior, stating that a number of delegates, 'qui par ordre du gouvernement provisoire ont parcouru les départements à l'époque des élections', were in a state of great poverty and insistently demanded payment of their expenses. The writer estimated that 4,000 francs would be necessary to satisfy them, and the reply was 'donner mais individuellement'. A.N. BB^{30} 319.

aroused so much opposition that the military delegates were withdrawn after eight days.[1]

The attempt to effect in a few weeks the political education of a whole nation achieved as little success as might have been expected. Moreover it was soon realized that the substitution of republican *commissaires* for Orleanist prefects was not likely to be sufficient to produce satisfactory elections, unless it was also possible to remove the influence of those who were described in

[1] Report of Ducos Commission, *Le Moniteur Universal*, April 26th, 1849, pp. 1553–1554; Calman, op. cit., 162–5. Evidence of the nature of the activities of one of these delegates to the army is provided by a letter from the *commissaire* for the Loire-Inférieure to the Minister of Justice, April 12th, 1848 (A.N. BB³⁰ 323), which seems interesting enough to deserve quoting at length:

'Hier le nommé Dieulouard (Antoine-françois) se disant domicilié à Paris, rue Neuve St Eustache no. 52, et envoyé par le *Comité révolutionnaire*, dont le siège est rue de Rivoli, no. 16, s'est présenté dans les casernes de Nantes pour demander aux sous-officiers des renseignements sur les opinions politiques de leurs chefs, et leur a remis les deux pièces ci-jointes, que je me hâte de vous transmettre, sans aucun commentaire ... Il résulte de ses explications qu'il aurait pour mission spéciale d'aller ainsi visiter toutes les garnisons de l'Ouest et du midi de la France, que sa mission aurait reçu l'approbation secrète du Gouvernement; et que M. le préfet de police, en lui délivrant le 7 de ce mois, un passeport *gratuit*, que j'ai sous les yeux, aurait fait remettre l'argent nécessaire pour subvenir aux frais de son voyage ... [He has with him a great many copies of the journal *La Commune de Paris*, issue of March 17th, and of an address by the *Comité révolutionnaire*. He is a jeweller by trade.] ' ... Le voyant disposé à partir pour Bordeaux, malgré la promesse qu'il avait faite au commissaire du département de retourner à Paris, je l'ai sommé de rester à Nantes jusqu'à nouvel ordre ... ' [The letter ends with a request to be told what should be done about him.]

An attached document gives the instructions of Dieulouard. He is to report at least every three days, stating:

1. The opinion of the regiment.

2. The names of the non-commissioned officers regarded as most suitable for propagating republican doctrines.

3. The ideas of the colonel and the officers, and if they are favourable or not to the Republic.

4. If there is any dissension between the officers and soldiers, and what are the motives of this dissension.

After various instructions on methods of propaganda, the document ends: 'Vous aurez soin aussi que l'armée vote dans le sens des listes dressées par les commissaires du Gouvernement – c'est un des moyens qu'ils auront d'obtenir ce que leur est due.

'Vous recommanderez le citoyen Manaud aux électeurs de Tarn-et-Garonne, Gadon aux électeurs de la Creuze. [The names are filled in by a different hand.]

'Correspondance avec le citoyen [illegible]

rue de Rivoli 16,
Ch. Emery [?]'

one indignant letter from the Vosges as 'gens autrefois privilégiés, gens electa, nourris au râtelier du budget, âmes damnés de l'ancien régime'.[1] Under the monarchy the local officials had become too habituated to 'making' the elections easily to lose the habit. A republican wrote from the Haute-Garonne : 'Parmi les plus fatales épreuves des temps passés, nous avons acquis cette conviction que le président d'un collège électoral influe considérablement sur le succès de tel ou tel candidat. Le choix de président provoque toujours le premier cri de triomphe.'[2] Now the presidents of the electoral bureaux were normally the local *maires* or *juges de paix*, men appointed to uphold the regime of Louis-Philippe. Hence the cry of despair that came in another letter from the Haute-Garonne : 'Que la République ne force pas les électeurs à déposer leurs votes entre les mains d'un homme qui était l'âme damné de Guizot.'[3] One of the tasks of the *commissaires* was therefore to remove officials whose influence was likely to be hostile to republican and democratic candidates in the forthcoming elections. They did not all carry it out with equal zeal or efficiency. The two *commissaires* for the Allier, who had taken possession of the *préfecture* on March 12th, voluntarily resigned on March 19th because of their unwillingness to apply the instructions of Ledru-Rollin in this respect.[4] Their successor issued a vigorous circular to the *maires* calling on them to organize the candidature of sound republicans and unmask 'des hommes à double visage qui, après avoir servi la royauté, se disent les serviteurs du peuple'.[5] This clarion call aroused protests in the Paris press but it evoked a letter of approval from Ledru-Rollin.[6]

The opposition that the *commissaires* met in attempting to

[1] A.N. F 1c II 97. March 18th, 1848.
[2] A.N. F 1c II 56. A. Pelleport, avocat à Saint-Gaudens, to the Provisional Government, March 15th, 1848.
[3] Ibid.
[4] E. Maure, *Le Bourbonnais sous la seconde république* (1909), 10. The letter from the *commissaires* offering their resignations is in A.N. F 1c II 97. March 14th, 1848.
[5] Ibid., March 24th, 1848.
[6] Maure, op. cit., 22.

carry out this policy may be seen in a letter from the *sous-commissaire* of Mirecourt in the *département* of the Vosges :

> Je crois de mon devoir de vous dire que la circulaire du ministre de l'Intérieur, interprétée généralement dans un sens trop littéral et trop absolu, a produit dans nos campagnes une émotion assez pénible. Je me suis attaché à détruire cet effet, en leur affirmant que l'administration ne se proposait pas le moins du monde de révoquer en masse tous les maires et adjoints des communes rurales (mesure qui mettrait le pays en feu et rencontrerait d'ailleurs des obstacles insurmontables).[1]

The mixture of sentiments with which the *commissaires* faced the task of promoting 'good' elections is well illustrated in a circular sent by Lorentz, *commissaire* in the Meurthe, to the *maires* of his *département* on April 12th :

> Tous vos efforts combinés avec les nôtres doivent donc tendre à un but commun : de bonnes élections. Faites en sorte que les choix de vos administrés tombent sur des hommes franchement dévoués à la cause républicaine ... Écoutez surtout notre voix, les autorités d'aujourd'hui ne ressemblent en rien à celles du Gouvernement déchu : celle-ci s'appuyaient sur la corruption ; nous, nous ne voulons agir que par l'influence morale de la raison.[2]

The trouble was that for the peasantry the moral influence of reason could hardly compete with the material influence of the *maires*, and many letters came in to the *commissaires*, or direct to Paris, protesting against the ill will of the *maires* of the rural communes towards the Republic.[3] A protest from the Sarthe, after the election, declared that the 'pauvres, naïfs et honnêtes gens des campagnes', under the eyes of their *maires*, 'les maires de Louis Philippe !', dared not vote against their wishes.[4]

[1] A.D. Vosges. 8bis M[4]. Police et sûreté générale, 1819–50.
[2] A.D. Meurthe-et-Moselle. M. Élection des députés, 1845–9.
[3] A.N. F 1c II 56.
[4] Ibid.

The more energetic of the *commissaires*, as has been suggested, took strong action to guard against such a situation. Thevenet, the leading member of the *Commission départementale* in the Isère, reported: 'Vous verrez par les propositions que nous ferons pour les nominations des maires et adjoints, que nous avons tout sacrifié en vue des élections des représentants.'[1] Similarly the *commissaire* for the Doubs wrote to his *sous-commissaires* on April 15th: 'Il importe que les fonctionnaires de la république soient des hommes du mouvement ... Tous les maires donc des communes de votre arrondissement dont vous ne croirez pas les sympathies acquise à la république doivent être révoqués de suite.'[2]

The revocation of officials in view of the elections was not confined to *maires*. Tax-collectors, *percepteurs*, 'gens si influents dans nos campagnes par leur rapports avec les petits propriétaires', as a letter of denunciation says,[3] had also been used under the Orleanist regime as political agents. A letter to the *commissaire* of the Isère, complaining that a *percepteur* had been threatened with dismissal unless he voted and canvassed for particular candidates, suggests that the new authorities expected them to continue to exercise an influence over the electors.[4] The municipal councils were purged. The *commissaire* of the Isère wrote to the Minister of the Interior on April 6th: 'Il était indispensable pour imprimer partout une bonne direction à l'esprit public et aux administrations communales de les purger dans bien des localités des hommes dévoués au régime déchue.'[5] In the archives of this *département* is a series of documents beginning 'Vu la nécessité de mettre l'administration des communes en harmonie avec les principes du Gouvernement

[1] A.D. Isère. M² Élections municipales, 1848.
[2] A.D. Doubs. 16 M 47. The extent to which the *maires* were changed varied greatly from *département* to *département*. In the Allier, it was alleged, some 200 *maires* were dismissed by the *commissaire*. *L'Ami de la Religion*, March 30th, 1848, vol. 136, p. 759.
[3] A.N. BB³⁰ 319. Letter from a notary of Monts, Vienne, to the Ministry of the Interior, March 25th, 1848.
[4] A.D. Isère. M² Élections municipales, 1848. March 10th, 1848.
[5] Ibid.

Républicain ... ', and proceeding to nominate a new municipal council.[1] Only in a few cases was the municipal council dissolved as a whole, but in one of the *arrondissements*, Vienne, out of 133 municipal councils sixty had their composition modified.[2]

The *juges de paix* were the object of similar measures. A memoir sent to the Provisional Government by a republican lawyer in the Haute-Garonne declared: 'Les magistrats de cet ordre sont pour la plupart le produit de la corruption et de la vénalité ... Les services qu'ils étaient forcés de rendre à la police politique étaient une condition presque essentielle de leur existence judiciaire. Plusieurs sièges ont été payés par la monnaie électorale.'[3] The writer drew the conclusion that it was necessary to replace most of them. Similarly the *commissaire* of the Loir-et-Cher reported: 'C'est dans les places de juges de paix qu'on trouve le plus d'agents corrupteurs, nommés par le gouvernement déchu.'[4] A *sous-commissaire* at Châtillon informed the *commissaire* for the Côte d'Or that a *juge de paix* 'pouvait influencer les élections d'une manière fâcheuse; j'ai obtenu sa destitution'.[5] A later report from a *sous-commissaire* in the same *département* says that in his *arrondissement* eight out of ten *juges de paix* have been dismissed, 'et c'était justice, car les anciens titulaires étaient les courtiers électoraux du Gouv^t déchu'.[6]

It is unnecessary to give further examples: long columns in issue after issue of the *Moniteur* announce the dismissal of existing officials and their replacement by new men. The process was sometimes carried very low down the administrative hierarchy, as witness a letter from the *commissaire* of the Côte d'Or to the *Citoyen directeur des postes* referring to the 'dispositions antirépublicains' of a *directrice des postes* and suggesting the name of a successor.[7] A letter from the same *commissaire* to a teacher at the École des Beaux-arts of Dijon ran: 'J'ai l'honneur de vous

[1] A. D. Isère. M² Élections municipales, 1848. March 10th, 1848.
[2] *La Révolution de 1848 dans le département de l'Isère*, ed. F. Rude (1949), 281.
[3] A.N. F 1^c II 56. March 15th, 1848.
[4] Ibid.
[5] A.D. Côte d'Or. M 6 51³. March 27th, 1848.
[6] Ibid., June 4th, 1848.
[7] Ibid., April 27th, 1848.

informer que pour me conformer aux vues de la République qui veut compter sur le zèle des citoyens qui lui sont dévoués d'ancienne date, je me vois dans l'obligation de vous révoquer des fonctions de professeur d'architecture.'[1] Even the village teachers were liable to be threatened with dismissal if they did not support the list of candidates put forward by the *commissaire*.[2]

These, it must be emphasized, are only illustrations of a widespread tendency. But though the efforts of the *commissaires* to purge all ranks of the local administration, as a preliminary step to the elections, are unquestionable, the success with which they were able to carry out this policy is more open to doubt. In the towns the political influence of the administration could be organized with some chance of success, but as the *commissaire* for the Bas-Rhin warned the Minister of the Interior: 'Dans les cantons ruraux, la guerre aux écharpes municipaux, de misérables petites vanités, l'appât des intérêts matériels, sont les seules préoccupations de la majorité des habitants.'[3]

A further problem was to obtain reliable information about officials. That this was not easy is indicated by a note from a *sous-commissaire* in the Côte d'Or: 'Vous ne sauriez croire combien j'éprouve de peine à obtenir des renseignements exacts sur les fonctionnaires de l'arrondissement. On n'obéit ici qu'aux ressentiments et aux affections personnels.'[4] More serious was the problem of providing competent replacements for the dismissed officials. The *commissaire* for the Dordogne said of his *département*: 'Le pays est très peu avancé, ignorant, et il nous est difficile de trouver parmi les vrais republicains assez d'hommes aptes à remplacer les juges de paix qui sont en général animés d'un mauvais esprit.'[5] Similarly, the *commissaire* for the Côte d'Or wrote on April 15th: 'Le travail sur les percepteurs est à

---

[1] A.D. Côte d'Or. M 6 52². Politique : sûreté générale, an VIII–1851. April 30th, 1848.

[2] Examples from the Puy-de-Dôme, Dordogne, Vosges, Marne, in *English Historical Review*, lvii (1942), 342.

[3] A.N. F 1⁰ II 57. March 14th, 1848.

[4] A.D. Côte d'Or. M 6 51³. April 14th, 1848.

[5] A.N. F 1ᶜ II 56. April 1st, 1848. With this letter was enclosed a list of *juges de paix* to be dismissed.

mon avis très sérieux. Il faut faire des changements sans doute; mais le service des contributions est dans ce moment si difficile et si chargé, que de nouveaux titulaires auraient de la peine à se tirer d'affaire.'[1] A *sous-commissaire* in the same *département* complained: 'Les maires en général nous sont hostiles et nous ne trouvons personne pour les remplacer.'[2] The same objection came from the *commissaire* of the Vendée: 'Il faut changer les maires; mais quand et comment? J'y ai pensé, j'ai frappé les hostiles et je n'en ai pas trouvé toujours à les remplacer.'[3] The *commissaire* for Finistère, sending in a list of revocations of *maires*, explained its shortness by his inability to find substitutes in a countryside where often not more than three persons could read and write in a whole commune.[4] The central government found the same difficulty in obtaining reliable republican *procureurs-généraux*, as appears in a plea from the Minister of Justice to the *commissaire* at Besançon: 'Avez-vous un candidat pour la place de procureur-général? Il m'est extrêmement difficile de trouver des hommes qui réunissent républicanisme, capacité, considération acquise. Éclairez-moi, aidez-moi avec votre patriotisme.'[5] The result was often that anti-republican officials managed to retain their offices for lack of competent successors. Even in the Côte d'Or, where considerable efforts had been made to purge the administration, a report from one district after the elections could say: 'Presque tout ce qui est employé en autorité a travaillé contre nous.'[6]

Whatever the degree of success, however, there can be no doubt of the effort that was made to secure local officials who could be trusted to support republican candidates. The necessity of this policy if the Republic was to have any chance of survival can hardly be doubted. Ledru-Rollin was to go much further, however, in compromising with hard facts. Besides appointing

---

[1] A.D. Côte d'Or. M 6 51³. To the *sous-commissaire* at Semur, April 15th, 1848.
[2] Ibid. From the *sous-commissaire* at Semur to the *commissaire*, April 1st, 1848.
[3] A.N. F 1ᶜ II 56. In a letter of May 9th, 1848.
[4] A.N. F 1ᶜ II 97. March 28th, 1848.
[5] A.N. BB³⁰ 327. March 19th, 1848.
[6] A.D. Côte d'Or. III M 52. Élections des 23 et 24 avril 1848. Report from Recey, April 25th.

republican officials to influence the electors, it was also necessary to have republican candidates, and their selection also presented considerable difficulties.[1] In Paris the *National,* the journal of the moderate republicans, organized a central electoral committee, put itself in touch with similar local committees and on April 10th published lists for all *départements.* Louis Blanc and the socialists who followed him issued the *liste du Luxembourg.* Conservative groups more cautiously began to organize candidatures. Local electoral committees, representing many different interests, sprang up all over the country, and a flood of potential candidates appeared, as many as 2,000 in Paris. The choice of candidates and drawing up of party lists by electoral committees, which is now taken for granted as a necessary part of democratic machinery, seemed in 1848 a usurpation of the power that rightfully belonged to the people. The moderate Catholic paper, *L'Ami de la Religion,* protested: 'Vous étouffez le principe du suffrage universel sous l'action des comités électoraux.'[2] On the other hand, as Garnier-Pagès asked, how was the choice to be made among thousands of candidates, or would-be candidates, by millions of uninstructed new electors, unless they had some guidance from above?[3] The peasantry was often content to follow the lead of the curé or the local landowner and in so far as they did this might indeed manage without other advice. It was those who were most in sympathy with the new Republic who most felt the need for guidance. The *commissaires* were inundated with demands for lists of genuine republican candidates. There is only space here for two quotations by way of example. A *maire* writes to the

[1] Many letters to the Minister of Justice in A.N. BB³⁰ 319, and there were doubtless similar letters to the other ministers, illustrate the expectation that the Provisional Government would play an important part in the choice of republican candidates. Among these is a letter from C. Renouvier, the philosopher, supporting the candidature of a friend and asking that the government should recommend him 'en sous ordre' to the *commissaire* for the Côtes-du-Nord. Renouvier adds: 'Veuillez recevoir mes vifs remerciements pour l'attention bienveillante avec laquelle vous avez lu mon petit livre que certains trouvent trop philosophique.' This is presumably a reference to his *Manuel républicain de l'homme et du citoyen.*

[2] *L'Ami de la Religion,* April 4th, 1848, vol. 137, p. 31.

[3] Garnier-Pagès, *Histoire de la Révolution de 1848,* vol. v, 230.

commissaire for the Var: 'Nous voilà à la veille des Élections, et sans savoir à qui accorder nos suffrages ... Je me permets, Citoyen Commissaire, de vous adresser ces mots pour vous prier de nous servir de gouverne en cette occasion, et nous désigner les candidats auxquels nous devons accorder nos suffrages.'[1] Another *maire*, in the Doubs, says of his villagers: 'Chaque jour ils me demandent sur qui est qu'ils devraient donner leur suffrage vu que nous ne sommes pas au centre du département, et que nous ne connaissons pas d'hommes vraiment républicains, capables de soutenir nos droits à l'assemblée nationale.'[2]

Although such letters came largely from republican sympathizers, conscious of the lack of notabilities in their localities who could be regarded as sincere supporters of the new regime, they doubtless reflected also the habit of regarding government as something that came from above.[3] At the same time, even among republicans they do not necessarily indicate a willingness to accept blindly whatever names were suggested. 'Les villageois', writes a *sous-commissaire* in the Côte d'Or, 'demandent partout des petites biographies qui leur fassent connaître les candidats, dont le plus grand nombre ne leur sont pas même connus de nom.'[4] Another *sous-commissaire*, from Cambrai, advises: 'Si vous avez des candidats qu'il faille populariser donnez-nous un mot de biographie et nous ferons bonne besogne. Il faut que les candidats soient la conversation de tous les cabarets qui maintenant ne parlent que d'élections mais à vide.'[5] Delay in drawing up official lists of republican candidates produced frequent complaints. On April 10th the Ministry of the Interior intervened with a circular to all the *commissaires*:

---

[1] A.D. Var. April 1st, 1848.

[2] A.D. Doubs. 6 M 10. The *maire* of Jallerange to the *commissaire*, March 15th, 1848. The *Archives Départementales* of the Côte d'Or contain a considerable number of such letters in III M 52.

[3] For example, letters to the *commissaire* for the Loiret asking for instructions for whom to vote. *La Révolution de 1848*, vol. ii, no. 12, pp. 309–10.

[4] A.D. Côte d'Or. 6 M 513. The *sous-commissaire* of Châtillon, April 5th. The demand is reiterated by the same *sous-commissaire* in a letter of April 14th.

[5] A.D. Nord. M 273. March 18th, 1848. Cf. H. Contamine, *Metz et la Moselle de 1814 à 1870* (1932), i, 422–3.

'Citoyen Commissaire, veuillez m'adresser sans retard la liste définitive des candidats choisis par les comités électoraux de votre département, afin que je puisse ... désigner à votre attention les noms de ceux sur lesquels vous devez plus spécialement appeler les suffrages des citoyens.'[1] In the end, lists of republican candidates were drawn up by the *commissaires* in every *département* and circulated in large numbers.[2]

L'Ami de la Religion said, cynically :

> Partout, en effet, les nouveaux chefs des départements dressent leurs listes de candidats à la représentation nationale. Le commissaire d'abord, ou bien deux ou même trois, si le département est assez heureux pour les posséder, puis quelques amis dont on répond, voilà la liste complète ... Les maires sont prévenus, des émissaires doivent veiller à la consigne ... Une telle combinaison est une atteinte au principe de la souveraineté du peuple.[3]

It was true that the *commissaires* often included their own names in their lists,[4] and this was a frequent source of sarcastic comment. There was also much criticism of the way in which the electoral committees were chosen. 'Qui est-ce donc qui a établi ces comités?' asked a curé who was very active politically in the Vosges,

> On dit que près de trois cents personnes se trouvaient réunics à Mirecourt. Je ne sais pas comment elles avaient

---

[1] A.N. F 1ᵃ* 2097.

[2] Thus the *commissaire* in the Nord says on April 22nd that 10,000 copies of his list have been sent to the *arrondissement* of Avesnes. A.D. Nord. M 273. For the *département* of the Moselle 20,000 copies of the *commissaire's* official list of candidates were printed at Saareguemines. Contamine, op. cit., i, 422–3. As this practice seems to have been general it is unnecessary to give further examples.

[3] *L'Ami de la Religion*, April 4th, 1848, vol. 137, pp. 31–2.

[4] On April 1st the Provisional Government decided to send a circular to the *commissaires* recommending them 'de ne point user, dans l'intérêt de leur élection, d'une influence qui ne doit servir qu'à la consolidation de la République, et d'attendre, sans le provoquer, le vœu des populations'. Garnier-Pagès, op. cit., v, 189. Whether they provoked it or not, the wish of the population did in fact elect 22 former *commissaires-généraux*, 53 former *commissaires* and 35 *sous-commissaires*. *La Révolution de 1848*, vol. vii, no. 42, pp. 420–1. This, however, is to some extent merely evidence that Ledru-Rollin had chosen men of notability in their *département*.

été convoquées, mais je sais bien que plusieurs hommes même de Mirecourt qui avaient intention de se trouver à cette réunion pour y donner leur voix ne surent pas du tout qu'on avait appelé les citoyens à cette opération.[1]

A particular ground for objection was the belief that the electoral committees were dominated by the *chefs-lieux*. A protest in a Dunkirk paper said of the local committee: 'Élu ... par 2,637 électeurs de la ville de Dunkerque seulement, comment a-t-il pu se croire le droit de déclarer ... au nom de l'arrondissement entier, composé de 104,000 habitants, que MM. tel et tel étaient les candidats du département à l'Assemblée nationale?'[2] Where committees were called into being in the communes it was for the purpose of carrying out instructions issued from the *chef-lieu* rather than initiating proposals. The *commissaire* of the Doubs instructed the *maires* of his *département*:

> Vous vous attacherez à convaincre les citoyens de la nécessité de s'unir *sous le drapeau de la République*, et de choisir des Représentants *franchement et loyalement dévoués* au Gouvernement républicain. Je compte à ce sujet sur votre propre dévouement au principe de la *souveraineté du peuple*, et sur l'ardeur de votre zèle pour faire triompher la vérité, faire prévaloir le mérite.[3]

After the list had been agreed on at the *chef-lieu* of the *département* by the central committee, delegates were usually appointed to convey it to the cantons. In the Pas-de-Calais over one hundred such delegates were sent out.[4] The procedure is described by the *commissaire* for the Moselle:

> Sous mon inspiration il a été décidé que des envoyés iraient dans chaque canton provoquer l'envoi de délégués qui viendraient prendre part aux discussions du club général

[1] A.D. Vosges. Collection Deblaye: Élection de la Constituante, du Président et de la Législature.
[2] *Journal de Dunkerque*, March 29th, 1848.
[3] A.D. Doubs. 6 M 10. March 25th, 1848.
[4] A.N. F 1ᶜ II 97.

de la ville. Echauffés, entrainés par l'ardeur des discussions, éclairés sur le mérite et les chances des candidats, ils retourneront dans leurs cantons pour y communiquer l'agitation électorale et guider les suffrages.[1]

The *commissaires* were not, however, alone in their desire to have good elections. The Orleanist political machine had disintegrated with the collapse of the central authority from which it derived its motive power. This did not mean that the wealthy classes who had monopolized political power under the July monarchy ceased to exercise political influence, but in the elections of April 1848 they had to exercise it as individuals or as small local groups, and not as the allies, agents or beneficiaries of the political machinery of the state. But while the Orleanist electoral machinery was disbanded, there was another political organization which was free from the Orleanist taint. In the course of the struggle against the anti-clerical tendencies of Louis-Philippe's government a *Comité électoral de la liberté religieuse* had been founded in 1846 by Montalembert. This met in Paris on the morrow of the Revolution for the purpose of organizing the defence of its interests in the new political situation. Its preparations included the publication of a periodical sheet called *L'Élection Populaire*, and the formation in the *départements* of committees to secure the election of representatives pledged to the principle of the control of all education by the Church. In the bishops and clergy it had the nucleus of a political machine in every town and village of France; and the Provisional Government could hardly complain if the clergy entered into the political campaign when, through its *ministre des cultes*, the Saint-Simonian Hippolyte Carnot, it had called on them to do so.[2] As *L'Ami de la Religion* commented: 'Nul ne sera surpris de voir le prêtre se rendre aux élections pour y donner son suffrage … Nul ne s'étonnera de voir siéger le prêtre dans l'assemblée nationale.'[3]

[1] A.N. F 1c II 56.
[2] *Le Moniteur Universel*, March 15th, 1848.
[3] *L'Ami de la Religion*, March 14th, 1848, vol. 136, p. 619.

The clergy flung themselves into the political struggle under the leadership of the Committee for Electoral Liberty and the bishops. Few were capable of seeing as far ahead as the bishop of Viviers, later Cardinal Guibert, who raised a note of warning:

> On se prépare aux élections de tout côté. Je n'aurais pas voulu que les prêtres se jetassent dans ce mouvement, mais j'ai fini par céder; comment les retenir ici, lorsque dans tous les diocèses on les a lancés? Je suis convaincu que nous faisons une chose imprudente, et que les quelques voix que nous pourrons envoyer à la Chambre favorable à la liberté religieuse ne nous vaudront pas la belle position que nous avons prise dans notre isolement des choses politiques depuis 1830. M. Carnot nous a tendu un piège dans lequel nous avons donné tête baissée.[1]

It is not necessary to describe the electoral campaign of the Church and its supporters. The attempt to draw up complete lists of candidates from its own ranks had to be abandoned by the clerical party in the face of the resentment it aroused. This was true even in a *département* like the Vosges, where the bishop of Saint-Dié had to recommend a more cautious line of action. He wrote on April 16th:

> Par suite de conseils qui nous ont été donnés ... nous avons dû renoncer au projet d'abord adopté de présenter une liste complète de 11 candidats ... Voici le nouveau plan qu'il a paru bon de suivre: c'est de présenter seulement six candidats; ce sont ceux qui sont en tête de la liste que fera paraître *l'Espérance* demain ... Ce système, qui offre à nos candidats des chances immenses, s'il est suivi avec entente, consiste donc en deux choses: 1° réunir sur nos candidats le plus de voix possible, 2° éparpiller les autre voix sur des hommes honnêtes, mais n'étant patronnés que dans la localité, de cette manière nous conservons toutes nos forces, et nous diminuons le plus possible celles des concurrents ...

[1] J. Paguelle de Follenay, *Vie du Cardinal Guibert* (1896), ii, 107.

Il faut donc que par l'emploi d'hommes discrets et dévoués, auxquels vous garderez bien de dire le fond du secret, vous fassiez adopter et suivre ce plan. Entendez-vous avec vos confrères [this letter was addressed to one of his curés] que vous mettrez dans le secret mais eux sculement et non les laïques ; pour ceux-ci il faut se borner à leur dire voici les six noms qu'il faut porter sur vos bulletins, vous choisissez les cinq autres comme vous voudrez ... on peut leur laisser mettre le maître d'école, un ouvrier estimable ... [1]

It is sad to have to add after this that of the six names on the bishop's list only one was elected. The activities of the clergy, like those of the *commissaires*, aroused intense resentment, though of course in different quarters; the chief agent of the bishop of Saint-Dié in the elections, the abbé Deblaye, confessed afterwards : 'On ne veut pas du clergé dans les élections ... Est-il un curé qui n'ait été calomnié à l'occasion des élections?' He refurred to 'cette effroyable tempête contre l'action du clergé dans les luttes électorales'.[2] Elsewhere, under more discreet guidance, clerical influence proved more successful. The clergy distributed voting lists in Brittany, it was said, at the confessional, and sometimes even checked the lists brought to the electoral bureau by their parishioners and tore up those that displeased them.[3] The bishop of Viviers was able to write to a fellow bishop: 'Je connais le merveilleux résultat de vos élections. Les nôtres ont été parfaites. Sur huit noms qu'avaient présentés les comités religieux, sept sont sortis, malgré les menaces, les intrigues et les violences indignes exercées par les commissaires et leurs agents.'[4]

The influence of the clergy over the Catholic peasantry of France was bound to be great. The *commissaires* of Ledru-Rollin regarded it as the principal danger, and tried to counteract it by such means as they had at their disposal. The *commissaires*,

[1] A.D. Vosges. Collection Deblaye.
[2] Ibid.
[3] A.N. F 1ᶜ III Finistère 9. Commandant of gendarmerie to the *commissaire*, May 4th, 1848.
[4] Paguelle de Follenay, op. cit., ii, 108.

or the central republican committees, as has been said, sent out delegates to engage in propaganda on behalf of the official list of candidates,[1] but for effective action in the countryside local men were needed, and these were lacking. Apart from the curés and landowners, the only other persons with a modicum of education in the countryside were the village schoolmasters. Hippolyte Carnot, in a circular of March 6th to the rectors of the universities, called on them to marshal the *instituteurs* for the task of educating the people in their new political duties.[2] The Provisional Government hoped to make use of them as republican propagandists. A school inspector wrote to the teachers under him: 'Chacun de vous aura la confiance de vingt électeurs *au moins*. Travaillez tous pour le même, votre triomphe est assuré.'[3] Alas, it was not. I have discussed elsewhere the attempt to use the *instituteurs* in the elections and need not here do more than refer to this aspect of the electoral campaign.[4] It was in any case a resounding failure and only resulted in the subsequent persecution of such unfortunate schoolmasters as allowed themselves to be carried away by these exhortations, or by their republican enthusiasm, to the point of joining in the political struggle.

In considering the efforts to limit the influence of the Church, the choice of Easter Sunday for the day of elections is also perhaps of relevance. 'Est-ce inadvertance?' asked *L'Ami de la Religion*, 'est-ce mépris? est-ce calcul? ... On aurait donc espéré empêcher les hommes religieux et le clergé d'allér aux élections, en les mettant dans la douloureuse alternative ou de manquer aux saints devoirs de leur conscience ou de renoncer à leurs devoirs de citoyens?'[5] In reply to a protest from the bishop of Nevers, Ledru-Rollin answered that in fixing on Easter Sunday

---

[1] For an example from the Haute-Garonne see A. Cayré, 'La Révolution de 1848 à Toulouse et dans la Haute-Garonne', in *La Révolution de 1848 à Toulouse et dans la Haute-Garonne*, ed. J. Godechot (1948), 214.

[2] *Le Moniteur Universel*, March 7th, 1848.

[3] *L'inspecteur des écoles de la Dordogne à MM. les instituteurs du département* (Périgueux), le 19 mars 1848.

[4] Cf. pp. 68 et seq.

[5] *L'Ami de la Religion*, March 28th, 1848, vol. 136, p. 738.

for the election the Provisional Government had above all been anxious to ensure against the possibility that the churches might be used for the purpose of electoral meetings.[1] This sounds a little disingenuous, but whatever the reason the decision aroused strong protests;[2] a number of *commissaires* were of opinion that it would in any case have a bad effect.[3] The *commissaire* for the Mayenne explained that the result of the choice would be precisely the opposite of that which the Provisional Government had presumably hoped for: 'Dans nos campagnes de l'Ouest, essentiellement religieuses, presque fanatiques, tous les habitants vont à confesser et communiaient en ce jour de grande solemnité. Vous comprendriez quelle influence cela peut donner au clergé.'[4] In the event the bishops arranged for the church services to be taken at an unusually early hour in order to enable the faithful subsequently to fulfil their democratic duty at the polls, and the warning of the *commissaire* for the Mayenne was to some extent justified.

Ledru-Rollin and the *commissaires* were fully aware, of course, that their greatest danger in the elections would come from the influence of the clergy and local gentry over the masses of the peasantry. Another and potentially more effective device for limiting this influence lay in the choice of the place of voting. The original directions of the Provisional Government, on March 5th, that voting should take place at the *chef-lieu* of the canton,[5] aroused a torrent of protests.[6] The concession that cantons with a population of over 20,000 might be subdivided was of little value. The *commissaires* of Ille-et-Vilaine, Lot-et-Garonne, Basses-Pyrénées, Haute-Saône and Seine-et-Marne, for example, pointed out that none of their cantons reached this population; the *commissaire* for the Haute-Loire said his *département* had only one, while the *commissaire* for the Manche,

---

[1] A.N. F 1ᶜ II 57.
[2] A collection of these protests has survived in A.N. F 1ᶜ II 56.
[3] E.g. those of the Bouches-du-Rhône, Var, Vienne, Seine-et-Marne, Aube. Ibid.
[4] In a letter of March 31st, 1848. Ibid.
[5] *Le Moniteur Universel*, March 6th, 1848.
[6] There are many of these in F 1ᶜ II 57.

arguing for the right to subdivide his cantons, said that though one of the richest and most populous *départements* of France it only had two cantons with a population of over 20,000.[1] Inhabitants of rural communes, it was complained, if they had to vote at the *chef-lieu* would often have to walk long distances to record their votes. The *maire* of a commune in the Meurthe protested that only the strongest or the aristocracy could make the necessary journey of 30 to 50 kilometres to the *chef-lieu* and back, 'et c'est alors que l'on verrait cette aristocratie passer en voiture à côté de leurs frères en les couvrant de boue ou de poussière.'[2]

In some cases a canton was divided by a river: there was not always a bridge, and where there was, crossing it might involve payment of a toll. It was presumably not often as heavy as in one case in the Vienne, where the *commissaire*, in a covering letter forwarding a petition from four cantons, added: 'L'impôt dont il est parlé est énorme. C'est un droit de 50 c. que chaque citoyen aura à payer pour aller déposer son vote.'[3] From the Marne and Maine-et-Loire came complaints that communes were cut off from their *chefs-lieux* by floods.[4] Another reason given why voting should not take place at the *chef-lieu* was the existence of local enmities, which, it was alleged, would make it impossible for peace to be preserved if two communes traditionally hostile to one another had to meet and vote in the same town. Thus the inhabitants of Laferté-Miron (Aisne) expressed their fear of the consequences if they had to encounter at the *chef-lieu* the voters from Neuilly St Front, for the canton which included both communes was 'pays disaine, ayant d'anciennes rancunes à exercer'.[5] From Puy-Laroque (Tarn-et-Garonne) came a plea that its inhabitants, having already had occasion to go to Montpeyat to exercise their civic functions,

[1] There are many of these in F 1ᶜ II 57.
[2] Ibid. *Maire* of Bourdonnay to Minister of the Interior, April 5th, 1848.
[3] Ibid. In a letter of April 4th, 1848. The toll for the use of the bridge at Criel in the canton of Poissy, Seine-et-Oise, was only 5 centimes, but the *maire* of Verneuil asked if this could be remitted on the occasion of the elections.
[4] Ibid.
[5] Ibid.

were 'horriblement maltraités'. 'Toute la population de Mont-peyat en masse, hommes, femmes et enfants armés de couteaux, de bâtons ou de toute autre manière, se rua sur eux avec un fureur indisciple.'[1] These were all more or less genuine reasons. It is justifiable to feel more doubt about a letter from the *maire* of Batignolles-Monceau, who wrote: 'Il faut considérer d'ailleurs qu'en cas d'incendie la sûreté de la ville pourrait avoir considérablement à souffrir de l'éloignement même momentané de ses habitants.'[2]

In one carton at the *Archives Nationales* there are appeals from the *commissaires* for as many as twenty different *départements* to be allowed to divide the rural cantons for the purpose of voting.[3] That these may in some cases have represented con-cessions to local opinion rather than the personal views of the *commissaire* is suggested by a letter from the *commissaire* for the Meuse, who, in forwarding petitions from his *départment*, wrote : 'L'origine de ces demandes me confirme dans l'opinion qu'un semblable fractionnement serait nuisible à notre cause, en facilitant les pressions des influences de fortune.'[4] Similarly the *commissaire* for the Aisne declared that in the communes, 'Nous aurons contre nous l'influence des anciens manieurs d'élections'.[5] Another *commissaire* declared : 'Dans la Vendée, les forces du parti républicain se trouvent dans les villes et les gros bourgs. Le fractionnement communal aurait pour effet de donner la prépondérance à l'élément campagnard qui appartient gén-éralement à l'opinion légitimiste.'[6] Similar views were expressed by the *commissaires* for the Moselle,[7] Tarn[8] and Loiret,[9] and

[1] Ibid.
[2] Ibid.
[3] These were the Allier, Basses-Alpes, Basses-Pyrénées, Charente, Eure, Eure-et-Loir, Haute-Loire, Haute-Saône, Haute-Vienne, Ille-et-Vilaine, Loiret, Lot-et-Garonne, Maine-et-Loire, Manche, Mayenne, Meuse, Seine-et-Marne, Tarn-et-Garonne, Vaucluse, Yonne. Ibid.
[4] A.N. F 1c II 56. March 22nd, 1848.
[5] Ibid., March 27th, 1848.
[6] Ibid., March 21st, 1848.
[7] Contamine, *Metz et la Moselle* ... , i, 422.
[8] A.N. F 1c II 97.
[9] Ibid.

there is no doubt of their correctness. They were put equally strongly by the conservative but anti-clerical Odilon Barrot, who declared:

> Sous le prétexte de mettre l'élection plus à la portée des gens de la campagne et de leur épargner les déplacements, ils réclamaient le vote à la commune : leur motif réel, bien facile du reste à reconnaître, était de soumettre ce vote à l'influence plus directe du curé et du grand propriétaire, et de le soustraire aux influences politiques des villes.[1]

On this point Ledru-Rollin was adamant against concession.

'Le plus grand nombre de vos collègues,' he wrote in a circular to the *commissaires* on March 26th, despite the many petitions and opinions he had received to the contrary effect, 'a été d'avis ... que le décret de 5 mars ne doit pas être modifié, en ce sens que le vote, pour être indépendant, pour être dégagé, autant que possible, des influences locales, doit avoir lieu au Chef-lieu de canton.'[2]

Another much debated issue was the question of the postponement of the date of the elections from April 9th to 23rd. Pressure for delay had come in the first place from the more advanced revolutionaries of Paris. Ledru-Rollin's secretary, Delvau, later defended the policy of postponing the elections on the ground that: 'Retarder les élections, c'était enraciner davantage la République; c'était permettre à tous de la comprendre; c'était concourir à la fonder solidement par une Assemblée nationale entièrement composée de républicains.'[3] These views were also expressed in the second *Bulletin de la République*, which included an address drawn up by the *Club des clubs* demanding the postponement of the elections for at least a

---

[1] *Mémoires posthumes de Odilon Barrot*, 3rd ed. (1875), ii, 437.

[2] To facilitate the execution of this decision the voting was to be continued from April 23rd to 24th where necessary. The remoter communes voted first, and in some of the more mountainous areas grants were paid for the expense of the journey to the *chef-lieu*. In addition the larger cantons, with populations of over 20,000, were divided into sections, to meet and vote at separate bureaux. Circular of the Ministry of the Interior, March 30th, 1848.

[3] A. Delvau, *Histoire de la Révolution de Février* (1850), 402.

year to give the revolution time to consolidate itself.[1] Blanqui, at the head of the *Société républicaine centrale*, on April 6th presented the Provisional Government with a petition urging postponement;[2] and Cabet with the *Société fraternelle centrale* and other clubs joined in the movement,[3] which culminated in the demonstration by the clubs on March 17th.

Ledru-Rollin at first sympathized with this demand. In a circular of March 17th he asked the *commissaires* whether they were of opinion that their *départements* could be sufficiently *éclairés* by April 9th to choose 'une représentation sérieuse, dégagée des traditions corromptrices, propre à établir solidement la république'.[4] I have found replies from fourteen *commissaires*. Four are favourable to postponement, but two of these only on the grounds, possibly justified, of the difficulty of technical preparation for the elections by April 9th. The *commissaire* for the Tarn employs this argument, but admits that the departmental commission is opposed to his view by 3 to 2.[5] The *commissaire* for Ille-et-Vilaine doubts if preparations can be concluded in time. In many of the communes, he says, the administration can only be given to peasants hardly knowing how to write, and the communes are too poor to be able to pay a secretary; but he does not explain how this difficulty can be remedied by a few weeks' postponement of the elections.[6] From the Haute-Garonne comes the view that public opinion cannot be prepared for republican elections before May 15th.[7] The *commissaire* for the Côtes-du-Nord favours postponing the elections to April 20th.[8] On the other hand the *commissaires* for the Moselle,[9] Aisne, Charente, Meuse,[10] Basses-Pyrénées,

---

[1] Garnier-Pagès, *Histoire de la Révolution de 1848*, vol. iii, 333–5.
[2] *Le Moniteur Universel*, April 8th, 1848.
[3] Garnier-Pagès, *La Révolution de 1848*, vol. iii, no. 17, pp. 252–5.
[4] A.D. Côte d'Or. II M 52. Élections des 23 et 24 avril 1848.
[5] A.N. F 1ᶜ II 97.
[6] Ibid.
[7] Cayré, op. cit., 204.
[8] A.N. F 1ᶜ II 97.
[9] Contamine, op. cit., i, 419.
[10] A.N. F 1ᶜ II 56.

Eure-et-Loir, Gard, Loire-Inférieure, Loiret and Mayenne[1] all write in favour of early elections, on the ground that the initial enthusiasm for the Republic will weaken as time goes on under the attacks of the revived conservative parties and the strain of continued economic crisis. The population, says the *commissaire* for the Eure-et-Loir, is awaiting the elections impatiently, and the *commissaire* for the Basses-Pyrénées, 'Il est très urgent de sortir du provisoire.'

Garnier-Pagès says that all the replies, except three or four, signified that the longer the delay, the less favourable the results of the elections were likely to be;[2] and the Provisional Government, in its proclamation of March 26th, announced that the almost unanimous opinion of the *commissaires* had been that the elections should be delayed as little as possible.[3] It was presumably not uninfluenced by the great wave of protests against the adjournment of the elections which emerged from the conservative *Comité central républicain* in Paris and from many cities in the provinces. On grounds of similarity of the arguments and language used it has been argued that these were artificially provoked by the Paris committee,[4] but there seems no sound reason for doubting that opinion in the provinces was overwhelmingly against postponement. In two cartons at the *Archives Nationales* there are a petition from Rouen with 17,928 signatures, 75 lists of petitioners from Paris, 67 from Lille and a large bundle from Bordeaux; in addition there are 102 other petitions from all parts of France.[5] These petitions almost invariably appeal for an early election on the ground that uncertainty is prolonging and intensifying the financial and commercial crisis. Ledru-Rollin admitted that the replies of the *commissaires* had convinced him that he was mistaken in his earlier opinion,[6] and in fact the delay that was eventually

[1] A.N. F 1ᶜ II 97.
[2] Garnier-Pagès, op. cit., iv, 61–3.
[3] *Le Moniteur Universel*, March 27th, 1848.
[4] *La Révolution de 1848*, vol. iii, no. 17, pp. 255–61.
[5] A.N. BB³⁰ 322, 323.
[6] Calman, op. cit., 135.

agreed to was necessary for practical reasons, to ensure the efficient conduct of the elections.[1] It seems very probable that the *commissaires* were right and that the earlier the elections had been held the less the initial republican enthusiasm of February would have declined. It has truly been said of the Revolution of 1848 that it reached its culmination at its commencement.

For the left wing of the republicans in Paris, however, February was merely a starting point; they realized the strength of reaction, even if they failed to realize that it was growing and not declining. The nearer they came to a democratic consultation of the whole nation, the less they liked the prospect. Yet it could hardly be avoided. The dilemma of democracy was already becoming apparent. It was put plainly in a letter that a friend, appointed to a post in the Ministry of the Interior, wrote to Ledru-Rollin. Recourse to arms, he said, could be contemplated only in one case :

Je ne l'admets que si la chambre veut renverser la *forme républicaine*. C'est un droit que je ne lui reconnais pas ; le peuple lui-même tout entier n'a pas ce droit. Il ne peut pas plus ne pas être républicain, qu'on n'a le droit de renoncer à sa liberté individuelle.[2]

An ingenious proposal put forward by an obscure *Comité révolutionnaire pour les élections générales* would have helped to prevent such a renunciation, if it could have been generalized. This committee adopted, by acclamation and unanimously, 'le projet de faire voter toute la population parisienne, réunie sur un seul point, tel que le Champ de Mars, le même jour et le même temps. Il considère cette mesure comme devant couper court à toutes les volées réactionnaires et de nature à assurer la sincérité intégrale des élections.'[3] The ideas behind this suggestion are patent.

Up to this point I have been discussing what might be regarded as the preliminary steps necessary for securing good republican elections—the changes in administrative personnel,

---

[1] Garnier-Pagès, op. cit., iv, 63.   [3] A.N. F 1c II 56.
[2] Calman, op. cit., 422.

formation of electoral committees and choice of candidates, the efforts to propagate republican and democratic views by official action, the attempted use of the *instituteurs* to combat the influence of the clergy, the fixing of the electoral bureaux at the *chefs-lieux* and the postponement of the date of elections. But when it came to actually 'making' the elections, Ledru-Rollin and his *commissaires* showed themselves, as indeed they were, novices compared with the prefects of Louis-Philippe who preceded, or those of Louis Napoleon who were to succeed them. They were not able to prevent the nomination of a host of candidates whose lip-service to the Republic very thinly veiled their real opinions. They did their best to exclude known opponents: the *commissaire* for the Aisne wrote to Ledru-Rollin that he hoped to secure a good number of republicans among the fourteen representatives of the *département*, 'mais nous ne pouvons empêcher la nomination de Monsieur Barrot, que nous combattons cependant de toutes nos forces.'[1] The principles of 1848 themselves stood in the way of thoroughgoing electoral management. As the *commissaire* for the Moselle regretfully wrote to Ledru-Rollin: 'Le souvenir de l'influence directe et mauvaise de l'administration déchue sur le travail électoral ne permettrait pas de voir avec faveur l'immixion officielle des représentants du Gouvernement dans les discussions à l'ordre du jour.'[2] However, he added: 'J'assiste aux assemblées par mes amis.' Similarly the *commissaire* for Maine-et-Loire wrote: 'J'estime que le gouvernement n'a pas de *candidats ;* mais comme citoyen je conserve mon droit de conseil et d'action.'[3]

We should not, therefore, expect to find a great deal of evidence of direct administrative pressure in the elections of April 1848. What we do find falls fairly easily under a limited number of headings. In the first place, besides drawing up lists of recommended candidates, the *commissaires* distributed these in large quantities through their *départements*. They were intended to be used as voting bulletins, though the *commissaire* for the Loire-Inférieure thought that the permission to use printed or

[1] A.N. F 1c II 56.　　　[2] Ibid.　　　[3] A.N. F 1c II 97.

lithographed lists[1] played into the hands of the enemies of the Republic.[2] The Ducos commission criticized the *commissaires* of the Allier, Ariège, Bouches-du-Rhône, Loir-et-Cher, Morbihan, Nord, Pas-de-Calais, Saône-et-Loire, Seine-et-Oise and Vosges for their expenditure on printing lists of official candidates, placards, electoral *avis*, voting bulletins and so on, but in fact these must be merely those *commissaires* who made the mistake of specifying such expenses separately in their accounts, as political activities of this nature were undertaken by practically all. Indeed, one cannot but suspect that the members of the Ducos commission would not have looked with disfavour on such expenditure if it had been for the purpose of propagating political views of a different complexion. The *commissaire* for the Indre had spent 12,587 fr. 35 c. on printing political propaganda, but as it was all marked by 'un grand esprit d'impartialité et de modération', they could not bring themselves to censure him.[3] Even in circulating the official lists a nice regard for democratic proprieties was observed by at least one *commissaire*, who instructed the *maires* : 'Bien qu'émanant du pouvoir central, ces bulletins ne doivent être considérés que comme une indication dont chacun peut faire tel usage qu'il voudra.'[4] On the other hand the official lists of candidates were almost invariably sent by the *commissaires* to their colleagues in garrison towns to be communicated to the troops, thus enabling them to record their votes for the right candidates in whatever *département* they possessed their civil domicile.[5]

[1] This was authorized on April 4th for the election at Paris and confirmed generally in a circular of the Ministry of the Interior of April 6th. *Le Moniteur Universel*, April 8th, 1848.

[2] A.N. F 1c II 56. April 18th, 1848.

[3] Report of Ducos commission, *Le Moniteur Universel*, April 26th, 1849, pp. 1555–8.

[4] A.N. F 1c II 56. The *commissaire* for the Loir-et-Cher, April 20th, 1848.

[5] The decision to postpone the elections was only known in some localities after the garrisons there had already voted in virtue of the circular of March 8th. The *commissaires* who received packets of votes from these garrisons were instructed to return them unopened. By the final arrangements the army was to vote on April 15th and its votes were to be transmitted to the *commissaires* of the *départements* at latest on April 18th. *Dépêche télégraphique* from F. Arago, Ministre de la Guerre, March 27th, 1848. A.N. F 1c II 57.

There are some indications that the printing of lists on paper of a particular colour, to frustrate the secret of the ballot, was occasionally resorted to. In Puy-de-Dôme the *commissaire*'s list of candidates was sent out on yellow paper, and a local legitimist journal commented: 'Quant aux conséquences qu'entraînera pour les fonctionnaires le vote sur tout autre papier que le jaune, elles se devinent aisément.' The allegation was added that in some villages it had been proclaimed *au son du tambour* that any elector who did not put one of the *serins* of the *commissaire* as the yellow voting papers were called, into the electoral urn would be considered an enemy of the Republic.[1] Similarly at Saarguemines the lists of official candidates were printed on red paper.[2] The use of coloured voting paper, was, however, a manoeuvre that both sides could employ. In the Mayenne, the *commissaire* complained: 'Il paraît que les légitimistes font imprimer les noms de leurs candidats sur papier vert.'[3] The *commissaire* in the Calvados suggested that only white paper should be allowed,[4] and it seems that in the *départements* of the Nord and the Pas-de-Calais the *commissaire* did in fact rule that only white paper would be accepted in the voting bureau.[5] In such cases at least it was clear that the *commissaires* thought the electors less likely to be afraid of the administration than of reactionary influences.

When we come to more direct interference with the freedom of the ballot it is surprising how few cases there are to relate. A later Minister of the Interior, the very conservative Léon Faucher, in a circular of April 23rd, 1849, declared that the freedom of suffrage was restricted in many areas in 1848:

Ici, le bureau était entouré par des individus qui repoussaient avec violence les électeurs qu'ils considéraient

---

[1] *La Révolution de 1848*, vol. xxiv, no. 122, p. 172. This allegation got into the Paris journals. It is repeated almost verbatim in *L'Ami de la Religion*, April 26th, 1848, vol. 137, p. 263.

[2] Contamine, op. cit., i, 423.

[3] A.N. F 1c II 56. April 16th, 1848.

[4] A.N. F 1c II 57. April 4th, 1848.

[5] A.D. Nord. M 271. Arrêté of April 21st, 1848.

comme contraires à l'opinion qu'ils désiraient voir triompher; ailleurs, le secret du vote était audacieusement violé, et trop souvent on a eu à reprocher aux fonctionnaires municipaux comme aux présidents des bureaux une blâmable inertie, si ce n'est même une coupable connivance.[1]

This may be true, but the assertion of Léon Faucher is not proof. The *préfet* of the Puy-de-Dôme wrote to his *sous-préfets*, and therefore presumably to men who knew the facts and without any intention of propaganda, in December 1848:

Vous vous rappelez que des faits regrettables signalèrent dans certaines localités les élections générales d'avril dernier et présentèrent un contraste affligeant avec le caractère imposant et calme qu'elles eurent sur presque tous les points de la France. En quelques lieux, on ne craignait pas d'abuser de l'ignorance et de la crédulité par des substitutions de bulletins; en d'autres endroits, des votes furent arrachés avec violence et une minorité égarée osa profaner l'urne électorale.[2]

This is by implication a testimonial to the general conduct of the elections, and in any case it does not say in whose interests the electoral misdeeds in the Puy-de-Dôme were perpetrated. Occasional local disturbance, such as the rioting reported at Villefranche and Villeneuve in Aveyron during the elections, does not indicate administrative pressure on the voters.[3] I have personally found no more than six complaints of deliberate interference with, or falsification of the voting, and in only one of these is it the suggestion that such action was in favour of the administration. This was a complaint that in one district of Toulouse the officials demanded to see the electors' bulletins, and when they did not approve of their choice tore them up and

[1] A.N. F 1c II 58.
[2] *La Révolution de 1848*, vol. xxiv, no. 1222, p. 182.
[3] A.N. BB30 323. *Commissaire* of the Aveyron, April 27th, 1848.

substituted others.[1] Even this, however, is only an allegation in a journal. A report on the conduct of the elections in Paris found that there had been some incompetence, and that the twelfth *arrondissement* had suffered from disorder, but only in one *arrondissement*, the seventh, accused the presiding officers of an attempt to interfere with the freedom of elections; and this evidently cannot be put down to the credit, or discredit, of the agents of Ledru-Rollin, for it consisted in the distribution on the stairways of the *mairie*, and on the second day in the electoral bureau itself, of voting lists from which the names of four members of the Provisional Government, Ledru-Rollin, Louis Blanc, Albert and Flocon, were excluded.[2] Again, the *maire* of Libourne in the Gironde was accused of using violence, intimidation, perfidious insinuations and calumny to secure the triumph of the party of reaction.[3] At La Flèche in the Sarthe it was alleged that reactionary officials took their voting bulletins away from the electors, saying: 'On vous trompe, vos bulletins ne valent rien, en voilà d'autres, ceux-là seuls sont bons.'[4] A petition against the election at Castel-Sarrasin, in Tarn-et-Garonne, alleged that it was conducted in a private house defended by armed supporters of one of the candidates, and that the electors were only allowed to vote for two candidates, the brother of one of whom controlled the bureau and inspected the votes. The voting was prematurely closed on the first day, electors from the rural communes being turned away, which provoked an affray in the course of which several voters were killed by the men defending the bureau.[5] This election was annulled by the *commissaire*, an action which evoked a protest from the president of the electoral bureau, who sent, along with a petition signed by some 200 electors, a copy of the *procès verbal* of the bureau, establishing rather disingenuously that in spite of certain

[1] *L'Ami de la Religion*, April 29th, vol. 137, p. 298.
[2] A.N. F 1ᶜ II 57. Le commissaire du gouvernement près les mairies de Paris et du département (Charles Rouvenat) au Ministre de l'Intérieur, April 28th, 1848.
[3] A.N. F 1ᶜ II 56. Protest from the editor of the *Journal du Peuple*, May 9th, 1848.
[4] A.N. F 1ᶜ II 56.
[5] Ibid.

undefined disorders in the 'rue', the bureau never ceased to function regularly.[1]

It is difficult to know how much credence to attach to allegations of interference with the freedom of voting, either by the supporters of the Provisional Government or its enemies; but it seems reasonable to suppose, given the strength of political feeling, that if it had been at all extensive we should find far more specific evidence of it, either in the press or in the form of petitions against the results, as distinct from vague complaints of undue influence, which each side naturally accused the other of exerting. All general statements in this matter by contemporaries are in the nature of things unreliable, the *commissaires'* denials of pressure as well as their opponents' accusations. There is little reason to attach weight to the claim of the *commissaire* for Saône-et-Loire, who boasted, in a telegraphic dispatch to the Ministry of the Interior : 'C'est moi qui ai fait les élections, et vous savez comme elles ont été bonnes.'[2] On the other hand it is not difficult to believe Émile Ollivier, who wrote to the Minister of the Interior : 'Nous pouvons nous féliciter bien vivement d'avoir empêché l'élection de Thiers et de Reybaud. Nous avons eu une peine infinite à y arriver.'[3]

Of corruption in the cruder sense of the word there is no evidence at all in the elections of April 1848, and no reason to suspect that there was any. The commission presided over by Ducos, which inquired into the expenditure of the secret funds of the Ministry of the Interior, could find no grounds for criticizing the administration of Ledru-Rollin in this respect. The only case of a money payment it found was that of a *maire* who was paid 300 francs by the *commissaire* for Saône-et-Loire, 'dans le but de le décider à renoncer à sa candidature de représentant du peuple'.[4] This expenditure was disallowed by

---

[1] A.N. F 1ᶜ II 57. Letter from the president of the electoral bureau of Castel-Sarrasin to Lamartine, May 1st, 1848.

[2] A.N. F 1ᵃ 19.

[3] A.N. F 1ᶜ III Bouches-du-Rhône. April 29th, 1848.

[4] *Le Moniteur Universel*, April 26th, 1849, p. 1556.

Ledru-Rollin, and it suggests a certain naivety on the part of the *commissaire* that it was ever put on record.

The ultimate criterion of the success of efforts at electoral pressure is the result of an election. In one respect this first exercise of universal suffrage was a triumph. In an electorate which had been expanded overnight from a quarter of a million to nine millions, 84 per cent voted. The elected candidates, apart from national figures, were nearly all men of the locality and mostly persons of standing in their communities.[1] In spite of the eloquent invocations of democracy and equality with which the Republic had been launched, the Assembly was overwhelmingly what Marat had called, many years before, *une aristocratie d'argent*. Lawyers, landowners, officers or retired officers, doctors, men of letters—such were its members.[2] The composition of the electoral lists is too heterogeneous to enable any very specific deductions about the political complexion of the new Assembly to be drawn from this source. Some indication of the results of the elections may be given, however. Of about 900 candidates elected, 350 were committed to the cause of the *liberté d'enseignement*[3] and therefore may be regarded as supporters of the clerical party, though only some sixteen ecclesiastics obtained seats. On the other hand, Félix Pyat's amendment to the constitution calling for the recognition of the *droit de travail* received a mere 82 votes, while only 110 voted against the *amendement Goudchaux* and in support of the principle of progressive taxation.[4] Seignobos summarizes the composition of the Assembly as roughly 100 legitimists, 200 former Orleanists, 500 rather undefined moderate republicans and 100 democratic and social republicans.[5]

[1] It has been estimated that some 676 out of about 900 were *hommes de terroir*, and most of the remainder, apart from the few national figures, had connections with the localities for which they were elected. *La Révolution de 1848*, vol. vii, no. 41, p. 292.

[2] Cf. Seignobos, *La Révolution de 1848–le Second Empire, 1848–1859* (1921), Lavisse, *Histoire de France contemporaine*, vi, 84.

[3] E. Lecanuet, *Montalembert* (1895–1902), ii, 396.

[4] *Biographie parlementaire des représentants du peuple à l'assemblée nationale constituante de 1848*, ed. M. Alhoy, s. d., 465–510.

[5] Seignobos, op. cit., 81.

If these results show anything it is that the efforts of the *commissaires* of Ledru-Rollin to 'make' the elections had been notably unsuccessful. This was perhaps only to have been expected. They lacked the experience of the prefects of Louis-Philippe, were opposed by the influential classes —landowners, employers, former officials, clergy—in their *départements*, and to some extent were hampered by their own democratic ideology. Their efforts to 'educate' the people in democratic republican ideas betrayed a naive idealism with little relation to political realities. As regards actual political pressure on the electorate, their efforts were for the most part negative — taking the form of attempts to check hostile influences by changing local officials and removing the elections from the communes to the *chefs-lieux* —rather than positive. Though it is not to be attributed necessarily to the purity of the intentions of Ledru-Rollin and his *commissaires*, the election of April 1848 was possibly freer from the political pressure of the administration than any other election in nineteenth-century France. Indeed, the fact that Ledru-Rollin may be said to have lost the election speaks for itself. Ministers of the Interior did not normally lose elections. It was a lesson that his successors took to heart, though it was to require one more demonstration, in December 1848. After this second proof that it was not safe for a government to rely on the force of reason, or at least propaganda, and refrain from the more material forms of administrative pressure, the history of the Second Republic becomes one of a steady return to the *candidature officielle*. But this was a process which will need to be examined separately.

4

THE INFLUENCE OF THE CLERGY AND THE 'INSTITUTEURS PRIMAIRES' IN THE ELECTION OF THE FRENCH CONSTITUENT ASSEMBLY, APRIL 1848*

THE struggle for the control of primary education is one of the major factors in modern French history. It constitutes an important element in that rivalry between Church and State which has played such an important part in French politics since 1789. The year 1848 witnessed one of the most critical phases in this struggle, although at first the revolution which broke out in February seemed likely to reverse the previous trend of events. During the reign of Louis-Philippe, for more than one reason, relations between the Church and the monarchy had been strained, and in 1848 clericals joined with republicans in welcoming the flight of the king. Moreover, the first half of the nineteenth century had been marked by a revival of religious feeling which even left-wing opinion, under the influence of writers such as Fourier and Saint-Simon, had shared. Hostility towards the Church was conspicuously absent at the opening of the revolution, and there was a favourable attitude to religion which found its most characteristic expression in the rather vague religiosity of Lamartine.

Even more surprising than the religious sympathies of some of the republicans was the revolutionary enthusiasm of many of the clergy. The chief clerical paper, *l'Univers*, came out, as early as February 27th, with an article entitled, 'Qui songe aujourd'hui en France à défendre la Monarchie?' The archbishop of Paris, Mgr Affre, paid an official visit to Dupont de

*This paper appeared in the *English Historical Review*, July 1942.

l'Eure, the head of the provisional government. Scenes of fraternization between revolutionaries and clergy were witnessed. Clerical symbols were respected and protected by the mob. Trees of liberty, planted all over France, were blessed by the priests. *L'Ère Nouvelle* was founded, with the collaboration of Lacordaire, to promote the idea of an avowed alliance between the Church and democracy.

Encouraged by such signs, Hippolyte Carnot, the Saint-Simonian Minister for Religion and Public Education, issued a circular to the bishops calling on the clergy to take their place in the political life of the country and exercise their functions as citizens in the electoral assemblies. After this, commented *l'Ami de la Religion*, no one will be surprised to see the priest taking part in political activities, or even sitting in the National Assembly.[1]

One section of the Church was already organized for political action. In the course of the struggle for what was called *la liberté d'enseignement*, an electoral committee for religious liberty had been formed in 1846. Its chief promoter, Montalembert, set it to work in the early days of the revolution. The committee met in Paris on February 28th, and on March 10th issued a private letter to the bishops calling on them 'se concerter, sans peur et sans bruit ... d'une part avec les curés de canton, et de l'autre avec les amis de la liberté religieuse ... à l'effet de reconnaître et de désigner les hommes les plus dignes, au point de vue sociale et catholique, des suffrages des honnêtes gens'.[2] The operations of this committee, and the political manoeuvres of such prominent figures as Montalembert and de Falloux, are familiar, and we do not propose to re-tell the history of the elections to the National Assembly from this angle. The reactions to their activities in the *départements* are less well known, however; in fact the history of the electoral campaign in the provinces has received little attention from historians, though it may reasonably be claimed that it was in

[1] *L'Ami de la Religion*, March 14th, 1848, vol. 136, pp. 618–19.
[2] E. Lecanuet, *Vie de Montalembert* (1895–1901), ii, 389.

the provinces that the election of April 1848, and indeed the whole fate of the Second Republic, was settled.[1]

Montalembert and the committee for religious liberty did not greet the revolution with the cordiality that some sections of the Church manifested, but their first steps were merely precautionary. The Church soon had real cause for alarm, however. At Lyons unauthorized but previously tolerated congregations were dissolved by the *commissaire*, whose actions were upheld by Carnot. The revolution had been the signal for a flood of extreme socialist propaganda, which inevitably aroused clerical hostility. A proposal to set up *écoles maternelles* was regarded as an attempt to extend the sphere of lay control of education to include even 'des enfants à la mamelle'.[2] A suggestion of the legalization of divorce evoked the comment, 'C'est la foi religieuse de la presque universalité des français que l'on outrage.'[3]

Under the stimulus of such provocations the clergy became all the more determined to make their influence felt in the elections. Thus a letter to a newspaper at Nancy declared, 'Sur divers partis des Vosges MM. les curés transforment leurs églises en espèces de *clubs* pour user de leur influence sur les électeurs.'[4] This is confirmed by the correspondence of a curé of the same département, named Deblaye, who was very active in organizing the clerical vote there. 'Quel est le prêtre dans une paroisse', writes one correspondent to him, 'qui ne puisse disposer de 10 ou 20 votes? Il en est qui peuvent en avoir des centaines ... J'apprends à l'instant que des comités secrètes sont organisés dans tout le diocèse par Mgr. ou pour mieux dire sur l'invitation de Mgr.'[5]

The bishops generally put themselves at the head of the electoral movement of the Church, and drew up lists of

[1] Very little of real interest concerning the elections of 1848 appears to have survived in the national archives. Cf. pp. 29 et seq.

[2] *L'Ami de la Religion*, April 30th, 1848, vol. 137, p. 307.

[3] Ibid., May 28th, 1848, vol. 137, p. 589.

[4] *Courrier de Nancy*, April 6th, 1848.

[5] *Archives Départementales, Vosges*, dossier entitled *Élections de la Constituante, du Président et de la Législature*; letter dated March 20th, 1848.

candidates to be sent to the clergy of their dioceses with instructions to recommend these candidates to their parishioners.

To take one example, a circular letter was issued to the clergy of the Vosges in the following terms: 'Je suis chargé *ex alto* de vous prier, vous et vos amis, de venir voter le jour de Pâques, sans compter sur le lundi. Voici une liste que je suis chargé de vous communiquer ... Veuillez, mon cher curé, faire ce que vous m'avez promis.'[1] The parish clergy, it is important to remember, were now in a much more dependent position than they had held in 1789, when, although poor, a large proportion of them had been *vicaires perpétuels* with a reasonable security of tenure. By 1848 nine-tenths of the churches were served by *desservants*, nominated and revoked at will by their bishop. A proposal in the *Comité des Cultes* to assimilate the *desservants* after five years' service to curés, who could only be removed for specified offences and after a fairly complicated process, was rejected by the strong opposition of the bishops. Thus the lower clergy had more than one reason for following the political lead given by their ecclesiastical superiors, and exercising in the direction indicated to them from above their considerable influence over the peasantry, who constituted the vast majority of the electorate of France.

The clergy in many cases read out lists of recommended candidates from the pulpit. They wrote out electoral bulletins for their parishioners.[2] As the election was held on an Easter Sunday—not, the clergy suggested, without some hope of keeping them away from the polls[3]—the clergy were allowed to say

---

[1] *Archives Départementales, Vosges*, loc. cit., letter of April 14th, 1848.

[2] A letter of denunciation to the commissaire of the Doubs alleges, 'Une grande partie des bulletins contenant le nom de Montalembert étaient écrits sur du papier à lettre, et d'une main plus habile que celle du paysan; ces bulletins, pour plus de certitude, étaient en grande partie cachetés.' It adds, however, 'Un grand nombre de citoyens paysans ont brisé les scellés, et substitué des noms plus ou moins démocrates' (*Archives Départementales, Doubs*, 16 M. 47).

[3] *L'Ami de la Religion* protested, 'Est-ce inadvertence? Est-ce calcul? ... On aurait donc espéré empêcher les hommes religieux et le clergé d'aller aux élections, en les mettant dans la douloureuse alternative ou de manquer aux saints devoirs de leur conscience ou de renoncer à leurs devoirs de citoyen?' (March 28th, 1848, vol. 136, p. 738).

Mass at an early hour in the morning. Subsequently the electors of many of the villages marched to the electoral assembly with the local priest at the head of the procession, where his rivalry with the *maire* sometimes produced an undignified conflict, in which the spiritual power did not always prove the weaker.[1] Ample testimony to the effectiveness in many parts of France of clerical influence in the elections exists, which it would be superfluous to cite. A letter to the *commissaire* of the Doubs sums up the bitter disappointment of the left wing at the result of the elections: 'Dans les campagnes, l'élection primaire, que nous avons tant désirée, n'est qu'un mensonge; les curés ont fait voter leurs paroissiens comme un seul homme.'[2]

The clergy were aware of the hostility their activities might arouse. Montalembert himself had advised caution, and at least one of the bishops was even more circumspect. The bishop of Viviers (later Cardinal Guibert), alarmed by the excessive zeal of his clergy, wrote that he had had to check their somewhat compromising enthusiasm by 'deux petites circulaires manuscrites'. The nomination of the nine deputies for the department, he believed, was in his hands if he wished; but, wiser than some of his colleagues, he resolved to abstain from exercising his influence unduly, for fear of the reaction it might provoke against the Church. In opposition to Montalembert, he said, 'Je suis convaincu que nous faisons une chose imprudente, et que les quelques voix que nous pouvons envoyer à la Chambre favorables à la liberté religeuse ne nous vaudront pas la belle position que nous avons prise dans notre isolement des choses politiques depuis 1830. M. Carnot nous a tendu un piège

---

[1] This rivalry is well brought out in a circular notice issued by the *commissaire* for the Côtes-du-Nord to the *maires* of the *département*: 'Par sa circulaire en date du 20 mars, M. l'évêque de Saint-Brieux prescrit à son clergé et aux fidèles des paroisses de marcher ensemble jusqu'à l'assemblée électorale ... Ne permettez donc, citoyens maires et adjoints, qu'aucune usurpation soit faite de votre autorité politique régulière; ceints de l'écharpe municipale, soyez à la tête de vos communes, et dans cette marche importante du peuple vers l'urne d'où doivent sortir les destinées de la patrie, déployez tout l'appareil que commande un acte aussi solennel' (*L'Ami de la Religion*, April 26th, 1848, vol. 137, pp. 255–6).

[2] *Archives Départementales, Doubs*, 16 M. 47.

dans lequel nous avons donné tête baissée, lorsqu'il nous a invités à user de nos droits.'[1]

Others among the clergy realized at least the need for secrecy. A letter to Deblaye says, 'Il fallait agir sans rien dire à ces gens-là [the government *commissaires*]. Maintenant encore évitez le bruit autant que possible. Ne dites point que vous organisez un comité ... '[2] Another advises that the names should not be put in the same order on the bulletins of all the electors.[3] There was considerable doubt about the wisdom of returning priests to the Assembly. 'Des prêtres à l'Assemblée Nationale, oui, mais pas beaucoup; nous sommes le sel de la terre, et tu sais qu'il n'en faut trop sur la soupe pour qu'elle soit mangeable.'[4]

Some of the alarms of the clergy were certainly justified. Their letters were opened in the post,[5] and the local authorities sometimes took energetic steps to check their political activities. Thus we find a *maire* writing to a curé, 'Demain à 7 heures du matin vous aurez la complaisance de nous attendre chez vous pour contester les raisons lancées à votre égard, et si vous dédaignez nous attendre il sera de suite procédé à l'enlèvement de vos meubles. Vous vous êtes trop exhaltés dans le temps, maintenant on se rappelle de vos antécédents et la liberté veut profiter de ce moment.'[6] Again, the *commissaire* for the Vosges warned a curé, 'Nous apprenons que vous vous êtes permis de prononcer en chair des paroles insultantes contre les membres du Gouvernement provisoire ... Vous ne serez pas surpris si, en vertu de nos pouvoirs illimités, nous prenons à votre égard des mesures de rigueur; en attendant, nous avons cru devoir

---

[1] J. Pagnelle de Follenay, *Cardinal Guibert* (1896), ii, 107.
[2] *Archives Départementales, Vosges,* dossier entitled *Élections de la Constituante, du Président et de la Législature.*
[3] Ibid.
[4] Ibid.
[5] One correspondent of Deblaye writes, 'P.S. N'écrivez plus ces lettres un peu suspectes, vous me comprenez, sous enveloppe; c'est trop aisé; on peut les lire à la poste, changer d'enveloppe et tout est dit' (ibid.). Another alleges, 'On dit que dans les bureaux on ouvre beaucoup de lettres, surtout celles qui sont adressées à des prêtres' (ibid.).
[6] Ibid.

retenir le mandat de la somme qui vous était due pour traite-ment du trimestre dernier.'[1] The *maire* of a village in the Puy-de-Dôme led a band of rioters against the *desservant*, locked up the church door, and barred it with ropes cut from the belfry.[2] Even in the Vosges Deblaye had to confess, 'On ne veut pas de clergé dans les élections', and he describes the opposition to the clergy as 'cette effroyable tempête'.[3]

At the same time it must be remembered that the Church was not incapable of defending itself. When one municipality dismissed various Church employees and seized a part of the curé's garden, the bishop of Viviers immediately withdrew the two priests from the parish. The deprivation of religious services had such an effect on the people that the leader of the attack, the *maire*, who was one of the richest landowners of the district, was obliged to let his properties and retire to Lyons.[4] Such an example does not stand alone.

In the towns there were plenty of bourgeois republicans whose activities counteracted those of the clergy, while the workers were largely under the influence of socialist propa-gandists. But in the rural areas the clergy, supported generally by the local gentry, dominated the political arena, and it soon became evident that the sentimental republicanism of the first weeks of the revolution did not represent the real political tendencies of the Church. Some counterbalance on the side of the republic was needed in the countryside. Now the only possible rival influence to which the republicans could turn was that of the village schoolmasters, the *instituteurs primaires*, who for this reason now for the first time enter the political struggle as an active factor. A republican journalist of the Charente had put this view of the situation already in 1845, when he declared, 'Au fond de nos campagnes, que les démocrates le comprennent

---

[1] *Archives Départementales, Vosges*, dossier entitled *Élections de la Constituante, du Président et de la Législature*.

[2] 'La Révolution de 1848', *Bulletin de la Société d'historie de la Révolution de 1848*, vol. 24, no. 118, pp. 961–2.

[3] *Archives Départementales, Vosges*, loc. cit.

[4] Pagnelle de Follenay, *Cardinal Guibert*, ii, 109.

bien, l'instituteur primaire est le représentant vivant de la Révolution.'[1] The teachers in the primary schools of the state had full cause for dissatisfaction with their lot. Their condition was generally wretched; they were paid a mere pittance and usually had to make up a living wage by acting as secretary to the *maire*, assistant to the curé, bell-ringer, and so on. As the humblest member of the bureaucracy of the university, the *instituteur* shared the hostility of the clergy, yet his position was largely dependent on the goodwill of the curé. The *Écho des Instituteurs* puts his situation in the words of an old teacher to a young one: 'Tout instituteur qui est mal avec son curé ne réussit pas dans sa profession et fait toujours une mauvaise fin.'[2] The rivalry of clerical and lay schools was acute already before 1848, and Guizot had been sufficiently alarmed by it to issue warnings against their growing antagonism. The possibility of turning this hostility to political ends was indicated two years before the revolution by a paper published in the interests of the teachers. 'Nous croyons', it wrote, 'à la générosité des sentiments du ministre actuel de l'instruction publique; mais c'est moins à cette générosité, qu'à la nécessité politique, qu'à la raison d'état, le mot n'est pas trop fort, qu'il cède en voulant relever la position des instituteurs. Quel autre moyen le gouvernment possède-t-il de résister à l'hostilité persévérante et indomptable du clergé, si ce n'est de mettre les instituteurs à même de conquérir, à son profit, une influence prépondérante sur l'esprit des populations?'[3]

February 1848 seemed to open a new age for the poor *instituteur*. *L'Émancipation de l'Enseignement Primaire* declared grandiloquently, 'Instituteurs, vos fonctions sont un sacerdoce. Vous êtes appelés à former cette génération future qui tiendra dans ses mains les destinées de la France et, peut-être, celles de

---

[1] G. Weill, *Histoire du parti républicain en France de 1814 à 1870* (1900), 293.
[2] *L'Écho des Instituteurs*, série ii, no. 12, June 11th, 1848, p. 853.
[3] *L'Écho des Instituteurs*, no. 22, October 1846, p. 340.

l'Europe.'[1] The *instituteurs* themselves were conscious of their new political importance, as is shown by innumerable letters in the departmental archives, expressing in exalted terms their republican enthusiasm. This was one of the forces on which Hippolyte Carnot confidently relied. In his apology he writes, 'Rallier autour du drapeau républicain la nombreuse armée des instituteurs primaires était un devoir facile à accomplir.'[2] Addressing himself to the rectors of the universities on February 27th, he said that the condition of the elementary teachers was a principal object of his consideration; and in a much criticized circular of March 6th he called on them to present themselves for the suffrages of their fellow-citizens.[3]

To assist the teachers to fulfil their new role in society, Carnot organized courses of lectures on civic duties, and appealed for the compilation of *manuels civiques*. Among the many *manuels* that were offered to the government, three were officially adopted, those by Ducaux, Henri Martin and Renouvier. The first two were eminently moderate publications which aroused little or no criticism; but that of Renouvier became the centre of a controversy which in the end brought about the resignation of Carnot. Most of the little book seems unexceptionable, even for 1848, but a question such as the following was certainly a little tactless: 'L'Élève: Existe-t-il au moins des moyens

---

[1] *L'Émancipation de l'Enseignement Primaire*, no. 1, May 6th, 1848. Similarly, a manifesto issued in the early days of the Revolution proclaimed, 'L'heure est venue, où la position de ces hommes modestes qui rendent de si éminents services à la patrie va changer de face, l'heure est venue où l'enseignment sera gratuit et uniforme pour toutes les classes de la Société. Oui, l'heure est arrivée où le Gouvernement accordera aux instituteurs un traitement fixe, proportionné à leurs nombreux et importants services' (*La Voix des Instituteurs*). Only the prospectus of this journal exists in the *Bibliothèque Nationale* (l.c.[5] 63). Probably no more ever appeared. A proclamation issued in the Bouches-du-Rhône urged the teachers to exercise their influence boldly: 'Instituteurs des campagnes ou des petites villes, votre influence sur les parents des enfants dont l'éducation vous est confiée est bien grande; vous n'avez à vouloir pour les réunir tous; mettez-vous à leur tête; assemblez-les tous les soirs; instruisez-les' (*Murailles révolutionnaires*, 17th ed. s.d., ii, 161-2). These are given by way of example; many similar appeals are to be found.

[2] H. Carnot, *Le Ministère de l'instruction publique et des cultes depuis le 6 février jusqu'au 5 juillet 1848* (1848), 15.

[3] Ibid., 24.

d'empêcher les riches d'être oisifs et les pauvres d'être mangés par les riches?"[1]

The organization of the *instituteurs* for their new political responsibilities was undertaken by the universities. At Dijon, for example, the professor of mathematics formed committees of teachers to organize their political activities in the Côte d'Or.[2] The rector of the academy of Nancy issued a circular couched in peremptory terms. 'Je vous invite', he wrote, 'au nom du citoyen Lorentz, commissaire provisoire du Gouvernement pour le département de la Meurthe, à vous rendre lundi prochain, à trois heures précises, chez votre collègue, l'instituteur Denis, à Nancy, où vous recevrez de la préfecture des instructions auxquelles vous aurez à vous conformer exactement.'[3] In the Moselle the *commissaire* called together the presidents of the cantonal conferences of teachers, reminded them of their duty to support the government, and granted them one day's leave to co-ordinate their political action. At Saareguemines a conference of teachers was held to counteract 'the intrigues of the priests'.[4] In the Aveyron the *commissaire* sent a circular to the teachers exhorting them to take the public welfare as their sole guide in the elections, and concluding, 'Je vous enverrai dix noms choisis par moi, de concert avec le comité électoral de Rodez, adoptez-les avec confiance, ils seront comme moi vos amis.' The clerical journal which gave publicity to this circular added that the list of ten names was naturally headed by that of the *commissaire* himself.[5]

The recommending of lists of candidates to the *instituteurs* was a common practice. The *commissaire* for the Meurthe wrote to all the *instituteurs* of his department, 'La liste que nous vous

[1] C. Renouvier, *Manuel républicain de l'homme et du citoyen* (1848), 2nd ed., 21.

[2] In one letter he writes, 'J'ai institué à Gevrey un comité particulier des instituteurs ... Ces braves pères de famille comprennent parfaitement bien que leur sacerdoce doit commencer avec la République et que la tyrannie des consciences est abattue pour jamais' (March 23rd, 1848, *Archives Départementales, Côte d'Or*, iii, M. 52).

[3] *L'Écho des Instituteurs*, série ii, no. 8, May 14th, 1848, p. 770.

[4] H. Contamine, *Metz et la Moselle de 1814 à 1870* (1932), i, 421.

[5] *L'Ami de la Religion*, April 9th, 1848, vol. 137, pp. 95-6.

adressons et que nous vous invitons à appuyer est composée d'hommes de cette trempe [i.e. energetic republicans]. Parlez donc aux habitants des campagnes en leur faveur, et écartez *toute* liste dont *tous* les noms ne seraient pas ceux-là.'[1] At Rouen the *instituteurs* were assembled in the *mairie* and made to give a written promise to vote for the candidates of the Central Democratic Club.[2] A correspondent of *l'Écho des Instituteurs* says that in a department bordering on the Meurthe a circular signed by the *commissaire* 'menace de *mesures de rigueur* les instituteurs qui ne voteraient pour les *candidats démocrates*, c'est-à-dire pour une certaine liste sur laquelle figuraient les noms de ces mêmes commissaires.'[3] Such threats are by no means rare. In the Dordogne we find a *sous-commissaire* reporting, 'Après avoir vu les instituteurs, je m'empresserai de vous signaler ceux qu'il sera utile et possible de remplacer sans inconvénient par des jeunes gens de l'école normale qui recevraient le mot d'ordre et consacreraient leur capacité, leur dévouement et leur énergie au triomphe de notre cause.'[4] The *commissaire* for the Vosges issued a warning that he had heard that several teachers were working in support of candidates recommended to them by the priests and against the democratic candidates. Such conduct, he said, would compel him to take vigorous measures against those guilty of it.[5]

The need for such pressure suggests that in fact the authorities had been somewhat too optimistic in counting on the republican enthusiasm of the teachers of the country districts. Those with democratic sympathies were undoubtedly in the majority, but examples of the influence of the *instituteurs* being exercised in an opposite direction can easily be found. For instance, at Châlons-sur-Marne they drew up so conservative a list of candidates that the *commissaire* summoned them to the prefecture for a repri-

---

[1] *L'Écho des Instituteurs*, May 14th, 1848, série ii, no. 8, p. 770.
[2] V. Pierre, *Histoire de la république de 1848* (1873), 252.
[3] *L'Écho des Instituteurs*, May 14th, 1848, série ii, no. 8.
[4] G. Rocal, *1848 en Dordogne* (1934), i, 73.
[5] *Archives Départementales, Vosges*, dossier entitled *Élections de la Constituante, du Président et de la Législature*.

mand.[1] In the Puy-de-Dôme an *instituteur* was expelled from his post because of his alliance with the curé.[2] No general statement would hold true of all the country, for the political reports of the *procureurs-généraux* show that the attitude of the *instituteurs* varied greatly from region to region.[3] We also find that there was a widespread reluctance on the part of the teachers to engage in politics.[4] They feared the hostility their intervention might arouse, and with reason. The thought that the teachers might be aspiring to improve their humble social position was not the least among the motives of the resentment which their activities caused, and which seems to have been on the whole more bitter even than that produced by the political action of the clergy.

The local authorities, where they were not republican in sympathy, joined with the clergy in the task of intimidating the lay teachers. *L'Écho des Instituteurs* summarizes some of the methods by which pressure was put upon them. 'On menace de réduire les traitements qui sont susceptible d'être réduits; on retire les élèves; un instituteur a été consigné dans sa maison, un fonctionnaire à sa poste, pendant les élections. Peu d'instituteurs ont osé lutter jusqu'à fin, et ceux-là ne sont pas sûrs d'échapper à la destitution.'[5]

[1] L. Charpentier, *L'instruction primaire et notamment l'enseignement mutuel à Rheims de 1831 à 1868* (1869), 159

[2] *La Révolution de 1848*, vol. 24, no. 118, p. 962.

[3] Ibid., vol. 4, no. 23, p. 310 (article by Ch. Seignobos).

[4] Thus, a democratic teacher, writing to the rector at Dijon, explains the passivity of his colleagues by the fact that 'les timides instituteurs' were under the influence of the local *percepteur* of taxes (*Archives Départementales, Côte d'Or*, M. 6. 51B). Another, from the same *département*, himself opposes the project of nominating a teacher as a candidate at the elections. 'Si l'instituteur, qui a toujours été un homme modeste, vise à la députation, il n'y aura pas de raison pour que tous les citoyens français n'aspirent, quelle que soit leur position sociale, à tous les emplois du Gouvernement.' (Ibid.)

[5] *L'Écho des Instituteurs*, série ii, no. 6, April 30th, 1848, p. 740. The feelings of many of the local officials are probably adequately expressed in a letter from the *maire* of a commune in the Côte d'Or to the *commissaire*: 'Il m'a été rapporté que le nommé Valanchez, instituteur communale de Chassagne, était allé vous faire une visite la semaine dernière, j'ignore pourquoi, mais tout ce que je peux dire, il ferait beaucoup mieux de suivre un peu mieux sa classe, et ne pas se déranger aussi souvent qu'il le fait' (*Archives Départementales, Côte d'Or*, M. 6. 51B).

It was particularly after the elections that the *instituteurs* had to pay the penalty for their temerity in venturing on the political stage. A director of an *école normale* says of this period, 'Les instituteurs primaires devaient expier cruellement, quelques mois plus tard, le crime d'avoir ajouté foi à ces recommendations du ministre de 48! On les incitait à faire de la politique, et quelques-uns en ont fait; et c'est sur eux tous que sont retombés les colères.'[1] On April 30th *l'Écho des Instituteurs* wrote, 'D'après les nouvelles qui nous parviennent des départements, il paraît que partout les instituteurs ont à se repentir d'avoir suivi les instructions de M. Carnot, relativement à la conduite qu'ils avaient à tenir dans les élections. Nous ne doutons pas que M. le ministre de l'instruction publique ne les défende énergiquement contre les persécutions dont ils sont menacés ou qui les atteignent déjà.'[2] Its hope was in vain, for a month later it had to quote from a letter it had received, 'Vous ne savez pas, cher concitoyen, quelle oppression nous souffrons aujourd'hui. Les tracasseries jésuitiques de la restauration et de juillet ne sont rien en comparaison des persécutions que nous avons à subir.'[3]

The election campaign had indeed ended in a decisive victory for the moderate parties. The extreme left won few seats outside the large centres of population. And in the struggle the spirit of union with which the revolution opened had vanished. The honeymoon between the Church and the Republic barely lasted beyond the first few weeks. As the fear of social revolution grew to be the dominant factor in the minds of the clergy and their supporters, they turned for aid to the other conservative elements in society. From the other side, the Voltairean *haute*

[1] L. Person, *J.-B. E. Person, instituteur primaire* (1884), 134. Many examples might be given. Thus a teacher from a commune near Orleans writes, 'Mon action m'a attiré toutes les vengeances qu'invente l'esprit ignare des comités locaux, quand le pauvre instituteur veut sortir de sa torpeur' (*L'Émancipation de l'Enseignement primaire*, no. 21, September 23rd, 1848). Another from the Pas-de-Calais complains that he has had his supplement of 150 francs stopped and many children taken away from his school because he supported the democratic candidate. *L'Écho des Instituteurs*, série ii, no. 12, June 11th, 1848, p. 853.

[2] Ibid., no. 6, April 30th, 1848, p. 750.

[3] Ibid., no. 11, June 4th, 1848, pp. 823–4.

bourgeoisie abandoned their war on the Church and welcomed an alliance against the new enemy. To secure this alliance, however, they had to compromise their secularist principles in education. University and secondary education they saw no need to give up, and these were left under the control of the university with its anti-clerical traditions. But primary education they were now prepared to hand back to the Church, as the most effective way of keeping the people in a state of social discipline. Thiers, the arch-enemy of the Church, put himself at the head of this movement, writing, 'Aujourd'hui que toutes les idées sociales sont perverties, et qu'on va nous donner dans chaque village un instituteur qui sera phalanstérien, je regarde le curé comme un indispensable rectification des idées du peuple; il lui enseignera au moins, au nom du Christ, que la douleur est nécessaire dans tous les états, qu'elle est la condition de la vie, et que, quand les pauvres ont la fièvre, ce ne sont pas les riches qui la leur envoient.'[1]

The Church had emerged victorious from the electoral campaign. The logical sequel to the attempt to introduce the *instituteurs* into political life, and to use them to undermine the political influence of the clergy, was the passing of the *loi Falloux*, by which elementary education was placed effectively under the control of the clergy. On the other hand, the Church had to pay in the long run for its victory. As a consequence of its political activities in 1848 and the following years, the Church became identified with opposition to the Republic, and the foundations were laid for the violent anti-clerical movement with which the century ended.

[1] Thiers in a letter of May 2nd, 1848, quoted in *l'Ami de la Religion*, June 18th, 1848, vol. 137, p. 793.

5

THE SECOND CHAMBER IN FRANCE*

FRANCE's new second chamber, the Council of the Republic, has so far played a subordinate and rather obscure part in the political life of the Fourth Republic, yet the history of its establishment and functioning is more significant than its apparently minor constitutional role would suggest. Even though the Council at first seemed a mere political mouse, the constitutional labours which produced it were intense and prolonged. The problem of the existence, composition and functions of the second chamber was indeed, along with the dispute over the mode of election and powers of the President, one of the two crucial issues in the constitutional debates.

The initial question, whether the Third Republic should be resuscitated, or France endowed with a new Constitution, was largely argued in terms of the merits and defects of the former second chamber, and when the decision had been taken for the latter course, the precedent of the Senate still overshadowed the debates. The significance of this issue will only be appreciated if we recall what the Senate had been, and the role it had played, in the course of the Third Republic. A member of the extreme right said of the Constitution of 1875, 'C'est avant tout un Sénat.'[1] The creation of the Senate, in fact, had made a conservative republic possible.

The immediate predecessor of the new second chamber of the Third Republic was the nominated Senate of the Second Empire. Behind this its ancestry could be traced to the Chamber

---

*This paper appeared in the *Political Quarterly*, xix, no. 4, Oct.–Dec. 1948.
[1] J. Barthélemy, *Le Gouvernement de la France* (1939), 68.

of Peers of the monarchy, itself modelled on the English House
of Lords. A substitute, however, had to be found for the heredi-
tary principle. Seventy-five life Senators, it is true, were
appointed, but this system was abolished in 1884, though existing members were allowed to retain their seats till death. The
essential and characteristic feature of the new Senate was
indirect election by the members of local governing bodies. In
its early years the Senate, chosen by electoral colleges to which
each local council sent one delegate, was the representative of
the smaller communites of France, or at least of those who
controlled them, often the curés and local gentry. The revision
of 1884 gave the dominant influence to the smaller towns. The
big towns, with their more advanced political views, were still
grossly under-represented. Thus Lille, with some 316,000
inhabitants, returned 24 delegates to the electoral assembly,
while twenty-four villages in the vicinity, with a population of
some 4,000, had the same number of delegates. Moreover, the
nine-year term of office of the Senate, added to the three years
of the local bodies which chose the electors, meant that at the
end of his term a Senator might represent primary electors of
twelve years earlier. The minimum age for Senators was 40,
and the average age much higher; in 1921 it was 63.[1]

The character of the Senate was reflected in its political
influence, which was uniformly conservative. Thus, for example, until 1913 it successfully opposed the passage of a bill
to safeguard the secrecy of the ballot by authorizing the provision of cubicles for voters to use when inserting their ballot
papers in the official envelope.[2] It held up pensions for railway-
men from 1897 to 1909.[3] Laws were sometimes delayed for
even longer periods. Texts can be cited that were voted by the
Chamber of Deputies and the Senate at forty years' interval.[4]
Admittedly, the Chamber sometimes counted on such senatorial

[1] J. Bryce, *Modern Democracies* (1921), i, 266 n. 1.
[2] D. Thomson, *Democracy in France* (1946), 186.
[3] Barthélemy, op. cit., 82.
[4] G. Burdeau, *Cours de droit constitutionnel* (1946), 185.

delay and passed bills in deference to popular pressure, knowing that the Senate would block their passage into law.[1]

The influence of the Senate was perhaps most important in the field in which it was supposed to be least, that of finance. A financial expert such as Joseph Caillaux, while he was president of the Financial Commission of the Senate, was a power in the state. The Chamber possessed the initiative in financial legislation, and as it habitually left the voting of the budget to the last days in the year, the Senate had normally only a short time for discussion, and on occasion had to stop the parliamentary clock in order to complete its work before the year officially came to an end. In spite of such disadvantages, it was often successful in insisting upon its point of view: for many years, for example, it resisted the imposition of an income tax.[2]

The Senate represented the centre more strongly than the ends of the political spectrum. The extreme groups, Monarchists and Socialists, were both weaker than in the Chamber. The smaller factions were also less well represented.[3] The Radical-Socialist Party, which had been the strongest opponent of the Senate in the earlier stages of the Republic, once it had captured the upper house turned it into a citadel against the newer parties rising on the left, while Socialists and Communists took up the attack. Under Radical-Socialist control the Senate became republican and anti-clerical, but continued to be intensely conservative on social questions.

Between 1884 and 1939 the mode of election and attributes of the Senate remained unchanged, while its influence increased. In its earlier years it was capable of being described as a mere 'theâtre de rive gauche'.[4] At the end of the nineteenth century Bodley could still comment on the public indifference that marked the Senatorial elections and the mediocrity of its membership. The country, he said, took little interest in its

[1] Bryce, *Modern Democracies*, i, 265.
[2] Barthélemy, *Le Gouvernement de la France*, 81 ; Bryce, op. cit., i, 265.
[3] Ibid., i, 263.
[4] Barthélemy, op. cit., 66.

conflicts with the Chamber, and it had small authority or prestige.[1] Not the power, but the advantages of membership of a house that only demanded re-election every nine years, gradually attracted the elder statesmen of the Republic, until on the eve of the war of 1914 the high command of the Republic sat almost exclusively in the Senate.

The strongest evidence of the importance of a political body, however, lies in its power to overthrow governments. On this point the constitutional laws of 1875 were silent. Ferry, defeated by the Senate on an important clause of his Education bill in 1880, never thought of resigning. In 1896, for the first time, the Senate forced the resignation of a ministry, that of Léon Bourgeois, though only after a struggle. Briand retired after a hostile vote in the Senate in 1915. Herriot yielded to a vote of censure in 1925. In the last years of the Republic the Senate's power seemed to be increasing. Tardieu's alliance with clerical elements in the Chamber brought about a hostile vote in the Senate in 1930, and this time a definite precedent was established, because before the vote the government had acknowledged its equal responsibility to both chambers. As party strife became more intense, the Senate twice overthrew the Popular Front governments of Léon Blum, in June 1937 and April 1938.

The last act of the Senate was not the least in the indictment that was drawn up against it after Liberation. On July 9th, 1940, by 225 to 1, the Senate voted in favour of constitutional revision, and on the next day joined with the Chamber to grant full powers to Pétain, thus killing the Third Republic and itself at the same time.

On the morrow of Liberation the triumphant left-wing parties were determined to have no more to do with the discredited institutions of the Third Republic. The Radical Party, which from its stronghold in the Senate had retained, though in a weakened form, its power to the end, emerged from the war as a pathetic relic of its former greatness. By a vote of over

[1] J. E. C. Bodley, *France* (1898), 301, 304, 306.

96 per cent the country refused to re-establish the pre-war Constitution. Sovereignty returned into the hands of the people. Now, since 1789, the classic embodiment of the sovereignty of the people had been a single representative assembly. In the first Constituent Assembly, Communists and Socialists together had a small majority, and these were the parties which upheld the revolutionary tradition of uni-cameral government. The prospect of the re-creation of an effective second chamber therefore seemed slight.

We need not attempt to follow through the long and weary constitutional debates, the unavailing struggle for a constitutional plan on which the three big parties, Communist, Socialist and Mouvement Républicain Populaire, could agree. The method of election and powers of the President, and the mere existence of a second chamber, were a permanent barrier to agreement. M.R.P. proposed a second chamber composed of representatives of local, regional and overseas communities, together with professional organizations, with a suspensive veto and a share along with the other house in the election of the President. The Socialist and Communist majority rejected this proposal and substituted for it a *Conseil de l'Union française*, with a purely advisory role and no effective powers of delay. The left-wing constitutional draft was passed by 309 votes to 249, against the opposition of M.R.P. and the right-wing parties. A vigorous Communist campaign for ratification was launched in the country, with the war-cry, 'Thorez au pouvoir!' Given, in effect, single-chamber government, this seemed no vain hope, and the prospect was sufficiently alarming to a large body of Socialist voters to swing the majority in the country on to the side of rejection by a vote of 53 per cent. In the new elections of June 1946, the joint Socialist-Communist vote fell correspondingly to 47 per cent. It was evident that in the next constitutional draft, concessions would have to be made to moderate opinion.

If the referendum had meant anything it had meant the rejection by the country of a Constitution which appeared to offer the possibility of the concentration of power in the hands of the Communist Party in a single sovereign assembly. By the mediation of Vincent Auriol, and the influence in M.R.P. of Georges Bidault, a second constitutional plan was worked out, which the three big parties reluctantly agreed to, and the country accepted with even greater reluctance, by 9 million to 8 million votes, with 8 million abstentions.

The new Constitution bore a much greater resemblance to the discarded institutions of the Third Republic than the first project had done. 'At the time of Liberation,' wrote M. André Siegfried in December 1946, 'it seemed as though nobody wanted to have anything more to do with the Constitution of 1875, but since then what a change has taken place! It has proved necessary, whatever the cost, to take up again the principal institutions of the previous regime.'[1] The points at issue, so far as concerned the second chamber, had been its mode of election and its powers. The parties of the left, haunted by the ghost of the Senate, had been striving to keep its powers to the minimum. To prevent it from attempting to claim the inheritance of the Senate it was given a new name, *le Conseil de la République*, while the other house was called by the title which traditionally carried the implication of full sovereignty, the National Assembly. Ministers were specifically not to be responsible to the Council (art. 48). It was to vote on laws sent up to it from the Assembly within two months. If the Assembly in discussing a law had voted for emergency procedure, the Council was to discuss under the same limitations of time, and in the case of the budget its time for consideration was to be no longer than that taken by the Assembly. If the time allocated were allowed to pass without a vote, the bill was to be promulgated without further reference to the Council. The Assembly was free to accept or reject its amendments, with the sole condition that if the Council of the Republic had voted on the bill by roll-call and by an absolute majority, the Assembly was to vote under the same conditions (art. 20). Propositions of laws

[1] *Le Figaro*, December 24th, 1946.

87

initiated in the Council were to be transferred without debate to the Assembly, and if they involved a reduction of revenue or new expenditure could not be received (art. 14). In addition to these slender legislative rights, the new second chamber had the right of joining with the first in the election of the President, providing 315 members out of 931 (art. 29), of appointing one-third of the metropolitan representatives in the *Assemblée de l'Union française* (art. 67), four, including the President of the Council, out of thirteen members of the Constitutional Committee entrusted with guarding against infringements of the Constitution (art. 91), and of forming, along with the Assembly, the body with the duty of constitutional revision (art. 90).

There was a more heated discussion over the mode of election of the Council than its limited powers seemed to justify. The idea of a corporate chamber being put on one side because of its connections with Fascism, and direct universal suffrage because of the obvious undesirability of creating two chambers each with the same title to represent the people, it was almost inevitable that they should fall back on something like the mode of election of the former Senate. The parties of the left did not to create a body which could be described in the terms which Gambetta had applied to the Senate, as 'le Grand Conseil des communes françaises', but a proposal by the Radical, M. Bastide, that the Council should be 'the representation of the communal and departmental collectivities' was only rejected by 275 to 273 votes. After this, the non-committal text of M. Ramadier, that it should be elected 'dans le cadre' of the communes, cantons, departments and overseas territories, was accepted by 426 to 126.

The actual mode of election was referred to a subsequent law, which settled, on October 26th, 1946, that for the first election to the Council of the Republic, 200 members should be chosen by the metropolitan departments, 14 by the Algerian and 7 by the overseas departments (Réunion, Martinique, Guadeloupe and Guyane), 44 by the other overseas territories,

8 by the Assembly to represent the French residing outside France (5 for the protectorates of Tunis and Morocco, and 3 for Europe, America and Asia); finally 42 were to be elected by proportional representation by the National Assembly. In all there were 315 members, whereas the former Senate, after the recovery of Alsace-Lorraine, had 314.

The detailed arrangements for the elections were highly complicated. The 200 members to be chosen by the departments of metropolitan France were divided into two groups. The departments elected 127, 68 by majority ballot in the 68 departments with only one member, 59 by proportional representation in the 22 remaining departments. The other group of 73 was to be allocated to the parties in proportion to the votes obtained by them in the elections throughout the country. Voting was by universal suffrage, but indirect. It was intended that the electoral colleges should be chosen from *maires*, and departmental and municipal councillors, but it proved necessary to extend greatly the range of eligibility in practice. It was calculated that throughout the country some 85,000 electors would be required, and if five lists were presented in each department this would mean about 420,000 candidates. Not without some reason did a critic in *Le Monde* comment on this electoral system — 'It is born of an hallucination with proportional representation and an obsession with the resurrection of Lazarus.'[1]

The first elections to the Council of the Republic, which began on November 24th, 1946, were bitterly contested. 'What has happened?' asked *Le Monde*, and replied, 'Nothing, except that life is stronger than the law. The Council of the Republic exists, and the wrappings with which it has been carefully swathed cannot turn it into a mummy. It exists, we repeat, even before being born.'[2] There was a little exaggeration in this. The political parties were more excited about the elections than the country proved to be. A week later *Le Monde* was complaining

[1] Jean Maroger in *Le Monde*, October 10th, 1946.
[2] *Le Monde*, November 15th, 1946.

that opinion was indifferent to the elections.'[1] There was an average absenteeism from the polls of 26 per cent, and at Strasbourg it was as high as 47 per cent. The country, it is true, had been satiated with elections during the previous two years, and the voters were not encouraged by the long lists of candidates, the vagueness of the titles under which the lists were presented, and the complicated coalitions, which varied from department to department.

In three cantons of the Meuse there was a Socialist-Communist coalition; in the Corrèze, Socialists and Radicals united; in Ille-et-Vilaine, Radicals formed lists with Socialists, with Communists and with M.R.P.; in some cantons of the Hérault there were joints list of M.R.P. and the *Rassemblement des Gauches*; in the Manche, M.R.P. joined with the right-wing P.R.L. and Independents; in the Aveyron the lists corresponded to the titles of none of the official parties. Finally, in some twenty departments lists of a more or less conservative character were put forward under the title '*union des maires*', representing an attempt to return to the local basis of senatorial elections.[2]

An army of delegates, or as they were usually called 'grand electors', was chosen by the primary electors. 'Are these "grand electors",' asked the M.R.P. journal *L'Aube*, 'anything more than mere party men bursting for one day into the political arena, disappearing again from the scene, without any real link with the communes and cantons which are our true political realities?'[3] The grand electors were chosen in the proportion of one for every 300 voters, or fraction of 300. To be a delegate it was necessary to be a municipal councillor of a commune or canton, to have been an elector for at least five years in the canton, or to have been domiciled there for at least the same period. *Panachage* (splitting the vote between different lists) was not allowed. The grand electors were naturally party men, who could be trusted to vote as their party told them. Absenteeism

[1] *Le Monde*, November 22nd, 1946.
[2] Ibid., November 24th, 1946; *Combat*, November 24th–25th, 1946.
[3] *L'Aube*, September 5th, 1946.

in the secondary elections amounted to only 0·4 per cent.[1] After the operation of the provisions for proportional representation, and the addition of the members nominated by the Assembly, the second chamber became a reflection of the first, with only the slight difference that the two biggest parties, M.R.P. and the Communists, were proportionately a little stronger. Membership had gone for the most part to little-known politicians, rewarded for their loyalty to the party.

How would the new Council function? The place in which it sat, with its opulent nineteenth-century decoration, was heavy with memories of the defunct Senate. The very first speech to be delivered in the hall in which so many of the great men of the Third Republic had spoken, the inaugural address by the *doyen d'âge*, recalled memories of the past. 'May I make myself today', he said, 'the panegyrist of the deceased, as is only courteous when one succeeds to the inheritance of the illustrious dead? In spite of those who are envious, believe me, the Council of the Fourth Republic will not be badly inspired if it remembers the lessons of the past, if it is not merely a reflecting mirror, but truly a chamber of reflection.'[2]

In the constitutional debates of 1946 the Communists had foreseen this challenge. 'The Council of the Republic is a perfect copy of the former Senate,' *L'Humanité* had declared: the door had been opened, it added, for this chamber, called a 'chamber of reflection', to turn itself into a new Senate, as had happened under the Third Republic.[3] On the other hand the M.R.P. *rapporteur*, in presenting the constitution to the Assembly, had argued strongly that the Council of the Republic was not a camouflaged Senate, while the right-wing P.R.L. regarded its legislative powers as quite inadequate.[4] M. Léon Blum's comment at the time was, 'The future Council of the Republic presents no real analogy with the old Senate, with that "*Haute Assemblée*" invented by the duc de Broglie, in

[1] *Le Monde*, December 10th, 1946.
[2] Ibid., December 25th, 1946.
[3] *L'Humanité*, August 21st and 23rd, 1946.
[4] *L'Aube*, August 21st, 1946.

which is to be seen the characteristic institution of the Constitution of 1875.'[1]

It is interesting to see how, subsequently, the controversialists reversed their positions. We find M. Blum, in November 1946, arguing that, 'Not only do the constitutional attributes of the Council of the Republic remain important, but if one refers to past experience, it is probable that its role in the totality of public life is destined to grow.'[2] The Communists, on the other hand, once the Constitution had begun to function, were anxious to belittle the constitutional role of the Council as much as possible. A Communist speaker, in January 1947, declared, 'The Council of the Republic is in no way comparable to the Senate.'[3]

It was natural, with so much dispute about its status, and with so little constitutional power in fact, that the Council of the Republic should begin very cautiously. The parties manoeuvred for position with an eye to the possible future importance of the Council, but were not yet ready for positive action. The balance between the initial Socialist-Communist alliance and the other parties was so even that in the voting for the first President of the Council the Communist and the M.R.P. candidates tied with 129 votes each, the latter gaining the post as the elder of the two. When the first President, Champetier de Ribes, died in March 1947, M. Monnerville, a councillor from French Guiana, and a member of the *Rassemblement des Gauches*, the moderate right-wing coalition, was elected by 141 votes to 131 for the Communist candidate, and in January 1948 he was re-elected by 194 to 75. The President of the Council, though he was not, as the President of the Senate had been, next in rank to the President of the Republic, was still an important person in the state, and his election a significant political event.

The offices of vice-president, secretary, and above all, the chairmanship of the more important committees, were also

---

[1] *Le Populaire*, August 24th, 1946.   [3] *Le Monde*, January 30th, 1947.
[2] Ibid., November 16th, 1946.

strongly contested. The Communists and Socialists, while their co-operation lasted, had introduced a standing order that the chairmanships of committees should be distributed by the presidents of groups in proportion to the size of the groups in the Council. Thus in 1947, Communists presided over some of the more important committees. At the beginning of 1948, however, they were eliminated from the presidency of the Committees of National Defence, Reconstruction and Industrial Production, which they had held. The struggle over these posts is some evidence that the committees were not without importance. Lacking effective legislative power, they had the right of inquiring into administrative affairs, and of summoning ministers and high officials before them for oral questioning, a practice which the Communists had challenged unavailingly.[1]

The influence of the Council of the Republic over legislation during the first year of its existence was practically negligible. A councillor, in June 1947, protested above all against the *'procédure d'urgence'*. 'I do not wish to associate myself with this parody of parliamentary discussion,' he said. 'Despite the care which we devote to our labours, the National Assembly takes no notice of our opinions. Only thirty-five per cent of our amendments have been accepted by it, and these only when they introduced merely formal alterations.'[2]

With the budget laws at the end of 1947, for the first time, the Council was able to make its influence felt effectively. The Spartan financial proposals of M. Réné Mayer had been watered down by an Assembly conscious of their inevitable unpopularity with the electors, and uneasily aware of the Gaullist pressure for fresh elections. The government proceeded to reintroduce the essential clauses in the Council of the Republic, which, torn between a similar reluctance to accept responsibility for unpopular financial measures, and the desire to seize this opportunity to increase its legislative role, re-inserted the contested clauses in the budget. The criticism of unconstitutionality was met on the grounds that as these clauses had originally been

[1] *L'Aube*, June 6th, 1947.   [2] Ibid., June 27th, 1947.

introduced in the Assembly, though defeated there, they could not be said to have originated in the Council.[1] However, a precedent had been set, and the second chamber had taken the first real step towards asserting its influence in the state.

Another interesting constitutional point emerged in the course of these discussions. If the Council of the Republic passed its amendments by an absolute majority, the Assembly, by the terms of the Constitution, required an absolute majority to reject them. Suppose it could only produce a simple majority of those voting? By the spirit and letter of the Constitution, the Council of the Republic could not have the last word. The Assembly could neither accept nor reject the amendments, and the result would be a total impasse. However, this difficulty did not emerge at this time.

It was evident that the political functions of the Council were only at their beginning. So long as the political composition of the Council remained an almost exact reproduction of that of the Assembly, it was not likely to enter into serious conflict with the latter. But this political parallelism was a consequence not of the Constitution but of the electoral system, which, being embodied only in an ordinary law, does not require a constitutional amendment for its alteration. A temporary constitutional provision, moreover, decreed that the first Council of the Republic should be renewed as a whole (and not by halves as declared in article 6 of the Constitution) within one year of the renewal of the municipal councils (art. 102). This renewal took place in the sutumn of 1947, and therefore the second chamber should be re-elected in or before October 1948.

The arguments that were employed in 1946 in favour of a different mode of election were to be revived by those who hoped to gain by a change. General de Gaulle continued the demand for a partly corporative second chamber – 'The activities of the French nation having been given coherence by

---

[1] The same argument had been employed to justify the re-insertion of financial clauses by the Senate during the Third Republic. Cf. W. L. Middleton, *The French Political System* (1932), 175.

the formation of associations, their representatives could and should have constitutional functions. Great importance would then attach to a Council of the Republic in which they would sit alongside the representatives of the local assemblies.'[1] While the Gaullists were flirting with the idea of a corporative second chamber, and the Communists wished the second chamber to remain what it is, or even less, the Centre parties increasingly looked back to what the Senate was under the Third Republic. 'The election of the "grand electors"', commented *Le Monde*, in November 1946, 'demonstrates the need for a second assembly, more independent of the parties and more dependent on the people, which shall represent not ideologies, but a synthesis of the local popular interests which emanate from the collectivities closest to the people.'[2] And M. André Siegfried, 'The French elector is only at his ease when he is voting for individuals he knows ... Communal life in France, which has its political roots in our remotest past, is for the most part healthy: there the conditions of good government are understood.'[3] The Senate, declared *Le Monde*, had one important quality, 'It knew what the people were thinking and expressed it. Deputies elected by universal suffrage do not know what the country is thinking: they know what their party, or its active members, think or want.'[4]

The motive behind such arguments was a little too patent. It was the belief that a second chamber, indirectly elected by the members of the local councils, would be able to take up again the conservative role of the former Senate. The mode of election was clearly the vital issue: parliamentary powers could be left to look after themselves. When the composition of the Council came up for reconsideration, in August 1948, these ideas were in the ascendent. Only the Communists, now isolated, stood by the existing system. It was a Socialist Minister of the Interior, Jules Moch, who now proclaimed that the Council of the Republic should represent, not individuals, but

[1] *La Seine*, January 5th, 1948.   [3] *Le Figaro*, November 28th, 1946.
[2] *Le Monde*, November 26th, 1946.   [4] *Le Monde*, October 10th, 1946.

des collectivités territoriales, above all the smallest local communities.[1] The new proposals involved the abolition of the complicated procedure of nation-wide proportional representation and Assembly nomination, by which it had been hoped to prevent the second chamber from acquiring a political complexion in any way different from that of the first. Even before the details of the new electoral law were settled, it had become clear that the experiment of 1946 had had its day. As *Le Monde* put it, 'On revint ainsi doucement à la conception constitutionelle de 1875.'[2] The further comment that there was no question of reviving the former Senate, but merely of introducing a tangible counterbalance to the *'fantaisies'* of universal suffrage, was perhaps more tactful than true. If the Fourth Republic survives, and the corporative ideas of the Gaullists do not, all the indications are that the evolution of the Council of the Republic will bring it, slowly, or possibly rapidly, into a closer resemblance to its predecessor. The institutions of the Third Republic were apparently more deeply rooted in the political habits of France than had been believed. Perhaps the conductor of the *autobus* which stops outside the big gates of the Palais du Luxembourg is the best constitutional prophet when he calls out not 'Conseil de la République', but 'Sénat'.

---

[1] *Le Monde*, August 14th, 1948. [2] Ibid., August 18th, 1948.

6

LAVAL AND THE THIRD REPUBLIC*

ONE by one the living and the dead are adding their testimony of the share they took in the tragedy of the second World War. Laval's posthumous apologia takes the form of the memoir and notes written by him for his defence before the High Court of Justice in September–October 1945.[1] He was not able to make use of it; the trial, which threatened to cast even more discredit on the judges than on the accused, was prematurely brought to a close with his condemnation and execution. There are no spicy revelations in what he wrote: he was composing a defence, not a confession, and its main lines had already been indicated by the evidence he gave during the trial of Pétain. Assuredly Laval could have said much more. Whether it will one day be said, or whether he has carried the secrets of his association with the seamier side of French politics to the grave with him, time will show. The importance of his defence lies not in the addition of new facts but in the revelation of the man himself and his fundamental political outlook. In reply to an act of accusation which was a general indictment of his whole political career, we have here the interpretation of his policy which he wished to present to France and to history.

Behind the special pleading and equivocation of a clever man struggling desperately to save his life and reputation, certain fixed ideas emerge. The most persistent and outstanding is an intransigent pacificism. Speaking to the *maires* of Cantal at Vichy, in November 1943, he had declared, 'Toute ma vie,

---

*This paper appeared in the *Cambridge Journal*, ii, no. 5, February 1949.
[1] *Laval parle*. Notes et mémoires rédigés par Pierre Laval dans sa cellule, avec une préface de sa fille, et de nombreux documents inédits (1948).

vous le savez, vous, a été un apostolat de la paix ... Chaque fois
que vous serez dans vos villages, je vous demande de vous dire
que, quoi qu'il arrive et quoi que je fasse, je le ferai toujours
parce que je pense ainsi essayer de sauver notre pays et assurer la
paix des foyers et la persistance de la civilisation dans laquelle
nous sommes nés et dans laquelle nous devons encore vivre.'[1]
Sentiments well calculated to appeal to an audience of Auver-
gnat local notabilities, of course, but not for that reason to be
dismissed straight away as conscious hypocrisy. The desire for
peace in all circumstances and at any cost is the theme which
knits his varied career together. At the very beginning, as a
young Socialist deputy in 1914, he opposed the three-year
military service law. During the First World War he was a
member of the defeatist group in the Chamber. After 1918 he
moved away from the Left and associated himself with Caillaux.
Subsequently he supported Briand's attempts at a Franco-
German *rapprochement*. He claimed that forms of government
and ideologies should not influence a realistic foreign policy —
'les régimes se succèdent, les révolutions s'accomplissent, mais la
géographie subsiste toujours.'[2] On the other side, he continued
the negotiations begun by Barthou for the Franco-Soviet
Mutual Assistance Pact, though in this case, in spite of his
alleged indifference to ideologies, he delayed ratification as long
as he could.[3] His negotiations with Mussolini were much
speedier. The frontier incidents between Italy and Ethiopia
were staged in December 1934. Ethiopia demanded the application of the Covenant of the League of Nations on January 3rd,
1935. The same day Laval visited Rome, and on January 7th
signed his agreement with Mussolini.

There was little hope of arranging such a deal with Nazi
Germany, and the German problem was beginning to dominate
the international situation. Laval does not touch, in his defence,
upon the possibility of having stopped Germany at this stage,

[1] *Laval parle*, 279–80.
[2] Ibid., 89.
[3] It was concluded in May 1935, but only ratified, after the fall of Laval, by
the Chamber in February and by the Senate in April 1936.

and says little of French acceptance of the remilitarization of the Rhineland, but for obvious reasons this was not mentioned in the charges against him. His reply to Hitler was the Franco-Italian understanding. His policy, he declared in a secret session of the Senate on March 16th, 1939, had been 'de faire la chaîne de Londres à Paris avec Rome, Belgrade, Budapest, Varsovie, Bucarest, Moscou'.[1] The keystone in this arch was Italy. 'L'Italie alliée de la France, c'était le pont jeté entre la France et tous les pays d'Europe centrale et orientale alliés de notre pays. C'était la possibilité pour nous, non seulement de bénéficier la France de tout l'effort militaire de la Yougoslavie, de la Tchécoslovaquie, de la Pologne et de la Roumanie ... '[2] That Italy could ever have played the role for which Laval cast her seems now very doubtful. In any case the rejection of the Hoare-Laval plan frustrated his policy by ruining what he claimed to be 'une véritable politique d'encerclement de l'Allemagne'.[3]

So far we have given Laval's own explanation of his aims. It is probable that he also had further hopes, which it was not discreet to mention in 1945. The evidence of witnesses to whom he expounded his policy in private at the time indicates a more complex, though not necessarily contradictory, line of thought. H. Torrès reports Laval as declaring to him, 'I need the friendship of Italy to reach an understanding with the Germans. And to achieve peace in Europe and in the world, an understanding with Germany is indispensable.'[4] Laval saw, and rightly saw, that the problem of Germany was the problem of peace. 'Do you see this big red patch right in the middle of Europe?' he said to Alexander Werth in November 1934. 'Do you really imagine that we can have peace and collective security in Europe as long as we haven't brought *this* into our peace system?'[5] Did he hope to buy off Hitler, as he thought he had bought off Mussolini? And did he imagine that peace could

[1] *Laval parle*, 255.
[2] Ibid., 245.
[3] Ibid., 196.

[4] H. Torrès, *Pierre Laval* (1941), 135.
[5] A. Werth, *The Twilight of France* (1942), 37.

be preserved by paying Danegeld to the Nazis? Whatever his hopes, they failed with the failure of the Hoare-Laval plan, and for the next few years he withdrew into the background, though he remained active in the Foreign Affairs Committee of the Senate, and in private established links with the Nazis through Fernand de Brinon, later Vichy ambassador to the German government in Paris. He opposed the declaration of war in 1939, and in his memoir bitterly reproaches those who were responsible for it—'Le crime n'est pas de s'être trouvé là quand l'humiliation est venue de notre défaite, le crime, c'est d'avoir lancé la France dans une guerre dont on pouvait prédire d'avance qu'elle était perdue, puisqu'on ne l'avait préparée ni militairement, ni diplomatiquement.'[1]

During the first year of the war Laval's mind seems to have turned towards the creation of a neutral Latin *bloc* with Spain and Italy, leaving Germany and Great Britain to fight out the war between themselves, but he could only exercise influence behind the scenes until the defeat of France. This gave him his opportunity. The first step was necessarily the elimination of those who had opposed his policy in the past, and his own establishment in the position to which his foresight entitled him. This involved the overthrow of the existing regime. The act of accusation against Laval laid the responsibility for the destruction of the Third Republic squarely on his shoulders: 'V. C'est incontestablement lui l'agent responsable qui, par ses intrigues et ses menaces jusque dans le cabinet du président de la République, empêcha ce dernier, les présidents des deux Chambres, les membres du Parlement et ceux des ministres qui avaient encore souci de la souveraineté nationale, d'aller en Afrique du Nord former un gouvernement à l'abri des pressions allemandes ... VI. C'est également lui qui, à force d'intrigues, de marchandages, de promesses et de menaces, amena le Parlement à remettre au Maréchal le Gouvernement de la République.'[2]

That Laval, as the leader of the anti-war party, was in a

---

[1] *Laval parle,* 195.　　　　　　　　　　[2] Ibid., 227-8.

strong position at this moment, and that he used it to side-track the Taurines compromise, which would at least have preserved the Third Republic in cold storage, cannot be doubted. But to attribute the whole responsibility for a parliamentary vote of 569 to 80, with 17 abstentions, to one man, with no armed force, and not much moral force behind him, goes beyond the bounds of probability, and suggests merely an attempt to find a scape-goat.[1] The prosecution, it is true, was merely presenting the version which, five years earlier, Laval himself had favoured. The account of the events at Bordeaux and Vichy, published in November 1940 by Jean Montigny, an ardent supporter of Laval, put him right in the centre of the stage and made him almost single-handedly responsible for preventing the transfer of the government to North Africa, and for the constitutional changes. 'Si vous quittez cette terre de France,' he is repre-sented as saying to the feeble President Lebrun, 'vous n'y remettrez jamais plus les pieds.'[2] And again, at Vichy, 'Puisque la démocratie parlementaire a voulu engager le combat contre le nazisme et le fascisme, et qu'elle a perdu ce combat, elle doit disparaître. Un régime nouveau, audacieux, autoritaire, social, national, doit lui être substitué.'[3] In his defence Laval tries to relieve himself of this now embarrassing honour by shifting the main responsibility to Pétain, who, he says, 'disposait alors d'une autorité morale qui, ajoutée à son autorité militaire, faisait de lui l'arbitre incontesté'.[4] The truth seems to be that Laval and Pétain were both, each in his own way, aiming at the destruction of the Third Republic, and if Laval was the more skilful intriguer, Pétain enjoyed by far the higher moral auth-ority. Moreover, the responsibility was not confined to them: it was widely shared.

Up to this point the charges against Laval are not fatal. He is hardly to be distinguished, except by his greater ability, from a

---

[1] Cf. *Laval parle*, 50–51.
[2] J. Montigny, *De l'Armistice à l'Assemblée Nationale, 15 juin–15 juillet 1940. Toute la vérité sur un mois dramatique de notre histoire* (1940), 28.
[3] Ibid., 62.
[4] *Laval parle*, 42.

host of other politicians and private persons in the last years of the Third Republic. The charge on which he was to lose his life came from the years of collaboration which followed. As early as July 1940 he advocated before the National Assembly a policy of 'loyal collaboration with Germany and Italy', adding that to speak thus afforded him no embarrassment, because he had already urged the same policy in time of peace.[1] The Montoire interview with Hitler, on October 22nd, 1940, laid the foundation for the policy of collaboration. Laval's defence is that such a policy was merely the logical sequel to the Armistice. 'Ce n'est pas Montoire qui a inauguré la politique de collaboration, c'est la Convention d'armistice qui nous l'a imposée.'[2] And Laval was not himself to reap the first fruits of his efforts at collaboration, for Pétain's influence in the government proved by far the greater, and in December 1940 the Marshal, who detested Laval, dismissed him. He only returned to office in 1942.

Laval presents his resumption of power as a grave sacrifice of his personal interests to the needs of his country. Possibly it seemed so in 1945, though altruism was not his most strongly marked characteristic. He was undoubtedly inspired by a conviction that he, and he alone, could deal with the Germans. The same confidence in his capacity to 'rouler' Mussolini, Stalin, Hitler and others, had been present in his diplomatic negotiations before the war. The object he set before himself now was to create 'un climat de confiance vis-à-vis les dirigeants allemands et leur faire croire que nous ne pouvions faire ni mieux, ni plus, que ma bonne volonté était garante, qu'on ne pouvait aller plus loin'.[3] He repeatedly protests that he had saved Jews and Freemasons, and Frenchmen in general, from the worst consequences of the German occupation, and that while he was persuading the Germans that no one could do more for them, in fact no one could have done less. One is bound to ask if the Nazis were quite as stupid as this implies,

---

[1] J. Montigny, *De l'Armistice à l'Assemblée Nationale*, 64.   [3] Ibid., 122.
[2] *Laval parle*, 70.

and if there was any other pre-war politician with a reputation, however bad, who could have served them as a tool as well as Laval did. The Swiss ambassador at Vichy, who was an admirer of Pétain, though not of Laval, formed the view that the Vichy government, lacking psychological insight into the German mentality, and convinced that in the end they would always have to give way, never made sufficient use of the single but powerful trump card they possessed, the great interest which Germany had in the maintenance of tranquillity and order in France.[1]

Laval certainly went a long way in the attempt to convince the Nazis of his good faith, even as far as the notorious broadcast phrase, 'Je souhaite la victoire de l'Allemagne', in June 1942.[2] The explanation offered in his memoir is that this broadcast was given before the American disembarkment in North Africa, when general opinion in France accepted the inevitability of a total German victory. He held that, given this assumption, it was to the interest of France to transfer her allegiance to the victors, at least in appearance. It is possibly true that in fact at this stage he did not wish for the victory of Germany, or at least not the complete victory. There is no reason to disbelieve his statement that, asked to declare war on 'les Anglo-Saxons' in November 1942 and conclude an alliance with Germany, he refused.[3] His pacifism, as well as his sense of what was possible, prohibited such a policy. Accepting the need for France to work her passage in the German New Order, he was not prepared to do it by war. There was also, as he pointed out in his memoir, a second part to the sentence — 'Je souhaite la victoire de l'Allemagne, car sans elle, le communisme s'installera partout en Europe.'[4] Some eighteen months later,

[1] W. Stucki, *La Fin du régime de Vichy* (1947), 63.
[2] In the course of Pétain's trial, Laval tried to shelter himself behind the allegation that the Marshal had seen and approved the phrase. This was one of the few points in the trial at which Pétain was aroused from his senile drowsiness. With emotion he declared that he was horrified when he heard Laval's expression, believing that it had been cut out of the speech. (*The Times*, August 4th, 1945.)
[3] *Laval parle*, 135–7.
[4] Ibid., 133.

in November 1943, explaining his policy, he argued, 'Je voudrais agir de telle façon que l'Allemagne ne soit pas trop forte pour nous étreindre, mais de telle façon que le bolchevisme ne puisse pas, lui, nous supprimer.'[1] In international affairs, as in domestic politics, he was the perpetual middleman, hating war—in war there is less scope for middlemen—with an eye always to the main chance, seeking personal or national advantage by playing off one side against the other, and able to do it so well because he was free from allegiance to any principles. 'Les traités,' he said, in one of many passages of unconscious self-revelation, 'ne valent pour les peuples que dans la mesure où ils consacrent leurs intérêts.'[2] He was politically sophisticated to the point of naivety. Perhaps he almost believed himself when he wrote, 'On m'a représenté comme un malin, comme un roublard, alors que j'ai toujours lutté avec l'intelligence vierge et simple d'un enfant du peuple.'[3] This was his last word to the world he was leaving, written on the eve of his death.

It is hardly likely to be the last word of history on Pierre Laval. For all the tragic circumstances in which it was composed, his memoir curiously fails to move the reader. It is clever, too clever: what is lacking is any spark of nobility or generosity of mind. Its author has not even the greatness of a real villain. It is difficult to believe that he exercised a decisive influence at any point, or that the course of events would have been very different had he never existed. The details of his life and intrigues, if they are ever recorded, will be of inconceivable insignificance. He will keep his place in the history of our time as a symbol rather than as an individual. As has already been said, the fundamental thing in Laval was the pacifism that was typical of a generation which, sickened by the wasted sacrifices of one world war, by an over-anxious desire to buy peace at any price, purchased a second war and still paid the price. It was a pacifism devoid of moral or religious values. The Lavals believed that they could use Mussolini to cast out Hitler, and

[1] *Laval parle*, 280.   [2] Ibid., 29.   [3] Ibid., 206.

Hitler to cast out Stalin, while they were left undisturbed in their weakness to profit from the struggles of their enemies.

Beyond this, what does Laval stand for? The answer is, nothing, except politics as an end in itself. All systems of government have their weaknesses, and all professions their characteristic vices. In the years between the wars, the weaknesses of parliamentarism were everywhere more evident than its strength, and the vices of the politician more prominent than the virtues of the statesman. Laval was a superb specimen of the genus Parliamentarian, for whom the acquisition and retention of power is an end in itself. The only object of policy is to be on the winning side, to climb in time on to the right bandwagon. For the pure politician, abstract ideas are meaningless, politics has ceased to have any connection with principle, and has become a mere pragmatism of self-interest. Power, acquired by political intrigue, is exercised by administrative intrigue. Laval was responsible for no positive acts of legislation except a badly drafted Social Insurance law which he inherited from a previous government. His name is associated with financial corruption, and he was certainly peculiarly successful in accumulating a fortune and concealing its sources; but it was not this, but the transformation of the political game from a means into an end which was the real sign of the degeneration of democratic politics between the wars. It was as evident in an incorrupt politician, like Baldwin, as in a corrupt one, like Laval. It was exhibited in the domestic and foreign politics of the present, and reflected in the general trend of historical interpretation of the past.

This estimate of the significance of Laval, however, is open to the criticism that it deals with results rather than with causes, and describes a symptom without analysing the disease. Behind the degeneration of politics some deeper cause must be sought. It would have been fashionable until recently to have looked for an explanation in terms of economic interests. Certainly no one could claim that Laval was indifferent to such considerations. But the economic interpretation which has historical significance refers to class and not merely personal interest. From this point of view it is more difficult to place Laval. He is generally said to have come from poor peasant stock, with a strong strain of gipsy. He exhibited the characteristic qualities of the peasant—tenacity, shrewdness, greed, courage and capacity for work. He began his political career as a spokesman for the working class. As he moved on into the world of finance and business, he shed his Socialism and came to be regarded as a representative of the French bourgeoisie. His later career, and indeed the whole political development of his time, has been taken as evidence of the decadence of bourgeois democracy. This interpretation is completely convincing, so long as we are content to take as our premises the definitions of the ideas of democracy and the bourgeoisie which are to be proved in the conclusion. Some difficulties require to be met, however, before we can regard Laval as satisfactorily pigeon-holed by this verdict.

In the first place, it must be observed that those who take this view are usually not content to leave well alone. Having condemned parliamentary democracy by describing Laval as a democrat, for other purposes they go on to call him a fascist. He was really neither. Democracy as it was practised by Laval meant the game of political and administrative wire-pulling and intrigue on the back-stairs and in the corridors of Parliament and the Ministries. His Fascism, if it can be given that name, was one not of *coups d'état* but of *coups de téléphone*. He is equally difficult to classify socially. If he is to be summed up as bourgeois, not only his peasant origins, but the fact that for forty years he represented the working classes of Aubervilliers and the peasantry of the Auvergne has to be explained away, as well as the slightness of his support in the country as a whole. His personal financial interests were in the press, the radio, and in a mineral water company whose product he was able to introduce on the state railways. Again, it must be asked, what was the bourgeoisie which he is alleged to have represented? He rose to power in a period during which inflation was steadily ruining the old bourgeoisie of France and a new wealthy class was emerging, one of shady financiers, war profiteers, newspaper proprietors, politicians, with no traditions or culture, a kind of lumpen-bourgeoisie, parasitic on society. It was a sign of the weakness of the French social structure that such a group should have acquired such influence. The source of the weakness is not to be found in the size or strength of the elements of corruption, and the economic interests they represented, but in the divided and mistaken policies of industrial workers, peasantry and employers, who constituted the real economic interests of the nation. It is important to note also that the fatal strains and stresses were as much within as between classes. The conflicts which were rending French society, and giving Laval and all that he stood for its opportunity, are not to be summed up simply in the form of the classic struggle of proletariat against capitalists. The most dangerous conflict, because the most fundamental one, which is as manifest in a communist as in a capitalist society, is that of town and country, of agricultural against industrial interests. The country, exploited for so long, had discovered that under the operation of universal suffrage it had a means of self-defence. The peasantry gave their votes to the Radical-Socialist Party—on conditions. Their economic enlightenment did not yet reach to a positive policy: their desires were simple, merely to escape taxation. But in a country which was still nearly fifty per cent rural, that was sufficient to ruin the national finances and make inflation inevitable. Finance and industry could also keep down their taxes by evading their legal responsibilities. Both agricultural and industrial wealth, in addition, were agreed on restricting government expenditure by preventing the development of social services, and on drawing the revenue as far as possible from indirect rather than direct taxation. The working classes of the towns were not as strong as in more industrialized countries, and their weakness was further increased by the ideological split between Socialists and Communists, the latter of whom were more concerned with advancing the cause of the world revolution than with the economic improvement of conditions for the masses. In addition, cutting across all classes, was the traditional conflict of clerical and anti-clerical, and the absurdly irrelevant war of the monarchists against the Republic. The conclusion must be that, on a realistic analysis, the weakness of France did not lie in the decadence of French capitalist society, but in its immaturity.

There is no space here for the further social analysis, and the more careful discussion of the interaction of economics and politics in France, which are obviously required to explain the degeneration of French politics. In concluding, however, there is one fundamental question which must be put. Was there not behind the economic and political troubles a more deep-seated disease, a spiritual malaise which was not peculiar to France, and which indeed did not reach its climax there? Here, perhaps, is the ultimate significance of Pierre Laval. In his small way, as Hitler on a larger scale, he represented that general disintegration of values and triumph of force and fraud, which is one sign of the breakdown of a civilization.

7

SECURITY AND SOVEREIGNTY IN FRENCH FOREIGN POLICY*

In France, with the theories of 1789 and the practice of the French Revolution, the idea of national sovereignty was first fully fledged, and it is in France that it has in recent time been most vigorously challenged. This development is primarily to be explained in terms not of the history of ideas, but rather of the material change in the position of France in the world. Up to the nineteenth century she was the European state with by far the largest population under a single government. In days when military strength depended mainly on available manpower, she was necessarily the greatest military power of Europe, only to be kept in check by coalitions of other powers or by internal weakness and divisions. This situation changed in the course of the nineteenth century, when the population of France rose only gradually, while that of other countries was multiplying rapidly. Neither France nor Europe properly appreciated the military effects of the alteration in the balance of population until after the Franco-Prussian War. Its effects were then to be intensified by the creation of a united Germany and by the progress of industrialization, which gave Germany greater material as well as human resources to draw upon than France. The growth of the French Empire during the nineteenth century helped to limit the effects of this situation but could not alter it. The consequence was that France had either to drop out of the ranks of the Great Powers, or else look for some other source of strength to redress the balance.

*This paper appeared in *International Journal*, the quarterly of the Canadian Institute of International Affairs, viii, no. 3, Summer 1953.

Her governments naturally turned to the idea of foreign alliance, in particular with Russia, on the supposition that only a power on the continent of Europe could come into action with sufficient rapidity to prevent the whole German military machine from being diverted against France in the opening stages of a war. This calculation proved correct in 1914, when the necessity for fighting on two fronts prevented the German military machine from overrunning France in the first days of the war.

The Communist Revolution in Russia altered the situation. France had to look for another European ally against a possible revival of German military strength. American isolationism and British fear of commitment in Europe intensified this need, but it would have existed in any case. The new answer took the form of the alliances with the states of the Little Entente. But no collection of weak states, whatever their number, can equal one strong state. Even in the 'twenties, it was becoming evident that the Little Entente was not the answer to France's problem. Right-wing forces in France clung to their belief in the efficacy of the military alliance with the small states of Central and Eastern Europe, up to and beyond the point at which it had patently become an illusion; but on the left there were politicians who had seen the need for a new approach to the problem. As early as 1925, after the electoral victory of the *Cartel des Gauches* in 1924, M. Herriot issued an appeal for a United States of Europe. This evoked no immediate practical response.

In 1929 the idea was revived in a more specific form, when Briand presented the idea of a European Union to the League of Nations. For Great Britain, Ramsay Macdonald replied that the idea might reasonably be discussed in ten years' time: in fact, other matters had a higher place on the international agenda in 1939. Inside France, nationalist forces were hostile to the initiative Briand had taken, and their hostility found expression even within his own government. The Communists also opposed the idea of European Union.

The same tacit alliance of extreme right and left was to appear against more recent proposals for a federal Europe. Briand's attempt to modify his proposal, to satisfy those who had criticized it as an attack on national sovereignty, weakened the plan without satisfying its critics. International developments soon robbed it of all relevance.

It would not be correct to say that the search for an international solution to the problem of the future of French foreign policy came to an end with the failure of Briand. In a sense the same theme was taken up, from the extreme left and right, by those who had just joined in denouncing it. The Communists looked to a Communist International, but even if France had been ready to follow the Moscow line, the alliance with Nazi Germany in the end seemed to the Soviet Government to offer greater possibilities, as in a sense it did. On the right the opposite idea of a Fascist International also found a measure of support. After the German victory of 1940 a not inconsiderable body of opinion believed that the future for France lay in a close collaboration with Germany; but the Pétain-Hitler interview at Montoire in October 1940 was followed almost immediately by the expulsion of the Lorrainers, and Nazi policy gradually reduced the collaborationists to a small faction of extremists. Meanwhile, moderate opinion, in the Resistance, was looking to a future close association with the democratic nations, while the Communists still clung to their faith in a world revolution to set up a universal union of Communist-controlled states. Thus by the 'forties practically all sections of political opinion in France had come to see the future in terms of internationalism, though the nature of the international association they envisaged varied through all the shades of the domestic political spectrum.

In the first stage after the Second World War French international policy was directed by General de Gaulle on more old-fashioned lines. His ideas were those of 1919 — a Germany divided into small states, with the Rhine as its western frontier, the Saar detached, and the Ruhr under international control.

The possibility that Russia might represent the real threat to French independence was left out of calculation in this scheme, for Russia had been the first power to recognize the French National Council of Liberation during the war and the Communists were still inside the tripartite coalition which governed France. Indeed, even if the fact was not fully appreciated, a Franco-Russian alliance was essential to the European plans of de Gaulle; but the prospect of an effective alliance was frustrated by the subsequent development of Soviet policy and this phase in French foreign policy came to an end.

All the previous solutions for the French dilemma were now ruled out for one reason or another. The idea of a Nazi-Fascist Europe was dead; the Little Entente states were now mere Russian satellites; the former ally, Russia, had itself become the chief menace to European peace; pacifism was discredited, though there remained a strong current of neutralism, finding expression in the columns of *Le Monde*. A new approach to the problem of maintaining the role of France as a world power, while recognizing its inability to stand by itself, emerged out of and ran parallel with the attempt by the middle parties to create a Third Force in French politics between Communists and Gaullists. In face of the increasing aggressiveness of Russian imperialism even the Gaullists accepted the idea of a federal relationship between the democratic nations of Western Europe. The Gaullist Conference of April 1948 called for an international constituent assembly to set up a federal council and assembly, with courts of justice and arbitration and a committee of chiefs of staff. Its resolution added, 'Economic union is clearly the indispensable basis of political union. It is Zollvereins which make federations.' All this, it was recognized, would involve sacrifices, even for the French economy, but it was the necessary bridge that the present generation had to cross.

The governments of the Third Force began to put such ideas into practice. The Brussels Pact of March 1948 between France, Great Britain, Belgium, the Netherlands, and Luxemburg offered a promising beginning. British ideas of a council and conference, in which each national delegation should vote as a unit, conflicted with the French readiness for an assembly with liberty of vote for its members. In this respect the French view prevailed. The other major problem was the future relationship of Germany with the federal institutions of Western Europe. In the face of the aggressive policy of Russia, the United States, and with some hesitation Great Britain, had drawn the conclusion that only a revived German state could redress the balance in Europe. The French plan for a Federal Europe was an attempt, taking up the earlier schemes of Briand, to render the inevitable revival of Germany harmless by fusing French and German policies and power to the point at which they could not effectively be directed against one another.

At the first session of the Council of Europe, in August 1949, M. Bidault recognized that a German delegation might be admitted in the not distant future. He linked this concession, however, with the condition that there should first be an agreed decision on the future of the Saar as an autonomous territory closely associated with France. French opinion was all the more determined on this because the autonomy of the Saar was all that remained of earlier French plans for ensuring the permanent weakening of Germany by its division. France had meanwhile been strengthening her ties with the West by the Dunkirk Treaty of Alliance with Great Britain in March 1947, and the Atlantic Pact of April 1949. These hardly went far enough to satisfy French opinion. It was impossible for the French to forget British and American policies between the wars and the part they had played in permitting, or even aiding, the rise of the Nazi military machine. The creation of international institutions which would prevent the repetition of this history, even if such an arrangement involved a close association with the Germans, seemed to them a sounder guarantee of future peace than looser Anglo-American promises. Political advance on the new line was rapidly followed up by economic moves. In May 1950, M. Schuman issued his declaration in favour of a

H 113

pooling of the coal and steel industries of the Western powers. In April 1951, the agreement was signed, and subsequently ratified by the governments of France, Western Germany, Italy, Belgium, Holland and Luxemburg.

The third and most decisive step was taken when M. Pleven, in October 1950, proposed the formation of a European Army under the authority of a European Minister of Defence and the Strasbourg Assembly. This proposal from the beginning had a more difficult passage than its predecessors. The Communist Left naturally opposed a plan primarily aimed at the defence of the West against Russia. Voices from the right were also raised against such a revolutionary step; and the Socialists urged that European political institutions should be further developed before an international army was created. M. Schuman did not attempt to conceal the implications of the Pleven plan when he presented it to the Council of Europe in November 1950. 'States', he said, 'must reconcile themselves to the abandonment of a part of their autonomy to a collective authority, in which they will participate but to which they will submit themselves in advance.' After a series of discussions, in February 1952 the draft treaty for a European Defence Community was drawn up by representatives of the six states which had already concluded the coal and steel agreement. Successively, thus, the political, economic and military instruments of an integrated Western Europe had been planned on paper. How far they would remain merely paper plans depended on the reaction to them of political opinion in each of the participating countries, and not least in France, where they had originated.

Communist Party opinion in France needs no discussion. For it the whole development was merely the first step towards war against the peace-loving governments of Eastern Europe. The Socialists were more hesitant. They had set up a committee to study plans for a socialist United States of Europe, and at first refused to co-operate with federalists of other shades of opinion. Subsequently they gave a limited and divided support to the movement for European Union. The Radicals were, for different reasons, equally cautious. The Right proper was even more suspicious of idealistic schemes and prepared to take its stand on a revived assertion of the principle of national sovereignty. The Gaullist position was equivocal. General de Gaulle's Rally, having blessed the idea of Federal Europe, denounced its execution, or perhaps it would be more correct to say, those who were executing it. The one party which was wholeheartedly behind the successive steps towards European Union was the *Mouvement Républicain Populaire*, the Catholic Democrats. Opponents even presented the whole scheme as a Catholic plot, got up between the three leaders of French, German and Italian Catholic Democrats—Schuman, Adenauer and de Gasperi—for what they called 'la petite Europe Vaticane'.

Party divisions in France are, however, not clearly enough marked to make an analysis of opinion based purely upon them very penetrating or accurate. A discussion of the main points at issue is likely to be more revealing. They all relate to the central issue of Franco-German relations. The greatest controversy has been over the future of the Saar. Undoubtedly the problem of European Union will not be solved without an agreed solution of the Saar question; but equally this question is not insoluble if it is viewed in a European context. Another and hitherto little considered aspect of the German problem has recently appeared. It is difficult to believe that Germans will reconcile themselves permanently to the rule of a large section of their population by Russia or its satellites. *Le Monde*, still with a strong hankering after neutralism, seized upon the natural French concern at the prospect of being dragged into a war with Russia at the heels of German irredentism, and this fear has been echoed in many quarters.

Thirdly, however, there is the general problem presented by the prospective revival of German military power. French critics of European Union envisage a situation in which France might be left, for all effective purposes, in an embarrassing *tête-à-tête* with Germany, and point out that there would be no remedy open to her if the Germans repudiated their obligations under the treaty. True, the Anglo-American declaration of May 27th, 1952, guaranteed: (a) that in the event of a breach of the integrity of the European Union the two powers would act in conformity with Article 4 of the Atlantic Treaty [but this was a mere promise of consultation]; (b) that they would keep their forces in Europe, including Western Germany, for so long as they considered necessary for the common defence of the area included in the Atlantic Treaty. The latter promise left the maintenance of their troops entirely at their own discretion and at the mercy of a sudden change in American or British policy. The British guarantee of April 15th, 1952, went further and promised automatic British assistance to any member of the European Defence Community that suffered aggression; but the experience of the inter-war years has shown that many preliminary steps precede open aggression, and Russian policy has confirmed the lesson. The French are to be excused if they ask for a policy which will give some guarantee that next time aggression will be challenged before it has reached the point of war, and they do not regard British and American guarantees so far as offering this.

There are other major problems involved in French participation in European Union. France, like Great Britain, has an overseas empire. Is this to be regarded as entering into the Union or not? Will France be left with full sovereignty over it? Will she be free to fix the proportion of her troops to be allocated to imperial defence, if her military budget is no longer under her undivided control? Moreover, will she be able to treat with a rearmed Germany on equal terms, when the German army is concentrated in Europe while important French forces are stationed overseas?

All these grounds for hesitation were summed up in the terms which the National Assembly laid down, in February 1952, as the conditions on which it was willing to approve the negotiations for a European Army. There must be an equal division of the burden of defence, making especial allowance for French commitments in Indo-China. Great Britain and the United States must offer a guarantee against a breach of the terms of the treaty by any member, this guarantee being made effective by the maintenance of British and American troops on the Continent for as long as necessary for this purpose. French forces available in Europe should be at least equal to those allowed to any other member of the Defence Community. National contingents should be organized on the smallest basis possible, to prevent the danger of the reconstitution of national armies. The European Army must be controlled by a supra-national political authority with limited but effective powers. The cases in which unanimity is required for the action of this authority should be clearly laid down and strictly limited. The military budget should be voted by the European Assembly and not subject to a veto. There must be no national German army or General Staff. Finally, every effort should be made to secure the participation of other democratic countries and especially Great Britain. Even with these conditions, the French Government only obtained the assent of the Assembly by 327 to 287 votes.

After this, the French Government proceeded with the negotiations for a European Defence Community. A draft treaty was drawn up in May 1952, but the question of ratification opened a national debate. Communist opposition to any form of Defence Community for Western Europe is, of course, a permanent fact, but this does not necessarily weaken its political prospects in France. What was to happen in the U.S.S.R. was more important. The death of Stalin and the subsequent reorientation of Russian propaganda in the direction of 'peaceful co-existence' slackened the sense of urgency. If the indications of a new line in Russian policy were to be confirmed by a real *détente* in the international situation, French foreign policy might be thrown into the melting-pot, and the European Defence Community along with it; for after all, the prime object of the Community is defence against an aggressive Russia, and if the Russian threat were to seem to diminish, the danger of a re-armed Germany, within or without a Defence Community, would grow larger in French eyes.

Apart from the Communists, the only other clear reaction to the E.D.C. plan came from General de Gaulle, who, while his Rally still remained an organized party, denounced the proposed treaty as involving the political and military hegemony of Germany in Europe and opening the perspective of a German-led twentieth-century crusade against the East. The French public may have been a little confused when, after this formidable indictment, the General went on to propose his own solution. This was, as in 1948, confederation of the peoples of Europe, in which Germany should have its place; the armies were to remain national armies, even if under a single command and a unified General Staff; and political control was to rest in the hands of a conference of heads of governments, meeting at regular intervals and in an organic manner, whatever that meant. He was, in fact, reopening the debate over the incompatibility of a real international fusion with national sovereignty.

At the same time, de Gaulle produced a red herring, which diverted many other politicians and which has done much to divert subsequent discussion into the rather unprofitable line that a European alliance should not be the mere work of irresponsible 'technocrats', but should receive the sanction of popular sovereignty by being made the subject of a national referendum. Indignant protests that this proposal is the only logical one, that if national sovereignty is to be alienated it must at least be with the consent of the nation, and that the referendum is not merely a device of the politicians for shifting responsibility from their own shoulders, or at least concealing the inability of the Assembly to come to any decision, do not quite carry conviction.

The dilemma in which French foreign policy now finds itself is partly the result of political changes since liberation. Largely under M.R.P. inspiration France set out on the path of a United Europe at a time when right-wing opinion was weak or even unrepresented. The steady recovery of the parties of the right, with more traditional ideas of national sovereignty, has weakened support for European Union. It might be asked why the whole policy of internationalism is not frankly abandoned and France does not return to a nationalist policy of 'notre drapeau, notre discipline, notre hiérarchie, notre esprit', to quote an appeal which recently came, ironically enough, from the lips of a war-time collaborationist mayor of Paris.

The dilemma is too real to be solved so easily. The more responsible opponents of European Union, and particularly of the European Army, on the eve of success, show signs of drawing back in face of the probable consequences of their own victory. If the military treaty, with whatever qualifications, is not ratified, the political institutions of the European Community will receive a blow from which it may be difficult for them to recover. In turn, the coal and steel plan will be seriously shaken. A dramatic failure of the attempt to create European institutions could only mean a revival and intensification of the separate nationalisms of the states of Europe, including amongst these, of course, Germany. German military power would then be revived as the weapon of a re-born German nationalism. This is precisely what the whole plan of Europeanization was intended to avert.

The argument thus comes full circle. French nationalism finds itself caught in a logical dilemma from which, within its existing terms of reference, there is no escape. Indeed, so long as Germany and France are left face to face, the fact of ultimate German industrial and military superiority cannot be avoided, whether it be partially concealed beneath the robes of federal institutions, or exposed in the stark nakedness of power politics. The theoretical discussion over the issue of national sovereignty has become, it seems to me, little more than an intellectual exercise which has little relation to actual facts. National sovereignty is a principle to which all parties appeal against any policy whose practical implications they dislike, but which they have all been prepared to forget, to a greater or less degree, when there seemed a chance of securing a solution which met their views in other respects. Thus, if Great Britain were to accept full membership of the European Defence Community, most of the objections raised against it would vanish. If Russian policy made the U.S.S.R. a possible ally, ideological differences would not stand unduly in the way of a Franco-Russian alliance. If neither of these avenues of escape is opened, France is left with a choice of evils. The cry of national sovereignty in danger may still be strong enough to sway the decision, but if so it will only be because it is allied with more practical considerations. French opinion, I believe, is ready for the necessary sacrifices of national sovereignty involved in taking its place in an international order, on strictly realistic grounds of national interests, but it must be an order which clearly promotes those interests. In one direction or another, for more than the last twenty years, French governments have been looking for that order, which still remains to be found.

8

FRANCE—A PEASANTS' REPUBLIC*

A HUNDRED years ago, de Tocqueville put the question 'Are
we on the way to intermittent anarchy?' It would not be out
of place today. One is often asked whether the government of
France is incurably unstable, whether the French political
kaleidoscope can stay in one position for more than a passing
moment. I never shared the pessimism of the last few years, but
the question is a natural one. The Government of M. Queuille
has survived for some six months — and already some observers
are proclaiming that it has come to stay, though others are
beginning to ask when it may be expected to succumb to
senility. The results of the local elections which are shortly to be
held may give some clue whether its position is becoming
relatively stronger or weaker. But I do not want to discuss the
prospects of this or that government but rather to take the
opportunity of this pause to put a more serious question. Will
the Fourth Republic itself survive?

In Paris there is a placard, which can be seen on every
underground station: it shows Marianne, the symbolic figure
of the Republic, or rather it shows four Mariannes, one succeed-
ing to the other. Behind them a painter is daubing a long fence,
and the inscription reads, 'Republics pass, but so-and-so's paint
stays'. Political cynicism of this kind is still widespread. Is it
justified? Will the Fourth Republic survive? I am tempted to
reply by denying the validity of the question, and to say that the
Fourth Republic is not now tottering into a premature decay, for
the simple reason that the Third Republic itself is not yet dead.

*A talk broadcast on the Third Programme of the B.B.C. in March 1949, and
published in _The Listener_, March 17th, 1949.

A few years ago it was generally believed that defeat and occupation had dug a deep gulf in the political life of France, a gulf in which the Third Republic had been buried. A new and better system was to take its place. 'La République est morte, vive la République!' The belief was mistaken. Political institutions and, even more, political habits die hard. It is becoming clear that the funeral ceremonies of the Third Republic were at least premature. As the veneer of newness on the so-called Fourth Republic wears off, beneath it the characteristic features of the Third are reappearing. The new National Assembly is indistinguishable from the old Chamber of Deputies. The second Chamber, the Council of the Republic, despite the provisions of the constitution, behaves more and more like the former Senate. The extreme parties of right and left play into one another's hands just as their predecessors used to, and a minority government of the centre struggles to prevent the state from disintegrating into civil war. Nothing is new in all this. Is it unreasonable, in the light of such facts, to conclude that the Fourth Republic is not a new beginning, not even the heir to the Third Republic, that it *is* the Third Republic?

This may seem a pessimistic view. The old evils are reborn and the sacrifices have been in vain. But it has an important corollary. If we want to know whether the instability of French governments is curable, and in what way, we have to look, not merely at the events of the last few years, but at the whole development of the Third Republic. The Third Republic had great achievements to its credit; but it had certain weaknesses which prepared the way for its fall. The most common charge was corruption. This was shockingly misused for party purposes, but no one can deny that it existed. Political corruption is a result before it is a cause, a symptom, not the disease itself. If shady politicians or their financial backers have been able to pull too many political strings, that is not because of their intrinsic importance in French society. It is because of the failure of those who should have ruled in their place.

France, let us remind ourselves, is a democracy. Where shall we look for the sources of the weakness of the French Republic but where the ultimate political power lies, in the masses of the people, which means the industrial workers in the towns, and the peasantry in the countryside? First the industrial workers: the political influence of the trade unions is naturally less in France, which has such a large rural population, than in Great Britain. But it might have been much more effective than it was, or is now, if it were not divided between Communists and Socialists. How much more effective was shown in the Popular Front episode before the war, and in the first phase after Liberation. Apart from these two brief interludes, for the greater part of the last thirty years, the Communist Party in France has subordinated practically every other objective in domestic politics to the attempt to drive the Socialist Party out of existence. It has failed, but the result has been that the political influence of the industrial workers has largely been nullified.

There is no such fundamental political cleavage in the countryside; in consequence the peasants—that is, the farmers of all grades, rich and poor—and the party that identified itself with their interests, the Radical Socialists, dominated French politics during the Third Republic, and are still very powerful. France, after all, is a rural country. Over half of the population lives in communes of less than 2,000 inhabitants. In the last resort, and at bottom, France is a peasants' Republic. That, I believe, is the key to understanding the fundamental facts of French politics. The strength and the weakness of France arise from this. The trouble with the peasantry is that, though they have learned the value of the vote to defend their interests, they have had no very enlightened conception up to the present of what those interests are. Their political programme can be summed up in two points—to preserve peace at almost any price, and to pay as little direct taxation as possible, preferably none. But apart from these two basic aims, their political consciousness hardly extended beyond local issues.

Thus, I must qualify what I have just said. Though ultimately the peasants ruled France, their rule was passive and negative.

Like the industrial workers, though for a different reason, they did not exercise the constructive political influence that their numbers would have justified, and into the vacant place stepped, not unwillingly, the professional party politicians. By their influence the political struggle was transformed from a means to achieving specific policies into an end in itself. No fundamental problems were solved, because none were tackled. It would not be fair, perhaps, to blame the politicians too severely for the disasters which struck France. They merely followed their nature. All the same, we ought to ask why the evil did not produce its own cure, why, ever since the war, France has continued to be ruled by weak and unstable governments. We must not expect too much from democracy, but why were French electors unable to apply the sanction of the polls effectively?

The explanation, I believe, is that the weakness became self-perpetuating. One result of the conditions I have just described is that France has rarely or never, since 1918, had a government strong enough to draw up a balanced budget. The almost permanent deficit was met by printing paper money. The resulting inflation intensified the cleavages of interest in society, and established a vicious circle of financial and political instability. Inflation was not the original cause of political weakness, but it provides a reason why political instability has become endemic. It is the running sore which has prohibited the restoration of health to the French body politic. If this analysis is accepted, one practical conclusion follows. The Gaullist remedy for the post-war difficulties in France, a change in the constitution, is not merely inadequate but almost irrelevant. The disease lies in the state of society, not merely in the structure of political institutions. We can even say in which section of society it lies. Not in the profiteers from inflation: they may have taken advantage of the situation, but they did not create it. Nor among the industrial workers and the trades unions: they are not powerful enough in France to be a decisive force; which is just as well, because their divisions result from communist world policy and are not likely to be curable, except in terms of the world situation.

The fundamental source of the political and financial weakness of France lies where, as I have already said, ultimate political power resides, in the great mass of the peasantry. That is the reason why I have emphasised that France is primarily a peasants' Republic. What follows from this? Political thinkers, it seems to me, have been slow to recognize the fact that the peasantry no longer plays its traditional role in the state. The peasant is no mere conservative: his kind of reaction is the foster-mother of revolution. An unintelligent clinging to customary abuses renders the peasant the ideal agent for exploitation by the most sinister forces in the community. The continuing influence of the peasantry is the chief reason why the so-called Fourth Republic cannot escape from the Third, and remains petrified in the past.

Yet surely something must happen? If the peasantry will not move of its own volition, can it not be made to move? There is one method of coping with the problem of the peasantry which is now becoming familiar. It is the communist method. The agricultural population is split by playing on the grievances of its poorer elements. The discontented section is combined with the industrial workers, and a revolutionary force is assembled, sufficiently strong to enable a left-wing coalition, led by the Communists of course, to seize power. Non-Communists who had gone along with the party are subsequently either absorbed or liquidated, and an economic policy is put into force which proletarianizes the peasantry. Henceforth the peasant, whether he wants to or not, shares the burden of the state in ample measure.

This solution is apparently workable in the conditions of eastern Europe. I do not believe it would work in France. The solution—if there is a solution—will have to come in France not by force but by consent. It will have to win the co-operation of the peasants. Is this as good as saying that there is no solution? I do not think so. The French peasantry is one of the most conservative classes in Europe. But it is beginning to be capable of change. In recent years the shortage of food has made the country wealthy at the expense of the towns. More important, the French peasant is beginning to demand a better standard of living for himself and his children. Anyone who has seen the conditions of life in many French villages knows that there is plenty of room for improvement. I believe the peasant knows it himself—and that is an important new fact. It means that he is beginning to be capable of playing a constructive, and not merely a passive, role in the political and economic life of the nation. The party that first succeeds in harnessing him to progressive social and economic policies will hold the future of France in its hands.

History may say that it cannot be done, that it never has been done. Well, I believe history may prove wrong. A new factor is coming into operation. Prices are beginning to fall. Unless there is an increase in the productivity of the land the French peasant will lose all his recent gains. The desire to keep what has once been won is a greater force than the hope of winning hypothetical benefits. With this desire in his mind, a desire only to be satisfied by increased productivity, the hoarded capital of the peasant may begin to emerge. Indeed, in the subscriptions to the recent loan it has already begun to do so. Even the tax collector may draw in rather more than he does at present, though perhaps not all he should, if the state can offer the peasant something, as well as taking it away.

How to increase productivity is matter for a more technical discussion. Obviously it involves a plan for the modernization and increased mechanization of agriculture. The need for this is undeniable. By way of illustration here are a few comparisons. An estimate for 1935–8 gives the productivity of agricultural labour in France as just half what it is in Great Britain. France has, including women, some 7,000,000 workers on the land; America has about 8,500,000 : but compare their food production. Even given the will, France by herself cannot modernize her agriculture. Marshall Aid will help, but here lies one of the most promising fields for Franco-British co-operation. The recent economic agreements between the two countries have already laid the foundations. French agriculture needs machinery and it will need a market. We can supply both. European economic co-operation has few more promising fields.

9

THE HISTORICAL SIGNIFICANCE OF MARCEL PROUST*

An appreciation of the historical setting is always valuable, and sometimes essential, for the understanding of any work of literature. This is a platitude. It is not quite so platitudinous to point out that in this connection history must be understood as including events to come, as well as the past and present. Great revolutions in human affairs have their harbingers in the world of letters. I am not thinking of the professional prophets of doom and destruction, but of those who, taking their *sondages* from far below the surface of national life, detect and respond to the movement of its deepest tides. Thus Beaumarchais mocked at a decadent noblesse and in the antics of Figaro exhibited the superiority of brains to birth. Rousseau foresaw the approach of 'a state of crisis and the century of revolutions'. At a deeper level, in the great Russian novelists a dying social system agonized. A host of German late-Romantics, from Nietzsche to Thomas Mann, foreshadowed the coming of the Nazi revolution of destruction. France, during the last generation, was also in a state of impending crisis, which eventually, under the shock of foreign attack, proved mortal to the Third Republic, and among those whose work can now be seen as an anticipation of social catastrophe, perhaps the greatest was Marcel Proust. In the light of subsequent history the *Recherche du temps perdu* has acquired a significance that could hardly have been suspected in the early 'twenties.

It may seem strange to discover historical significance in a writer who, as he himself often declared, never concerned

*This paper appeared in the *Cambridge Journal*, i, no. 10, July 1948.

himself with politics, and for whom reality consisted in the inner world of the subjective consciousness. But if Proust was the most subjective of novelists, he was also one of the keenest observers of the world around, with a preternatural sensibility to the impressions it offered. The impressions to which his mind most often reverts may seem to be merely trivial physical sensations. He recalls with almost painful reality the most insignificant memories — the taste of a madeleine dipped in his great-aunt Leonie's coffee, the sight and scent of the hawthorn hedges in spring, the unevenness of the paving-stones at Venice — but these are part of his private magic: they are the incantations which bring to life a lost world. Things are not real, he seems to tell us, nor do we really possess them, when we experience them for the first time, but only when they have sunk into our consciousness and are re-lived in the memory. This, the discovery of lost time and its restoration to consciousness, is the essential theme of his book.

It would not be fanciful, therefore, to say that Proust was in his way undertaking the same task as the historian. The period he covers stretches from the closing years of the nineteenth century to the end of the First World War; his novel was in composition between 1905 and 1922. Beginning at a time when the echoes of the Dreyfus case and the struggle against clericalism still aroused the bitterest feelings in France, he died, writing to the last, when these great conflicts had become almost historical memories, and the country had emerged victorious from a titanic struggle. His book, therefore, might have been expected to have begun with doubts, and fears, but to have ended with a triumphant assertion of difficulties overcome and dangers past. In fact we discover precisely the opposite development in his mind. There can be no doubt that he thought of the later years of his life as the beginning of the end for the France he had known and loved as a young man. Mr Edmund Wilson, writing in 1939, says, 'We are always feeling with Proust as if we were reading about the end of something — this seems, in fact, to be what he means us to feel.' A very short time was to pass before it was discovered that Proust had not been entirely wrong. It really was the end of something, of the social and political compromise on which the Third Republic had rested, and—he believed—of the charm of that society which had flourished under its protection. For, and this, it seems to us, has not been adequately recognized, Proust gives us both sides of the picture. The degeneration of so many of his characters, their almost inevitable progression from good to bad, or from bad to worse, has been seized upon to the obscuring of the fact that if there is degeneration it must be from something better. The gloomier pictures were not the only ones that Proust painted, nor did they furnish the impressions that recurred with most persistence to his mind.

To understand the significance of Proust we must begin where he began, with the France of *Chez Swann*, its focal point in the little town of Combray towards the close of the nineteenth century. Innumerable memories of childhood and youth went to the composition of an enchanting picture of *la douceur de la vie* in a small French provincial town. Not that Combray is to be identified with Illiers, where Proust spent much of his childhood. All his places, like almost all his characters, are composite portraits, drawn from many different originals. He takes particular care to confuse his geographical references, so that the reader shall never be able to say here is this or that particular place. Combray is not Illiers: it is the quintessence of all the little towns of France, distilled and redistilled with loving care, and, as touch after touch is added, the design, composed at first of apparently chance details, gradually takes shape—silent streets in the summer sun, cool evening gardens, hedgerows bestowing the revelation of hawthorn in spring, the two familiar walks—the *côté des Guermantes* with the companionship of the ever-changing little Vivonne, and the *côté de Méséglise* along a typical straight road across the plain. Appearing and reappearing, over the roofs, between the trees, seen from innumerable angles, ever changing yet always the same, the church spire of Saint Hilaire presides over Combray and the surrounding countryside and draws the wanderer back as if by an invisible chain. Volumes in *À la recherche du temps perdu* are devoted to the portrayal of a series of salons, nor should we forget the long lyrical passage on the street cries of Paris, yet in the whole book the rural atmosphere predominates, as indeed it should, for France is a land of country towns and villages. It is rural and not urban France that holds Proust's strongest affections. A nostalgic love of the country and idealization of its inhabitants is one of the strongest characteristics of the book. It appears in innumerable touches, in the pleasure, for example, with which the narrator listens to the peasant accents of the maid, Françoise, and in the ever-present feeling that life is lived out of doors, under the sun or the stars.

We do not get to know many people in Combray. Its spirit emerges more subtly from the description of externals, the slow tempo of the scenes in which its reality is re-created out of the impressions stored up in the mind of the child. But we see through the eyes of Marcel the home of his parents, and meet the faithful Françoise, her unattractive qualities as yet unrevealed. We hear echoes of the life of the town as they penetrate to the ears of great-aunt Leonie, ruling and passing judgment from her bedroom sanctuary. We sit in the dusk in the garden, waiting for the tinkle of the bell that will announce the coming of M. Swann, known to Marcel's parents as a friendly, cultured and modest neighbour, only later to be revealed as the man of society, member of the Jockey Club and associate of the Prince of Wales, as Swann in love and frequenter of the bourgeois Verdurin salon, finally to decline into the husband of Odette, *déclassé* and racked with jealousy.

After a long pastoral introduction, the appearance of Swann introduces the theme of love and jealousy, to be repeated with innumerable variations in the relationship of Marcel and Albertine. Already in the story of Swann romantic love is recognized as an illusion, but the illusion is still there, and jealousy, which is presented as wrapped up with love, is, after all, strongest in youth. And nothing happens — nothing ever will happen—to spoil the idyllic, almost Rousseauist charm of Combray, which is destined to remain, stored up in the mind of Marcel, like a Platonic idea in heaven.

Just outside the orbit of Combray, hovering over it as the medieval castle guarded and overshadowed the medieval scene, is the great house of Guermantes, its ancient titles glowing for the young boy like the colours in a stained-glass window, enduring witness to a past of chivalric love and knightly deeds, symbol of the greatness of the ancient aristocracy of France. And once, to bring it all to life, he is granted a vision of the lovely duchess herself, Oriane—Proust had a genius for names—inheritor of all this splendour and embodiment of an unattainable ideal.

Incorporate in this peaceful scene, as the soul in the body, are the two watchful angels whose love surrounds and protects the young boy, his mother and grandmother, moving together in such perfect harmony that his mother seems only an echo, an octave higher, of the deeper note struck by his grandmother. Whereas to compose practically every other character Proust drew upon more than one model, here he has enlarged a single model to provide two separate characters. It is hardly an accident that he should seek to enhance the effect of perfect goodness by reduplicating it in the two women to whom the Marcel of the book looks up with love only this side of adoration, striking here a chord in unison where so much else is to be a chromatic discord. An ingenious device, moreover, adds a sense of depth in time, as though far-off notes were reverberating in harmony. His mother reads to him George Sand's pastoral romance of *François le champi*, the foundling adopted by the peasant girl, who finds when he grows up that, after absence— the transition is very delicately effected—his affection has changed in nature, and from a son he has become a lover, and who ends by marrying his Madeleine. The choice of tale is most significant psychologically, but the important point for our thesis is the skill with which the France of George Sand's Berrichon romances is brought in to give a patina of age to Proust's picture of Combray. A similar motive leads to the introduction, as the constant theme of his grandmother's conversation, of the letters of Mme de Sévigné. Proust recalls from the past the memory of the woman who had loved and most beautifully described the French countryside and its traditional way of life, and the writer in whom goodness was combined with intelligence in the highest degree.

All this, it is to be observed, is never lost. There is no going back on Combray and all it stands for. Whenever any aspect of this scene returns to the mind of Proust's Marcel it is with the same affection, the same implicit faith in its unchangeableness, its unalterable goodness. This is the standard by which the remainder of his life was to be judged, and it can only have been through failure to appreciate his book as a whole that the presence of this point of rest, this note of perfection, can ever have been missed.

The idyllic picture of Combray was not intended, of course, to represent a permanent state. Proust's object was to tell a tale of transformation and decay, and especially to illuminate social history by showing the meeting of the two ways of his childhood, the fusion of the old aristocracy with the new, wealthy bourgoisie. From the beginning he was conscious of the impermanence of all that is loved — 'look thy last on all things lovely, every hour' — which intensifies their apprehension. But it would be wrong to conclude from the belief that the transient is the all, that Proust's is an entirely pessimistic philosophy. All that ever really was for us, and exactly as it was, lives on in us. Things and persons change and fade, but the subjective impression persists. A chance sensation can bring the hawthorn on the hedges into bloom again and renew the springtime, not as it is now but as it was then. If we can keep the child's intense awareness, loveliness is not lost for ever. One of the objects of Proust's novel was the recovery and immortalization in art of a world whose transience was its reality.

Between 1914 and 1918, however, something happened to Proust which led him to attitudes of mind deeper than this romantic nostalgia, and caused him to make a total revision of his book, with the exception of the first two volumes, which were already in print. Albert Feuillerat, in a most valuable contribution to the study of Proust,[1] examined in detail the nature of this revision, and although his interpretation has been challenged, it is doubtful if it can be overthrown in its broad lines. He shows that Proust undertook a systematic blackening of his characters. Odette is made more vulgar and at the same time more successful in her social ambitions. Gilberte, the little girl played with and loved in the Champs Élysées, becomes older and harder. Françoise, the devoted servant of *Chez Swann*, is converted into almost a pathological specimen of petty domestic vices. Saint-Loup's mistress, Rachel, even becomes ugly. His mother, Mme de Marsantes, at first apparently the embodiment of maternal affections, reveals herself as the complete egoist and hypocrite. Bergotte, a modified version of Anatole France, had formerly appeared as the ideal of the literary man. Now Proust reflects the increasing impatience of the war generation with what seemed his incurable frivolity. Swann, the cultured, kindly aristocrat, had constituted a conspicuously high representation of the Jewish element in French society. Now Proust brings the odious Bloch family to the fore, covers them with ridicule, and lavishes on them vices unalleviated by any grace of manner or generosity of spirit. So we might go on. The author's mother, his grandmother and Saint-Loup alone escape the universal denigration.

From the healthy, traditional life of Combray, from the seascape of Balbec with its frieze of *jeunes filles en fleur*, Proust turns in his later volumes to the study of a society in decay. He concentrates his attention on an aristocracy which combines the vices of the Court with those of the courtyard. The bourgeois life of Combray disappears except as a memory. As Swann's Way merges with the Guermantes' Way, the bourgeois characters acquire all the vices of the degenerate aristocracy without its charm. Proust, by his own statement, saw himself as the Saint-Simon of his age. He has been criticized for his concentration

[1] *Comment Marcel Proust a composé son Roman* (1934).

on the degenerate elements in the community and the domestic class dependent upon them, and his indifference to all that made the real strength of the people, but—and here we return to the point from which we started—subsequent events have provided him with something like a posthumous vindication. His justification was to come after his death, when his choice of material was to be revealed as the result not of mere chance, or if it were an accident, of the kind of accident that happens to genius.

It is true that the whole of French society was not decadent and corrupt. It is equally true that less than twenty years after Proust had died the elements of corruption had gone a long way towards spreading through the whole social fabric and that much of it came from the sources of infection so cruelly satirized by Proust. The classes which suffered the bitterest of his implied criticism were undoubtedly the most dangerous elements in the fabric of the Third Republic. He does not write a word of politics. His judgment on society is not the direct indictment of a Rousseau, though there is much of Rousseauist criticism implied therein. As the reader draws to the end of each of Proust's long conversation-pieces, it is difficult for him not to sense an echo of the pessimism of Renan's phrase, 'l'impression qui me reste en sortant d'un salon, c'est le désespoir de la civilisation.' Written as a satire, his book became also an epitaph. The aristocracy, which the young Marcel had almost idolized, becomes the target of his bitterest shafts. His youthful idealization of the Guermantes gives place to contempt. The illusion of aristocratic exclusiveness disappears in a welter of mixed marriages. Saint-Loup marries, for her money, the half-Jewish Gilberte. The niece of Jupien, tailor and pimp, adopted in return for her uncle's services by the haughty Charlus, is wedded to the Marquis de Cambremer, and social climbers, unacquainted with the world of the old aristocracy, advertise their familiarity with high society by spreading reports of her elevated birth. At the end, in *Le temps retrouvé*, all social standards have vanished in the general disintegration after the war. The very titles of the aristocracy have become meaningless. The odious and bourgeois Mme Verdurin reappears under the guise of Princesse de Guermantes. Rachel, first offered him for twenty francs in a second-rate brothel, is now the bosom friend of the lovely and witty Oriane. The corrupt old republican politician has become an elder statesman, high in the favours of the Faubourg St Germain. Morel, sink of all vices, has a new-made reputation as the model of upright conduct. Charlus, prince of the Holy Roman Empire, and symbol of almost insane aristocratic exclusiveness, bows with pathetic senility to a woman whose existence he would formerly have ignored, and is himself despised by a jumped-up new society to which the genealogy of the Guermantes is meaningless.

Besides revealing the general collapse of social standards, Proust's satire goes deeper. Were they ever, he leaves it to us to ask, other than an illusion? The 'marquise' who keeps the *cabinets de toilette* in the Champs Élysées, whose snobbery towards her patrons provides a farcical commentary on 'social standards', gives us his answer. And ultimately even such standards vanish. Wealth is left as the only social criterion. Again Proust makes no open comment. Critics have been led, rather undiscerningly, to suppose that it was his own standard, and to attribute this *conception marchande* of human relationships not to the society he was satirizing but to his own personality. The memory of his grandmother, of Saint-Loup and of Combray rises up in protest against such a verdict.

We might, more plausibly, have supposed that Proust was at least unconscious of the social implications of plutocracy, were it not that in one passage he surprisingly lifts the curtain and betrays an awareness of the world outside his restricted circle that we might not have expected to find. He does it, of course, indirectly. Looking through the window of his luxury hotel at Balbec, he suddenly becomes conscious of another world, that of the *petit peuple* of workers and lower middle classes, moving in the gloom outside with expressionless faces. As always, there is no comment.

Proust, in fact, was intensely aware of the class structure of society. It was not the class conflict, however, but the war and the spirit that had come in with it that was the source of his deepest pessimism, and the central point in his diagnosis of social degeneration. It seemed to him that the war, as he wrote to his friend, the painter Jacques-Émile Blanche, had inaugurated a *'crise d'âme'*, which was to be the end, not only of the France, but of the Europe of his youth. It is difficult not to feel that Charlus, although he represents the ultimate degeneration of the aristocracy, is speaking for Proust himself when, as scion of a cosmopolitan aristocracy, he makes his futile demonstrations against the vulgarities of triumphant nationalism. We must not, however, identify the writer with the ill-concealed philo-Germanism of Charlus – another significant and prophetic stroke. Proust's patriotic spirit is undeniable. It appears in the affectionate portrait of Saint-Loup, modelled on his friend Bertrand de Fénélon, killed at the front in 1915, whose picture Proust, even in his latest mood, could not bring himself seriously to blacken. He made a half-hearted attempt to do so, but the story of the *Croix de guerre*, lost by Saint-Loup, and found by Marcel in Jupien's unsavoury establishment for gentlemen, is perhaps the only episode in the whole of Proust which does not ring quite true.

It is not easy to quote Proust except at immoderate length, but one passage, in its touching simplicity, calls for citation here.

Or, on avait vu cette chose si belle, qui fut si fréquente à cette époque-là dans tout le pays et qui témoignerait, s'il y avait un historien pour en perpétuer le souvenir, de la grandeur de la France, de sa grandeur d'âme, de sa grandeur selon Saint-André-des-Champs, et que ne révélèrent pas moins tant de civils survivant à l'arrière que les soldats tombés à la Marne. Un neveu de Françoise avait été tué à Berry-au-Bac qui était aussi le neveu de ces cousins millionnaires de Françoise, anciens cafetiers retirés depuis

longtemps après fortune faite. Il avait été tué lui, tout petit
cafetier sans fortune qui, à la mobilisation, âgé de vingt-
cinq ans, avait laissé sa jeune femme seule pour tenir le
petit bar qu'il croyait regagner quelques mois après. Il avait
été tué. Et alors on avait vu ceci. Les cousins millionnaires
de Françoise, et qui n'étaient rien à la jeune femme, veuve
de leur neveu, avaient quitté la campagne où ils étaient
retirés depuis dix ans et s'étaient remis cafetiers, sans
vouloir toucher un sou ; tous les matins à six heures, la
femme millionnaire, une vraie dame, était habillée ainsi
que «sa demoiselle», prêtes à aider leur nièce et cousine
par alliance. Et depuis plus de trois ans, elles rinçaient
ainsi des verres et servaient des consommations depuis
le matin jusqu'à neuf heures et demi du soir, sans un
jour de repos. Dans ce livre, où il n'y a pas un seul fait
qui ne soit fictif, où il n'y a pas un seul personnage «à clef»,
où tout a été inventé par moi selon les besoins de ma
démonstration, je dois dire, à la louange de mon pays, que
seuls les parents millionnaires de Françoise ayant quitté
leur retraite pour aider leur nièce sans appui, que seuls
ceux-là sont des gens réels, qui existent. Et persuadé que
leur modestie ne s'en offensera pas, pour la raison qu'ils
ne liront jamais ce livre, c'est avec un enfantin plaisir et
une profonde émotion que, ne pouvant citer les noms de
tant d'autres qui durent agir de même et par qui la France
a survécu, je transcris ici leur nom véritable : ils s'appellent,
d'un nom si français, d'ailleurs, Larivière.

One would have expected his patriotism to have called
Proust to rejoice in victory, but the great military and political
events of 1918 and 1919 are passed over in silence by his book.
Was this also a verdict on a victory which seemed to him to
bring few laurels with it, and those soon faded? Proust was no
nationalist, but he foresaw little good from the Peace settle-
ment. 'Ah!' he wrote to an American friend in 1920, 'notre
Paix ; je sais bien que ce n'est pas de votre faute si on l'a

sabotée ... mais quelle souffrance en pensant à mon pays.'
During and after the war his pessimism became truly fundamental, and to express it he made use of a theme which had
perhaps not originally been intended to fulfil this purpose.
Personal interest, and the passion for psychological analysis,
were probably the initial motives for the introduction as a leading theme of the homosexual illusion, but it now came to take
on the larger significance of a symbol, and to provide the most
poignant expression of his pessimism. It would be a profound
mistake, we believe, to class Proust – at least as he is revealed in
À la recherche du temps perdu – with the immoralists. Of course, he
never advocates or condemns. He describes, analyses, satirizes,
and the picture that emerges is all the more devastating. It is
important to note that as the novel proceeds the treatment of
this subject radically changes. The inhabitants of Sodom and
Gomorrah, when they first appear, are lonely *isolés*, wanderers
in a foreign land, specimens for the sociologist or the psycho-
logist. Gradually, however, Proust comes to see them, not as
individual eccentrics, as Charlus, Mlle Vinteuil's friend, or the
actress Léa had seemed, when first the revelation had burst
upon him, but as a growing and conquering army. It slowly
dawns upon the reader that Proust does not mean him to continue to think of them as what they had at first seemed, unhappy
alien types. They are everywhere. Sodom and Gomorrah are no
longer foreign lands, but Paris, France, Western civilization.

Proust's subject in the end becomes something more universal
and profound in significance than the transformation and
degeneration of French social classes he had originally planned
to describe. So long as Marcel's relations with Albertine are the
dominant subject the symbol remains tied to its individual
representation and therefore limited in its scope. But with
Albertine fled, and his love for her, after jealousies and agonies
that long outlive their object and victim, finally dead, a note of
sweetness and normality, which in spite of everything she had
carried with her, comes to an end. All that he had loved is now
lost. The satire becomes fiercer, with fewer idyllic interludes.

To the accompaniment of the bombardment of Paris the macabre comedy of Charlus-in-chains is enacted. Horror and madness take charge of the plot. What had earlier seemed mere incidental vices have become the characters themselves, stripped naked and tied down for merciless dissection. We are presented, in the closing episodes, no longer with men and women, but with dehumanized puppets. The last great reception of the Guermantes is hell on earth. Figures bearing the names we are familiar with perform a grotesque dance of death in life, stiffly repeating their customary gestures as though at the command of an infernal puppet-master. All are in varying stages of mental and physical decay. It is no accident that his mother and grandmother, Saint-Loup and Albertine, whom, when all is said, he had loved, are spared from sharing this ultimate degradation at the hands of time by the kinder hand of death.

Proust, it has been said, set out to be the Saint-Simon of the Third Republic. He succeeds in being something more. He assumes at the end the mantle of an Old Testament prophet, an Isaiah or a Jeremiah without the consolation of religion, with no messianic hope. The only faith left to him, the one thing standing like a rock above the destroying waters of time, is artistic creation. Bergotte, Elstir, Vinteuil, apparently insignificant, petty men in their lifetimes, find their true lives in the immortal forms of art they have created. That he must abandon the unreal world he has lived in and join these in the real world of poetry, painting and music, this is the lesson that the Marcel of the book learns at last. So perhaps Proust's gospel is in the end one of salvation, but it is salvation for the few : the rest must live out their lives in the Cities of the Plain, waiting for the fire that will destroy but not purify. Where are Combray, Madame de Sévigné, the Berry of George Sand, his grandmother in the garden, Swann at the Jockey Club, Gilberte in the Champs Élysées, the *jeunes filles en fleur*? They belong to a France we knew in our youth and shall know no more.

In 1922 Proust's pessimism may have seemed the expression of an individual eccentric. Less than a generation later the

Cities of the Plain were burning all over Europe. History, which sits in judgment on the works of man, and condemns some to oblivion, has vindicated the pessimism of Proust, though not, perhaps, his despair. That something was rotten in the state not only of France but of the Western world, that the society he knew was fast decaying and would soon be dead, he saw with agonizing clarity. What he did not see, or, at least, seldom if ever said, was that all was not dross, that there were elements in Western civilization that would stand the fire, that France itself was capable of rebirth. What absolute pessimism failed to allow for was the toughness of a society and a way of life that had been a thousand years in the making. In the Guermantes and Verdurins and Blochs, and all their hangers-on, the stink of decay is strong, and we can believe that Proust was a true prophet in foreseeing their destruction. But Combray can be rediscovered in every corner of France. The magnanimous ardour of Saint Loup, the loving irresponsibility of Albertine, the artistic integrity of Elstir, the analytic intelligence and intense sensibility of Marcel himself, above all the grace and devotion of his grandmother, embodiment of all the classic virtues — these are not dead, nor will easily die. Through them Proust escapes the limitations of his historical pessimism and enters into a broader inheritance.

10

AN AGE OF REVOLUTIONARY WARS:
AN HISTORICAL PARALLEL*

THERE is one point on which both sides in the present world conflict are agreed. Each may denounce the leadership of the other side, but neither supposes that a change in leadership would make any difference, because both believe that it is a conflict not of persons or governments, but of principles, or of systems of society. The commonly accepted explanation of the conflict, in short, is that the world is now divided between communism and capitalism. At the risk of seeming paradoxical it must be asked what this explanation explains, and whether, in fact, it does anything but provide convenient labels for the opposing forces. The implied assumption that states with differing economic systems must necessarily be hostile to one another is at least unproved, and goes against historical experience. It would be easier to explain the conflict as a religious war, and communism certainly exhibits many of the features of a militant religion, but can we be quite content to dismiss Communists and Capitalists as the Protestants and Catholics of the twentieth century? And if we are, can we find many religious wars in which secular and political interests did not provide as strong or stronger a motive than religion?

Because of the difficulty of accounting for the conflict in purely ideological terms, some students of the contemporary world fall back on the view that all hostilities between states are mere conflicts of power politics. The fact that we normally tend to resent the reduction of the motives of our states to simple Machiavellianism is no disproof of this interpretation.

* This paper appeared in the *Review of Politics*, xiii, no. 2, April 1951.

Historians are willing enough to allow the mere rivalries of power politics to account for many of the wars of the past, why not for the present struggle? If this view is accepted, the whole ideological apparatus on both sides must be dismissed as a gigantic smoke-screen, produced for the purpose of concealing the machinations of self-interest. Such an explanation seems to put human capacity for cold-blooded calculation at too high a level. The discussion thus wanders from one extreme to the other indefinitely: neither the ideological explanation, nor the explanation in terms of power politics, seems adequate by itself. The purpose of this study is to suggest that there is another line of approach to the problem, which takes us a good deal farther towards understanding the nature of the conflict. It may be suggested that a weakness in contemporary political analysis is the tendency to see each issue on too short a scale, or sometimes on none at all. Looking at the major struggles of our day, beginning with the last phase of the First World War, it is not difficult to see that they fall into a single historical category: they are essentially revolutionary wars. Now this is not an entirely new phenomenon, and to understand it we cannot do better than turn back to the history of the greatest of all revolutionary wars of the past.

At the end of the eighteenth century, Europe, as today the world, was split in two by the existence of a great revolutionary state. When the French Revolution burst on an astonished world it came with the promise of liberty and peace. The rulers of the other states of Europe did not exactly welcome it, but they had no intention of interfering in the affairs of France. The government of Great Britain, which was to prove the most enduring enemy of revolutionary France, was profoundly pacific. The younger Pitt, in his budget speech of 1792, uttered the famous prophecy that 'There never was a time in the history of this country, when we might more reasonably expect fifteen years of peace than at the present moment.' Why were these hopes of peace disappointed? Why did such a deep-seated opposition develop between Britain and revolutionary France that instead of fifteen years of peace, over twenty years of war followed? If the question is put in more general terms—why was a revolutionary state unable to live at peace with the rest of Europe?—its contemporary relevance will easily be seen.

It is worth pointing out, because the fact is often overlooked, that however much the other powers disliked the Revolution, the declarations of war did not come from them: it was France which declared war in turn on Austria, Prussia, England, Holland, Spain. But the question of responsibility for the beginning of the war is not the essential issue. The important question is not even whether there was any factor in the Revolution which was likely to lead to war—there are always plenty of causes of war—but whether there was anything which made peace impossible. Those who lived at the time thought there was. The first point that strikes one, in considering the causes of the long continuance, rather than the origins, of the Revolutionary War, is the fear of propaganda. The revolutionaries aimed at establishing direct relations with all peoples over the heads of their governments. In those who sympathized with their principles they had a Fifth Column everywhere. 'The genius of the French Revolution marched forth,' said Pitt, 'the terror and dismay of the world.' Its aim was to bring liberty to all nations. But to quote Pitt once again, 'They will not accept under the name of Liberty any model of government, but that which is conformable to their own opinions and ideas; and all men must learn from the mouth of their cannon the propagation of their system in every part of the world.' While such a combination of ideas and policies prevailed in the Revolution, the other powers saw no security in peace with France.

Even at the time, however, it was realized that revolutionary propaganda by itself was not a sufficient motive for war. The other countries of Europe, if left to themselves, were quite capable of suppressing their own Jacobins without undue difficulty. To Fox's charge that he was making war on opinion Pitt replied, 'It is not so. We are not in arms against the opinions of the closet, nor the speculations of the schools. We are at war with *armed* opinions.' The power of French armies was what made revolutionary opinions dangerous. Though we must not underestimate the great wave of genuine idealism with which the Revolution began, those who controlled the actions of the revolutionary armies were not moved exclusively by idealistic motives. When, early in the Revolution, the French Assembly passed a decree repudiating all conquests, it was undoubtedly sincere. But this idealistic frame of mind did not remain undiluted for very long. Revolutionary dynamism was not to be confined within the narrow limits of a single state. The revolutionaries soon learned to rationalize their aggressive instincts, and imagined that they had thereby moralized self-interest.

With the military genius released by the Revolution, with the military tactics adapted to make use of the enthusiasm of the early volunteers, and with the solid weight of manpower provided by the *levée en masse*, it was not long before war meant victory. As it went on, annexation followed occupation, and the plebiscites which at first accompanied liberation by the revolutionary armies rapidly came to be omitted as unnecessary formalities. The frontiers of France swelled, satellite states formed excrescences on the new boundaries, and the pretence of liberation wore thinner and thinner. The French armies brought many good things in their train: they brought a more humane and rational legal system, more efficient administration, opportunities for the middle classes. But the conquered countries had to pay a heavy price in government by small pro-French cliques, whose authority rested on French bayonets and the secret police, and in furnishing continual supplies of men and money for the French armies. As early as 1795 the dominant aims of French foreign policy, which can be traced without any disguise in the records of the Quai d'Orsay, were reduced to two: first, to obtain strategic frontiers and a glacis of dependent territories in front of them. These were to protect the gains of France from counter-attack, and to provide a jumping-off ground for further aggression. Secondly, France required economic advantages—money, corn, cattle, clothing, boots—requisitioned by the generals or legally obtained by treaties of peace and friendship. Bonaparte had nothing to teach the Republic in the arts of aggression and confiscation. The Revolution was aggressive abroad even before it became tyrannical at home, and Pitt was right in believing that the only limit on French conquests was the strength of the resistance opposed to them.

Of course, we must not exaggerate the novelty of much of this. Sorel has pointed out that practically every crime in international relations with which the Revolution has been charged could be found in the repertoire of the *ancien régime*. The difference is that the Revolution did on principle what the *ancien régime* had done from lack of principle. What is the explanation? Is it just the normal decline in the idealism of a political movement under the temptations of power? 'Tout commence en mystique,' wrote Peguy, 'tout finit en politique.' We might believe this to be the explanation, if it were not that the Revolution turned into something which went far beyond the normal aggressions of international politics. It developed into a bid for universal empire and changed war from a limited struggle between governments into an almost unlimited struggle between nations. The French Assembly even passed a decree—not put into practice—that no British or Hanoverian prisoners should be taken. The speeches and propaganda of the revolutionary leaders, denouncing their enemies as nations of cannibals, inhuman beasts of prey and so on, have a very modern ring. Their opponents retaliated in kind and the result was the first draft—admittedly a very imperfect one—of totalitarian war, war without restriction in its methods and without limit in its ends.

Such a war did not arise merely out of the customary rivalries of power politics, but from the introduction of some new factor. It is suggested here that the new factor was the development of an ardent opposition of ideas. This opposition was one which played so little part in most international conflicts during the nineteenth century that we tended to forget that it ever could be a cause of conflict. International struggles came to be interpreted as simple clashes of material interests, with which principles had nothing to do. More recently the reaction produced by the exaggerated propaganda of the First World War increased the tendency, particularly among historians, to look with suspicion on the alleged role of ideas, or principles, in the struggles of the past. History, reviewed in this light, became a mere conflict of interests, and the politics of the present a glorified intrigue. In the course of the last thirty years Communists and Nazis have taught us, at a heavy price, that ideas do matter in history. We could have learnt the same lesson more cheaply from a study of the French Revolution; for what was the Revolution?

In what I have to say, I hope I shall not be suspected of attempting to sum up a great movement in terms of a single formula. The Revolution was many things. It was an attempt to reform the government of France, a revolt against well-known abuses, a struggle for power between the bourgeoisie and the privileged classes, and much more. But it was also, and this is what concerns us here, the embodiment of a great idea, the idea of the sovereignty of the people, or nation. For a clear statement of the meaning of this principle of popular or national sovereignty there is no need to go farther than to the little abbé who in 1789 was the oracle of the *tiers état* in France, Sieyes. 'The Nation,' Sieyes wrote, 'exists before all things and is the origin of all things. It is sufficient that its will is manifested for all positive law to vanish before it. In whatever manner a Nation wills, it is sufficient that it does will: all forms are good, and its will is always the supreme law.' This was the essence of the revolutionary creed, and this was what turned an ordinary political conflict into a major war of ideas.

The theory of popular sovereignty is different in one particular from every other theory of government. It is a theory according to which those who exercise power, and those over

whom it is exercised, are one and the same. The People rules—
whom does it rule?—it rules itself. Popular sovereignty, according to its exponents, is self-government, and therefore freedom.
The argument is plausible. I think it is fair to say that many,
asked to define democracy, would define it in some such way,
and would refuse to believe that the definition differs from the
normal Western conception of democracy. But it *does* differ, and
differ fundamentally. Can anyone in his senses really believe
that the people actually, concretely, rule this or any other
country? Are *we* the government? Do *we*, the people, impose the
taxes on ourselves and decide how to spend them? Do *we* pass
and carry out the laws on military service or tariffs or capital
punishment? Do *we* appoint our Secretaries and Ministers, or
any of the civil servants who manage our affairs? Of course we
do not. What we mean by saying that we are a democracy is
not that we *are* the government, but that through the process of
election and representation we *control* the government. This is
quite a different thing, as Burke saw when he was first con-
fronted with the revolutionary theory. 'The people', he said,
'are the natural control on authority. But to exercise and to
control together is contradictory and impossible.' The identification of the government with the people, Burke realized, was
the new thing, and in the long run the fatal thing, in revolutionary theory. The Revolution ended many evils and introduced many reforms, but in letting loose this principle on the
world, it released a spirit perhaps more potent for evil than
even those that it had exorcized.

The idea that the rulers can be identified with the ruled, the
government with the people, and that this is the meaning of
democracy, was, is and must be fatal to liberty. That may seem
a sweeping statement, but it will hardly seem exaggerated if
we consider the implications of the belief that government and
people can be one and the same. The identification is, as I have
said, impossible; but the mere *belief* in such an identification
makes any constitutional device for attempting to control
government in the interests of the people unnecessary and

irrelevant. A government has only to assert that it is the government of the people to be automatically emancipated from all restraints. Whoever lifts a finger against it, or utters a word of criticism, is an enemy of the people. He is guilty not of *lèse-majesté*, but, in the words of Robespierre, of *lèse-nation* or *lèse-peuple*. Even under the most despotic regimes, at any rate in Western Europe, it was admitted that the individual had rights. Before the new theory of sovereignty those rights faded away like snow in summer. Whatever the government had the power to do, it had the right to do: any crime was permissible: if it was done in the name of the people it was not a crime.

Internally the theory was a justification of tyranny, externally of aggression, for in the conditions of the modern world popular sovereignty inevitably means national sovereignty. It was because he saw this in the French Revolution that Burke opposed it so bitterly. He had no doubt what the theory of popular sovereignty would come to mean in the end, and he lived to see his fears justified. 'What now stands as government in France', he wrote, 'is struck out at a heat. The will, the wish, the want, the liberty, the toil, the blood of individuals is as nothing. Individuality is left out of their scheme of government. The state is all in all. Everything is referred to the production of force, afterwards everything is trusted to the use of it. It is military in its principle, in its maxims, in its spirit, and in all its movements. The state has dominion and conquest for its sole objects; dominion over minds by proselytism, over bodies by arms.' And who exercises this vast power in the name of the people? The common sense of the younger Pitt saw the answer as clearly as the more theoretical mind of Burke. 'In what is called the government of the multitude,' Pitt said, 'they are not the many who govern the few, but the few who govern the many. It is a species of tyranny, which adds insult to the wretchedness of its subjects by styling its own arbitrary decrees the voice of the people, and sanctioning its acts of oppression and cruelty under the pretence of the national will.'

The justification for this excursus into history will now, I hope, be apparent. Its extraordinary relevance to the problems of our own times hardly needs to be underlined. Change a few of the circumstances and have we not a picture of the division in the world today? Modern revolutionaries, promising peace, have similarly brought about a climate of war, which like the French revolutionaries they have attributed to war-mongers abroad. Neighbouring states have been swallowed up, or puppet governments established in them. Revolutionary propaganda has created a Fifth Column throughout the world. Wherever, by arms or propaganda, the revolutionary creed has been able to seize power, a government on its own model has been set up. The expansive pressure is continuous, for like the Napoleonic Empire the modern revolutionary state has no principle of limitation within itself. Its dynamism demands a continual forward movement. Held back in one quarter it breaks out in another, for it lives on the political, economic and psychological conditions of expansion.

The cleavage, moreover, as a century and a half ago, is between opposed conceptions of government, and one as then based on the principle of the sovereignty of the people, which in practice means the government, and the other today recognizing the rights and interests of the individual. In both, government is in the hands of the few, as it always is, but in liberal democracy it is subject to free criticism and periodic control. In popular democracy criticism is ruthlessly suppressed and the machine of government is organized to prevent control over it from being exercised from any quarter outside the government circle. Of course, though I believe both interpretations of democracy to be sincere — attributions of insincerity, such as are usual when two sides to an argument use the same term in contradictory senses, seem to me out of place here — I cannot believe them to be equally valid. The test of political liberty, as much as anything else, is whether the people, if they are dissatisfied with those who rule them, can freely and peacefully cause their government to change its policy, or themselves change their government. The answer, in Soviet Russia as in revolutionary France, is that they cannot. And one reason why they cannot is the operation of the principle of popular sovereignty.

There is a conclusion of great practical importance, it seems to me, to be drawn from this parallel between the consequences of the French and Russian Revolutions. It suggests that a single historic force is at work in both great revolutions of the eighteenth and twentieth centuries. On both sides of the Iron Curtain it has been assumed too easily that the cause of the cleavage is to be sought in the economic theories and practices of communism. At the beginning of this paper it was suggested that this form of the ideological explanation was unsatisfactory. It is also unnecessary. The example of the French Revolution suggests that the principle of popular or national sovereignty, pushed to the extreme limit, by itself is capable of producing an unbridgeable gap between a state and the rest of the world. Soviet Russia has undoubtedly been to school to Marx and derived much from him. But if what is called communism in Russia were a faithful expression of the principles of the author of *Das Kapital*, it would be the first time in history that an idea had been translated into an ideology without suffering a radical change. In fact one of the ironies of the modern world is that in the name of Marx, whose theoretical pattern was fashioned with a view to the ultimate 'withering away' of the state, the state should have reached its apogee.

If the argument so far has any validity, it follows that the world is not quite so clearly divided ideologically as we have been apt to think. For all modern states have been influenced by the theories of the French Revolution, and all, to a greater or less degree, assert the principle of national sovereignty and base it on the claim of the government to embody the will of the people. The conflict, therefore, is not one of absolute opposites and there is no law of the excluded middle to apply. Undoubtedly, the state, being, as Marx saw, the embodiment of power, if it has complete sovereignty, tyranny at home and conquest abroad will be unrestrained. The result of freeing the state from control, by pretending that the people can themselves be the government, was shown between 1789 and 1815. The same experiment has been made in our own day, with similar results. Leviathan lives and moves before our eyes, all the more dangerous because in infancy he was called liberty.

I might end at this point, but the resulting impression would be a false one, based on an artificially simplified antithesis. In what has already been said, indeed, there is the implication, which needs to be made explicit, that the cleavage of principle between the Soviet regime and the Western democracies is one of degree, though so great that it has almost become one of kind. If this is the case there is no reason for supposing that even the inflated sovereignty of the Soviet state is incapable of modification in the course of time. And meanwhile whether it leads to open war depends not on ideas but on the balance of opposed forces. France, once her strength had been released from the bonds of the old regime, was by far the greatest of the land powers at the end of the eighteenth century. A long struggle was needed before the combined weight of the other great powers could put an end to her aggression. Today the balance is much more even, and the weight of the United States, behind Britain and Western Europe, has so far proved adequate to deter Soviet Russia from an open challenge by arms. China, in an earlier phase of revolutionary psychology, is less likely to be deterred, but cannot by herself start a World War unless Russia also comes in.

The present situation is in this respect a novel one. There is even a possibility that we may witness, for the first time, a state based on the totalitarian principle of popular sovereignty working out its destiny to the end without having its career cut short in the battles its aggressions have provoked. The history of revolutionary France offers some guidance here also. Its internal development, even while it was pursuing its foreign conquests with unparalleled success, suggests that a country cannot live permanently in a state of high political fever. Already in 1794 Saint-Just was saying, 'la Révolution est glacée.' The

Napoleonic system kept up the urge for conquest, but behind the military and bureaucratic façade the people of France increasingly longed for peace and tranquillity. Corruption and inefficiency were spreading on all sides. Enthusiasm was dying. Propaganda had ceased to exercise its former effect. All the energy had to be supplied from above. The Revolution was dead at its centre long before the fatal disease had spread to the periphery. Will the Revolution in Soviet Russia similarly become ice-bound?

Such a development would not necessarily weaken the impetus to aggression, though it would sooner or later affect the efficiency with which it was pursued. A more important conclusion to be drawn from the operation of the theory of national or popular sovereignty in the international field is that it is a theory which is very difficult to reconcile with any kind of imperial hegemony, as Napoleon found in Spain. The revolutionary Spanish juntas fought bitterly against the French armies and against a reforming French king, Joseph Bonaparte, and in support of a reactionary Church and monarchy, which stood for everything they hated most, except French rule. The principle of national sovereignty, which the Revolution had done so much to inculcate, proved stronger than all its other principles and in the end defeated them. There are signs of a similar development today. National sovereignty won a decisive victory in Russia when Stalin defeated Trotsky. It was a source of great strength to Russia in war; but it has become a source of weakness in the Russian attempt to create a combination of nations under Soviet leadership. Of that the Yugoslav revolt is the proof.

In the opposed camp, though of course the principle of national sovereignty is not absent, the situation is very different, and in spite of difficulties a voluntary association of nations has gradually been drawing together. The division in the world today is that between the spheres of American and Russian influence. Is it unreasonable to hold that it is marked by the differences between a moderate policy which attempts to influence its allies by persuasion rather than by force, and which leaves them freedom for the manifestation of their own separate sovereignties, and on the other hand a policy which effectively destroys all national independence and every expression of it which conflicts in any way with the will of the dominant power?

It is not our purpose here to discuss the relative balance of power, but in the present uneasy impasse moral factors are more important than they might be if there were an obvious preponderance of power on one side. From what has been said, and indeed from the simple facts, one important conclusion emerges. The Soviet imperium, based on the assertion of extreme rights of national sovereignty by the Russian state and the denial of the same rights to its satellites, is founded on a contradiction, which must become increasingly evident as time goes on, just as the same contradiction did in the history of revolutionary and Napoleonic France. On the other hand, the American policy of international co-operation has the virtue of self-consistency. This policy also is not without its historical antecedents. It was the reaction, however slow and reluctant, of old Europe to the Napoleonic domination, and one may see the United States as in this respect an inheritor of the traditional British policy of the Grand Alliance. It is a policy which Sorel described, with reference to Richelieu, as 'la modération dans la force'. It has proved itself many times in the past, in war and in peace, as against the policy of national hegemony, and will, I believe, do so again.

11

THE AGE OF THE
DEMOCRATIC REVOLUTION*

THERE has recently been a tendency among modern historians
to pay increased attention to the movements which transcend
national boundaries. Thus the revolutionary wave which swept
one country after another in the later years of the eighteenth
century is now seen as in some respects the inroads of a single
great tide. To write the history of such a movement is a difficult
task. A mastery of the available literature in various languages,
the basic research necessary to explore at least a few of the
crucial gaps in our knowledge, a fundamental re-thinking of the
political developments and an exploration of the social structure
out of which they arise, are all necessary. The courage of
Professor R. R. Palmer of Princeton University in launching on
this colossal enterprise deserves all the more admiration. Where
other historians have ventured only to suggest international
influence and affiliations, he has attempted for the first time a
connected history based on an integrated pattern.

The Age of the Democratic Revolution : a Political History of Europe
and America. 1760–1800 : Volume i, The Challenge,[1] is even more
than this. With greater frankness than many other historians,
who also have their prejudices, exhibit, Professor Palmer in
writing of the struggle as one between (using the terms broadly)
the aristocratic and the democratic conceptions of the community,[2] asserts his own predilection for American democracy
as against the inequalities of the European monarchical and

*This paper appeared in History, xlv, 1960.
[1] Princeton University Press, 1959; Oxford University Press. 1960. ix + 534 pp.
[2] p. 22.

155

aristocratic systems.[1] He also divorces the eighteenth-century democratic from the modern Marxist revolution, writing, 'It is permitted to believe that a better society, more humane, more open, more flexible, more susceptible to improvement, more favourable to physical welfare and to the pursuit of higher concerns, issued from the democratic revolution of the eighteenth century than from the communist revolution of the twentieth.'[2] At the same time he insists that the eighteenth century did indeed witness a revolution. To the European reader his argument that 'opposition to one revolution is no reason for rejecting all revolutions'[3] may seem superfluous; but he reminds us that 'there was something in the atmosphere of 1755 ... which made it important, for some, to dissociate the American Revolution from other revolutions'.[4] Admittedly, in present-day historical writing 'there is no agreement on what the American Revolution was';[5] and he tells us that 'those who discount the revolutionary character of the American Revolution seem to be gaining ground'.[6] Against this, he presents an interpretation of the American War of Independence 'on the analogy of revolutions in Europe'.[7] This is an interesting and profitable parallel, though Professor Palmer possibly carried it a little too far. What happened in America, he suggests, was even more revolutionary than what happened subsequently in France, tested by two 'quantitative and objective measures': first, the percentage of those who fled from the colonies as loyalists, which was 2·4, whereas the percentage of émigres was only 0·5, in relation to the whole population; secondly, the compensation paid to the émigrés in 1825, which was only twelve times as large as that paid earlier by the British government to the loyalists though revolutionary France was ten times as large as revolutionary America.[8] It would be easy to play this game with other sets of figures, but we shall have no difficulty in agreeing that the American was a real revolution without going into perhaps not very convincing statistical comparisons.

[1] p. 4.   [3] p. 10.   [5] p. 186.   [7] p. 186.
[2] p. 11.   [4] p. 188.   [6] p. 187.   [8] p. 188.

On America Professor Palmer seems to rely on the most recent historical work. On France he faithfully follows the interpretation of Lefebvre, and if this is to be quarrelled with it can be only on the basis of new research. On Great Britain his step seems unsure. At the very beginning he tells us, in a footnote, 'It will be evident to the alert reader that I do not share the revisionist admiration shown by L. B. Namier for the old House of Commons.'[1] No historian is obliged to share all the views of Sir Lewis; I do not myself. But it might have been preferable not to dismiss the work of the leading historian of the period in a single footnote, even if it represents a tendency with which Professor Palmer does not sympathize and if its interpretation of British politics runs counter to his own. One historian cannot, of course, be equally familiar with the history of all countries, and the analysis of British developments here sometimes suggests a subject 'got up' for the occasion but not really understood.[2]

The importance of occasional confused statements should, however, not be exaggerated. On Professor Palmer's history of the political developments in Sweden, Russia, Poland, Bohemia, Hungary, the Austrian Netherlands, the Swiss Cantons and so on, it would need as many different historians to comment adequately. Since he is writing on a broad scale it is almost inevitable that there will be statements that a historian with

[1] p. 45n.
[2] I am thinking of statements such as the following: 'In England men of the same kind ["wealthy men, whose grandfathers had been bourgeois, and who still owned and managed their wealth in bourgeois manner"], while they could rarely become peers because the peerage was so small, belonged in many cases to the higher levels of aristocracy' (pp. 68–9). 'The social distance between landed and commercial classes had perhaps never been greater in England than in the days of Jane Austen and the eve of the First Reform Bill' (p. 72). 'On June 2 Lord George [Gordon] entered the House of Commons (of which he was a member, being the son of a duke)'—this may be a joke (p. 299). We are told that in the Gordon Riots 'whole Catholic neighbourhoods were burned' (ibid.). 'In 1771 a group of Cambridge undergraduates petitioned for relief from the Thirty-Nine Articles' (p. 318). Undergraduates were not quite so important in the eighteenth century; this presumably refers to the famous Feathers Tavern petition. Apparently on the strength of a remark by Lady Holland, we are assured that 'with Pitt in office the aristocracy was kept at a distance' (p. 302). I wonder if Professor Palmer has looked at a list of Pitt's cabinets.

more detailed knowledge would want to modify or delete. But this does not affect the validity of his thesis of a single great democratic revolution dominating this period, or diminish his belief in the value of that revolution. In both respects I would go a long way with him. I think there was such a revolution, and when the ideals of the revolutionaries are compared with the facts of the various social and political systems against which they were revolting, my sympathies are certainly with them.

On the other hand, while agreeing with Professor Palmer's basic thesis and ends, I find it difficult to follow him all the way in his methods. He makes extensive use of parallels, which seem to me sometimes rather far-fetched. To fit Great Britain into the pattern, George III's political activities are likened to those of Louis XV, Maria Theresa and Gustavus III.[1] With Pitt in office he finds that 'as in the days of the Stamp Act, there was a remote and ludicrous English analogy to the enlightened despotism of the Continent, which the Whiggish traditions of English history have perhaps concealed'.[2] The British House of Commons is compared with the *parlement* of Grenoble because it had a large proportion of young members in its ranks.[3] Pitt's reform bill of 1785 is likened to the Maupeou reforms in France.[4] Burke is 'an eloquent writer, a man of feeling, and an expatriate, in many ways surprisingly like Jean-Jacques Rousseau'.[5] When France, Zurich and Berne employ their treaty rights to intervene in Geneva, there is 'a premonition of the Holy Alliance and the Protocol of Troppau'.[6] Admitting a difference in scale and intensity, this time I think on the side of France, Professor Palmer finds the France of the Reign of Terror foreshadowed in detail by the America of 1776 — a revolutionary government, committees of public safety, representatives on mission, paper money and forged paper money, price controls, oaths, delation, confiscations, Jacobins who wind up as sober guardians of the law — 'how much it all suggests what was to happen in France a few years later!'[7] It seems to me that

[1] p. 152.   [3] p. 77.   [5] p. 308.   [7] p. 199.
[2] p. 302.   [4] p. 307.   [6] p. 359.

to push the parallel into such detail is to weaken rather than strengthen the case.

When Professor Palmer finds, on the contrary, a parallel which runs counter to his own ideas, he has no difficulty in detecting differences. Thus his most prominent theme is that of an aristocratic counter-revolution, accompanying, following or even preceding the democratic revolution. He sees it in France, Great Britain and Ireland, Geneva, the Dutch Republic, Russia, Sweden, Poland, Prussia.[1] Some American historians have also seen a kind of 'aristocratic resurgence' in the United States after independence, but Mr Palmer patriotically protests, 'My own view is that, while a new upper class was undoubtedly growing up in the United States, it was clearly more dynamic, more oriented to the future, more receptive to change than the aristocracies of Europe.'[2] Elsewhere he tends to subordinate the differences to the similarities. His approach is well represented by what he writes of the French Revolution: 'So much being said for the uniqueness of the French Revolution, the pattern used in foregoing chapters will be applied to it in the following pages.'[3] Since, I suspect, the pattern was originally derived from a study of the French Revolution, it naturally fits very well in this case.

Another danger involved in his method is the temptation unconsciously to omit those facts that do not fit the pattern. Thus we are told that the aristocratic parties in the smaller countries 'showed a strong tendency to depend on foreign aid'.[4] This is true, but the fact that so also did their democratic opponents, though not ignored, emerges rather less emphatically. We are also told that 'the leaders of democratization showed an affinity for France'[5] as against Great Britain. Indeed they did in America and the Dutch Republic. But why omit to say that in Geneva it was the oligarchy who called in France and their opponents who looked to Britain? It is mentioned that among the Genevan democrats Clavière settled in France,[6] but

[1] p. 286.   [3] p. 447.   [5] Ibid.   [6] p. 361.
[2] p. 366.   [4] p. 367.

at first, like most of the leaders of the Genevan movement, he fled to England and obtained financial aid from the British Government. It is true, as Professor Palmer observes, that 'not everything can be told'.[1] Perhaps the Corsican struggle for independence, which also looked to Great Britain, is not relevant to his thesis. But in discussing enlightened despotism, why Sweden and Russia, and not Spain, Naples or Denmark? In the case of Spain it is frankly admitted that material to support the main thesis cannot be extracted from its history.[2] Moving closer home, Professor Palmer speaks of the 'rough kind of equality' in the colonies.[3] Twice he adds, 'except for slavery',[4] but are two perfunctory references enough for such a prominent feature of the American scene?

This raises a further difficulty. No doubt it could be argued that slavery, and other matters that are omitted, are irrelevant to the argument. And obviously if we allowed exceptions to dictate our interpretations we should never be able to detect any general tendencies in history at all. Professor Palmer has made a gallant attempt to break away from the concentration on individual trees which during the last generation seems to have made it impossible for many historians ever to recognize a wood. If a major and essential aspect of a subject were to be excluded, that would be a different matter, and unfortunately I cannot help feeling that this is what has happened here. Since Professor Palmer entitles his book a 'Political History' it would be grossly unfair to criticize it simply on the ground that it is not something else. The problem is whether the democratic revolution of which he writes can be understood in purely, or even predominantly, political terms. Thus he seems, in writing of the French Revolution, to want to draw a distinction between the Revolution, which was political, and its results which might be social. He says, 'It remained primarily political ... But in its effects on society and social and moral attitudes, it went far beyond the merely political.'[5] I wonder if this is a possible

[1] p. 374. [3] p. 191. [4] p. 191, 235. [5] p. 441.
[2] p. 398.

160

distinction. And if the results of the democratic movement extend far beyond the political, do not also its causes? One can see the difficulty : the material for a synthesis on social evolution in the second half of the eighteenth century hardly exists. Lacking this, a general history has to be political or nothing. Where some serious work has been done on social analysis, as it has in the history of America, Professor Palmer does in fact make good use of it. This may be why his discussion of the American Revolution seems so much more substantial than what he has to say of the democratic revolution in other countries. It may also be the reason why the American Revolution is the one which, in his picture, breaks away farthest from the generalized pattern.

There is another aspect of the democratic revolution which also still lacks fundamental research. This is the development of the idea of popular sovereignty and its progress from theory to practice. Professor Palmer curiously (but inevitably, given the present state of work on the subject) devotes far more space to aristocratic than to democratic theory. The latter seems to boil down to Rousseau's *Contrat social,* 'the great book of the political revolution'.[1] This is a subject for endless controversy, which need not be explored here; but Professor Palmer weakens the case when he tells us that Sieyes 'translated the ideas of the *Contrat social* into the language of 1789'.[2] The opposition between *Qu'est-ce que le tiers état?* and the *Contrat social* is glaring, and if Sieyes adequately represented the ideas of the tiers état of 1789, the political influence of the *Contrat social* on them must have been negligible. But the history of the political ideas of the period requires much further investigation.

If we end on a series of questions, this should not diminish our gratitude to Professor Palmer for being the first to venture on the bold synthesis which forces them upon our attention. We are beginning to have some idea who and what the American revolutionaries were. But who were the Dutch Patriots? What kind of merchants were these who are said to have rioted in the streets of Amsterdam, and what was the 'amorphous populace'[3]

[1] p. 119.　　　　　[2] p. 489.　　　　　[3] p. 340.

that shouted *Oranje boven* through The Hague? Because of the valuable work of Susanne Tassier we know about some of the Vonckist democrats in the Austrian Netherlands, whose leaders at least seem to have been largely professional men, but the social composition of the French revolutionaries of 1789, and how far they can be called democrats, is evidently still a matter of controversy.

Since Professor Palmer throughout his book emphasizes that the democrats in America, Holland, Geneva and elsewhere looked to France, one might have expected to learn something of the democratic movement before 1789 inside France itself. Instead we are taken straight from the Aristocratic Revolt to the 'revolutionary psychology' of 1789, and whether this is to be regarded as essentially democratic is not clear to me, though at the end of the book, in an appendix, it is argued that the Constitution of 1791 was 'somewhat more "democratic", and somewhat less "bourgeois", than has been commonly said'.[1] More than this is needed if the democratic revolution in France, when it comes, is not to be produced, surprisingly but unconvincingly, like the card one originally thought of, out of the conjurer's pack. Professor Palmer does indeed tell us that 'France before 1789 was full of Dutch, Belgian, Swiss, Irish, and even English political expatriates'.[2] I cannot identify any English or Irish political refugees at this time, but that may be mere ignorance. The point is, that for a French democratic revolution it would be useful to have some Frenchmen.[3] I am not suggesting that antecedents for 1793 and 1794 might not be found in France if they were looked for, but only that until they have been looked for there is a fatal gap in Professor Palmer's thesis.

Again, whether the reformers in England were democrats in Professor Palmer's sense of the term, and whether the English Protestant dissenters and the Irish Catholics fall into the same category, if 1780 in the British Isles were indeed a French Revolution *manqué*, what roots there were, in towns like Sheffield

[1] pp. 522–8. [2] pp. 367–8.
[3] Brissot is mentioned as an example of American influence.

and Bristol before the 'nineties, for the later growth of the Corresponding Societies — these are questions which it is easier to ask than answer. What do we know of democracy in Sweden, or Poland, or Austria? It is no criticism of Professor Palmer to say that his book does not answer these questions, for the research has not been done that would enable them, and many others like them, to be answered. Really his 'Age of the Democratic Revolution', which used to be called the Age of Enlightened Despotism, could, on the strength of his analysis, with much more appropriateness be called the Age of the Aristocratic Revival, for this is the subject to which the greater part of his book is devoted. It is far better documented (outside America) than the democratic movement, but is this because it was a much more widespread and substantial movement, or merely because we lack the knowledge of the democratic movement that would reveal its real shape to us? The function of the historian is not necessarily to answer all questions. One sign of a good history is that it should incite us to ask them. This Professor Palmer's *Age of the Democratic Revolution* does in ample measure.

12

THE NEW IMPERIALISM*

THE Empire Theatre in Leicester Square opened its doors in 1884. Its name was a new one, calculated to appeal to a new generation. The Empire, evidently now entering into the public consciousness, was not so new. It is not the Empire, however, as an oustanding fact of the reign of Queen Victoria, but late-Victorian imperialism which I want to talk about. And I must begin by admitting that while it was in the Victorian age, it was not quite of it.

What had the Empire meant to Cobden or Bright, to Dickens and Trollope and their readers, to the young Victoria and Albert? But then the Empire in their day had been different: pioneer settlements in the empty lands, a network of trading stations and forts, strung along the coasts and waterways of the world. It could not be more, until it became possible to open up the interiors of the great continents and link them together. Steam started the wheels of Empire turning. Power created power. Technical inventions, in fact, made the new imperialism possible.

At the same time, increasing foreign competition with Britain made it desirable, because by the fourth quarter of the nineteenth century British industrial supremacy was being challenged. Economic rivalry stimulated a search for new sources of raw materials, new markets, more profitable outlets for investment, and in this way the new imperialism was born.

The economic motivation is plain, though at the same time imperialism had to be presented in a form capable of appealing to the moral and religious conscience of Victorian England.

* From *The Listener*, May 13th, 1948.

'There are forty millions of people beyond the gateway of the Congo,' declared the explorer Stanley to the Manchester Chamber of Commerce, 'and the cotton spinners of Manchester are waiting to clothe them. Birmingham foundries are gleaming with the red metal that will presently be made into ironwork for them and the trinkets that shall adorn those dusky bosoms, and the ministers of Christ are zealous to bring them, the poor benighted heathen, into the Christian fold.' Other countries, unfortunately, were also moved by the desire to extend the blessings of civilization, so that political rivalry complicated the economic drive towards empire. Many forward steps were taken by late-Victorian statesmen for the purpose of forestalling or counteracting the extension of other empires, themselves moving forward under the impulsion of the same hopes and fears. When the Russians occupied Merv in north-west Afghanistan in 1884, or again when they moved into the Pamirs, though the country still separating them from India was rather diffi-cult military terrain, alarm in England went as far as talk of war.

If one date is to be given for the beginning of imperialism as an effective force in British politics, it is June 24th, 1872, when Disraeli, in a speech at the Crystal Palace, adopted imperialism as one of the three main planks in the Conservative platform. Two years later he became Prime Minister. The Suez Canal shares and the Imperial Crown of India, peace with honour, Cyprus, the annexation of the Transvaal, the Zulu and Afghan Wars, redeemed his pledge. Why did Victorian pacifism and the cult of little England give way to this bellicose imperialism? Before attempting a fuller explanation, it is necessary to ask what imperialism was, apart from a term of abuse. Economic and political rivalries may explain the fact of Empire. But every important political fact demands its theory. Imperialism was an assertion of the right of government over other lands and peoples, and behind this assertion, in the last resort, lay a theory of human destiny, an interpretation of history.

Yet if we look to the historians of the nineteenth century for a clue to the nature of the new imperialism we shall not at first sight find one. History has to be the history of something. The nineteenth century being an age of nationalism, historians naturally wrote the history of nations. The historian was the schoolmaster of nationalism, which seems to be the very opposite of imperialism. But opposites sometimes turn into one another. Nationalism involved a belief in the identification of the nation, as a community with a traditional culture of its own, and the state. Where the identity was not perfect, it had to be made so. Hence the attempts by ruling nations to assimilate by force any minorities unhappy enough to find themselves in their power. In movements such as Germanization, Russification, Magyarization and so on, European nationalism developed into a kind of petty imperialism. Empires have existed in many periods, and taken many different forms. I want to suggest that, paradoxical as it may seem, the imperialism of the late nineteenth century, for all its economic origins, acquired its peculiar colour and tone from the emotional nationalism which prevailed in the Europe of that day.

England inevitably was affected by this trend towards national aggrandisement, but with a difference. England was not in a situation, and did not inherit traditions, for which nationalist ideas had much practical significance. Her unity had been achieved long ago. She had no memories of foreign oppression, no irredenta beyond her own boundaries to rescue. Moreover, England was only a part of the United Kingdom, which was not, and never had been, even in idea, a nation-state. The existence of the Channel Isles, of the conquered but not assimilated principalities of Wales, the freely united Kingdom of Scotland, with its own laws and institutions, the subject but unreconciled Irish, forbade any attempt to conceive of the British Isles as the home of a single nation. There was *no* British nation. Hence the intensification of emotion resulting when nation and state coincide, when political loyalty and cultural inheritance reinforce one another, could not be more than a temporary aberration in British conditions. The national enthusiasm of English historians could not, therefore, have quite the effect such enthusiasms produced elsewhere.

This is not to say that it had no effect. But it did mean that the kind of bastard imperialism which is merely nationalism writ large, was a peculiarly artificial and temporary phenomenon in Great Britain. Certainly there was an Empire, and economic and political circumstances were promoting its growth. Late Victorian imperialism might be interpreted as an attempt to translate this Empire into terms of nationalism. The point I am trying to make is that it was a hopeless attempt.

To take a specific example, Seeley, in 1883, wrote the history of the Empire under the title *The Expansion of England*. His book sold 80,000 copies in two years, and is said to have converted Lord Rosebery to imperialism. Excluding India, the Empire, Seeley said, 'is a vast English nation', with 'a population which is English throughout'. This was a little difficult to reconcile with the facts. Scots, Welsh and Irish, even if they were regarded as junior partners in the Empire, and this might hardly have stood the test of statistics, were in any case there to protest against the conception of an English Empire: it had to be British. Even this was not very satisfactory. What was a Briton? A barbarian, dressed in skins or supplying his inadequacy with large quantities of blue dye, waving a battle-axe, and perishing heroically, but rather inefficiently, at the hands of the Roman legions. Definitely not a ruling nation. Born to be conquered—by Romans, by Angles and Saxons, by Danes, by Normans—and not even speaking English. But one had to stop somewhere. Language was the favourite test of nationality. Anglo-Saxon attitudes prevailed in art and literature. The Norman conquest could be explained away. Kingsley had written of the great deeds of Hereward, the historian Freeman of Godwin and Harold. Later, Kipling's Norman knight, by marrying a fair Saxon, showed the way to redress the balance.

But now this game is the other way over —
But now England hath taken me!

The term Anglo-Saxon therefore came into fashion as a more convenient adjective for the new imperialism than English. It had the advantage of being jargon. It fitted in with the new racial ideas. 'I believe in this race,' proclaimed Joseph Chamberlain, 'the greatest governing race the world has ever seen; in this Anglo-Saxon race, so proud, tenacious, self-confident and determined, this race which neither climate nor change can degenerate, which will infallibly be the predominant force of future history and universal civilization.'

Pseudo-Darwinian conceptions of the struggle for existence and the survival of the fittest helped to promote this interpretation of imperialism as an expression of racial conflict, and the new trend of thought won widespread acceptance, although it involved a breach with earlier Victorian ideas of political morality. Force and fraud were perhaps now a little more respectable, required rather less decent veiling. If trade followed the flag, did it bring a more commercial morality with it? A Stanley trod in the steps of a Livingstone. Something was gained, doubtless, but something else was lost, when the generation of Henry Lawrence of Lucknow was replaced by that of Cecil Rhodes.

There was always, of course, a current of opposition. Gladstone strove against the flowing tide unceasingly. But by 1895 the voice that had so long been Britain's conscience was soon to be heard no more. In 1895 Joseph Chamberlain went to the Colonial Office. The new imperialism, of which he was the chief spokesman, made its appeal to all sections of society. The ruling classes found an outlet for their sons in conquering and governing India, or administering the new lands. The rapidly growing public schools provided a training which specially fitted their pupils for the governing of 'lesser breeds without the law'. The great financial houses of the City of London shifted their allegiance to the Conservative Party, or attached themselves to the Liberal imperialists. For the lower middle classes the idea of Empire provided an emotional satisfaction and an assertion of their status as members of an imperial nation.

Imperialism, indeed, was a peculiarly urban though hardly urbane phenomenon. Something in the gathering of large agglomerations of individuals in the big cities, for the very reason that it destroyed the traditional social groupings, seemed to create a need for newer and more artificial stimuli. The political parties had not yet become big mass movements. Organized sport was only in its beginnings. Imperialism filled a gap in the social development of the masses. Its voice was the voice of the music halls. 'We don't want to fight, but by Jingo if we do', gave a name to the new movement. A long series of popular songs followed, with ennobling invocations of 'Tommy Atkins', the 'Dear Old Flag', and the 'Soldiers of the Queen'.

But imperialism did not reach its heights in the music halls, or in the politics of trade and territorial aggrandisement. If, as I believe is true, it was partly a response to an emotional need, its most revealing manifestations are more likely to be found in literature than in politics. In the later decades of the century the literary possibilities of the Empire were discovered by popular writers. The call of the wild was heard in City office and country rectory. Even before Kipling, romance was bringing up the nine-fifteen. Scott's Highlanders and Crusaders were too remote, Tennyson's Knights of the Round Table too unreal. The Empire was a fact. One could throw up one's job and join the Canadian Mounted Police, explore the Congo with Stanley, relieve Lucknow with Havelock, sit, with imagined nostalgia, in the shade of the old Moulmein Pagoda, or adventure in search of a Treasure Island or King Solomon's mines.

There is no time to elaborate this theme. It will be best to concentrate for a moment on the writer who was the Poet Laureate of Empire, Rudyard Kipling. Time is winnowing his writings. Phrases like the 'white man's burden', a certain streak of brutality, led critics of his own day, and later, to identify him with the crudest jingoism. Here is a passage from the *Athenaeum*, the most distinguished literary journal of his day:

> Mr Kipling only voices a drift of ethical speculation which is becoming articulate at more than one point ... Such speculations attempt to translate into ethical language the biological formula of the 'struggle for existence'; and although they do not commend themselves to minds which have enjoyed the advantages of a philosophical training, they certainly do to a group of brilliant, persistent, but, so far as philosophy is concerned, somewhat shallow journalists of whom Mr Kipling is the most striking representative.

If this were all there is in Kipling, his books would now be gathering dust in the back shelves and cellars of Charing Cross Road. But there is an India in *Kim* which Birmingham never knew. When we read 'On the City Wall' or 'Without Benefit of Clergy' we are a long way from the Simla of Mrs Hawksbee. Old Testament morality is much in evidence in Kipling, but the racial theory, and the Chosen People, the Anglo-Saxons, do not make as frequent an appearance as might have been expected. His Jungle is one which at least is ruled by law. His State is the servant, not the master of man. In Kipling's stories we meet soldiers, administrators, doctors, nurses: the economic motive is conspicuously lacking.

There is something in Kipling's imperialism which reaches beyond the jingoism of the age. When, in *Puck of Pook's Hill*, he tries to recover the spirit of the greatest empire of the past, he looks for it, not in the records of a great cosmopolitan capital, but in the lonely garrisons scattered along the Wall, the thin line behind which the settled populations teemed, and civilization flourished and declined. And the maturer Kipling chooses not the moment of triumph but that of decay, when Rome is falling.

Cities and Thrones and Powers
Stand in Time's eye,
Almost as long as flowers,
Which daily die.

When Kipling wrote this, and when he wrote the 'Recessional', was he already writing, in advance, the epitaph on the aggressive imperialism he seemed to embody? It *was* the epitaph. For jingoist imperialism did not last. The Diamond Jubilee of 1897 was the grand parade of Empire; the Boer War its most characteristic achievement; its last political triumph, the General Election of 1900.

But the trend of the public mind was soon to change. The Boer War proved to be rather more than the military picnic so light-heartedly anticipated. It was not a masterpiece of political or military art, and it delivered a shock to the public conscience from which jingoism never really recovered. It was difficult to represent the victory of a great Empire over a tiny nation as a glorious triumph. The strong vein of humanitarianism in the country made any permanent acceptance of the doctrine of blood and iron impossible. Mafeking was a popular but transient outburst of emotion. The *Annual Register* for the same year wrote that 'the outlook at the end of the year which closed the nineteenth century could hardly fail to arouse misgivings as to the future in all but the imperviously self-satisfied.'

The imperialism of the Jingos, then, illuminated the last days of the Victorian age, but only with an evanescent coruscation. If the only inspiration of Empire had been this, it would have been dead within a few years of the ending of the Boer War, with the ending of the social and political conditions which had made jingoism possible. For all its popularity and nation-wide influence, late-Victorian imperialism was an abnormal growth, alien to the deeper political habits of thought of the country. There was something different and more permanent in the idea of the Empire and Commonwealth, which outlived jingoism, something which, being a living force, grew and changed, in ways remote from the imaginings of those who had nursed or neglected its infant years, which had its roots far deeper in the traditions of the British nations, and survived storms to which the Boer War had been a summer breeze.

13

THE OPEN SOCIETY:
A RECONSIDERATION*

PROFESSOR Karl R. Popper's book, *The Open Society and Its Enemies*,[1] attained almost the standing of a classic with its first appearance. Such a book, in its second edition, demands a careful and critical re-examination of its major premises and conclusions, even though this may involve an apparent lack of proportion, in taking for granted the many points of agreement, and singling out for discussion those on which doubts still remain in one reader's mind.

To Professor Popper, it is clear, certain ideas, or attitudes of mind, which might have been adjudged safely dead a generation earlier, revived with a sinister and menacing life in the years that led up to the Second World War. These were the ideas that are summed up in the word totalitarianism, and he saw in them not a purely contemporary phenomenon but a tradition as old as our civilization. Their chief prophets, in his opinion, were Plato and Hegel, followed, though not to quite the same degree, by Aristotle and Marx. His book is thus a response to the challenge of contemporary politics and should be judged as such.

He forces us also to estimate his work as history. He does not say: this is what the ideas of Plato on politics amount to in a modern setting, and it is an evil thing; but rather: this is what Plato was attempting to do in his own day, and these are the consequences which flowed from it. This is an historical judgment,

*This paper appeared in the *Political Science Quarterly*, lxix, no. 1, March 1954.
[1] Second edition (revised). London: Routledge & Kegan Paul. 1952. 2 vols. xi + 318 pp.; v + 375 pp.

and in employing this line of argument Professor Popper is relying on the accuracy of his historical interpretation, which, it might perhaps be thought, is to weaken his case unnecessarily.

Fundamentally, I take him to be concerned with establishing the danger, or worse, of a particular way of looking at the problems of society. This way he takes to be that of Plato, and it is certainly one which plausibly can be attributed to the author of the *Republic*. He devotes a great deal of learned and profound discussion to establishing the correctness of this interpretation, but to me, at least, it seems that for his main thesis this is a secondary issue. Similarly, the discussion of the motives of Plato, of which Professor Popper often takes rather a low view, is surely of minor significance unless we are to suppose that good intentions necessarily go with sound political ideas and vice versa. Moreover, it is to be remembered that the influence of a writer, and the relation of what he said to what men made of it, is a highly speculative subject. In appearing to base his argument on his interpretation of the historical role of Plato, therefore, Professor Popper lays himself open to the criticism of those who are unable to accept his description of Plato as 'a totalitarian party-politician, unsuccessful in his immediate and practical undertakings, but in the long run only too successful in his propaganda for the arrest and overthrow of a civilization which he hated' (i, 169–70).

This interpretation of Plato is only the first step in a general historical argument. 'The conflict between the Platonic-Aristotelian speculation and the spirit of the Great Generation, of Pericles, of Socrates, and of Democritus,' writes Professor Popper, 'can be traced throughout the ages' (ii, 22). Thus Christianity was, in the beginning, 'in part, a protest against what may be described as Jewish Platonism in the wider sense' (i, 22); and he detects a close 'parallelism between the creed of the Great Generation, especially of Socrates, and that of early Christianity' (ii, 23). Admittedly this might not be quite so easy to say of medieval Christianity, but the official recognition of the Christian Church, it is suggested, may have been 'an ingenious political move on the part of the ruling powers, designed to break the tremendous moral influence of an equalitarian religion'. With Justinian's persecution 'the dark ages began', and after this 'the Church followed in the wake of Platonic-Aristotelian totalitarianism, a development that culminated in the Inquisition.' Professor Popper has some scathing things to say of 'the medieval conversion of Christianity into an authoritarian creed', though even this 'could not fully suppress its humanitarian tendencies' (ii, 58). With these opinions I have much sympathy, but is there not something a little arbitrary in a definition of Christianity which seems to confine it to those aspects of the religion which coincide with one's own ethical principles, regardless of the actual manifestation in history of the Christian churches? Similarly, some of the methods of Athenian imperialism, as well as the acceptance of slavery, though admitted, are not allowed to be an integral part of the picture of the 'Great Generation'.

The historian will be still more shaken when he reads that, while 'medieval authoritarianism began to dissolve with the Renaissance', 'on the Continent, its political counterpart, medieval feudalism, was not seriously threatened before the French Revolution' (ii, 30). These phrases suggest a very personal usage of the terms 'authoritarianism' and 'feudalism'. I should have thought there were reasons for holding that authoritarianism in Church and state was throughout most of Europe a good deal more extreme in the sixteenth century than it has been earlier; and certainly in most of Western Europe medieval feudalism had completely changed its nature long before the eighteenth century. It is by neglecting the latter fact that Professor Popper is able to declare that 'the fight for the open society began again only with the ideas of 1789'.

The ancient struggle now reappears in the modern world. 'Just as the French Revolution rediscovered the perennial ideas of the Great Generation and of Christianity, freedom, equality, and the brotherhood of all men, so Hegel rediscovered the Platonic ideas which lie behind the perennial revolt against freedom and reason' (i, 30). I find this interpretation a little difficult to reconcile either with the facts of revolutionary history or with the theories propounded by the revolutionaries. Take, for example, Sieyes' *Qu'est-ce que le tiers état?*, the most famous expression of the ideas of 1789: 'La Nation existe avant tout, elles est l'origine de tout. Sa volonté est toujours légale'; 'de quelque manière qu'une nation veuille, il suffit qu'elle veuille; toutes les formes sont bonnes et sa volonté est toujours la loi suprême.' Such opinions were not mere abstract theories. Sieyes spoke for a France that was soon to be the France that guillotined Lavoisier, the France of the Committee of Public Safety, of the Directory and of Napoleon. Was he the herald of the open society that, according to Professor Popper, the Revolution proclaimed, or the prophet of nationalism and totalitarian democracy? Professor Popper sees the principle of the national state, or nationalism, as born (he says revived) in Germany, out of the writings of Herder, Fichte and Hegel. I think it is arguable that the description of Hegel's theory of the state as nationalism is misleading, but whether this be agreed or not, the close link between nationalism, 'totalitarian democracy', and the ideas of the French Revolution can hardly be seriously questioned.

Professor Popper's historical pattern is based on the antithesis between the 'open society' achieved by the Athenians of the 'Great Generation' and by the French Revolution in modern times, and the 'closed society', or the 'return to tribalism' advocated above all by Plato, and in modern times by Hegel, as a remedy for the strains of freedom. It is not difficult to see that the modern antithesis does not correspond to historical facts. On the 'open society' of fifth-century Athens our knowledge is so patchy and indirect that there is more scope for speculation.

In making these comments from the point of view of an historian, I am not, of course, quarrelling with the assertion that each generation has the right to interpret history in its own way—it will do so whether it has the right or not. Nor would I suggest that 'under the influence of an inapplicable idea of objectivity', we should refrain from presenting historical problems from our own point of view (ii, 268). I am only suggesting that there are features of the important judgments I have quoted which are 'not really in keeping with the accepted records' (ii, 266).

It is a pity that Professor Popper has chosen to present his argument in an historical form, because in fact it is not dependent for its validity on historical evidence. It is really an impassioned indictment of a series of what he believes to be wrong, indeed immoral and dangerous, approaches to the problem of politics. The most important of these are, to summarize them briefly: historicism—the belief that there are laws discernible in history, which enable us to prophesy the course of future events (i, 3); and 'essentialism'—'the view, held by Plato and many of his followers, that it is the task of pure knowledge or "science" to discover and to describe the true nature of things, i.e. their hidden reality or essence' (i, 31). The main object of Professor Popper's book is to subject historicism and essentialism to a close examination: his criticism of both as methods of social thought seems to me convincing. Plato is the archpriest of these heresies and his theories are discussed with great thoroughness. What is said of Aristotle is much slighter.[1] It is concentrated mainly on the deficiencies in his approach to science, and this can hardly be questioned. But in even an avowedly slight treatment, the description of Aristotle's 'Best State' as a compromise between 'a romantic Platonic aristocracy, a "sound and balanced" feudalism, and some democratic ideas' (ii, 3) is not really adequate. Here, as elsewhere, I am in some doubt as to what 'feudalism', which after all is a term of art and not of abuse, signifies for Professor Popper.

From Aristotle we proceed to Hegel, whose opposition to the

---

[1] Incidentally, Professor Popper's references to Aristotle as a mediocre writer and to his 'dry systematization' (ii, 2) are curiously contradicted by the 'golden flow' of eloquence attributed to Aristotle by Cicero, no mean judge of a literary style. The explanation, presumably, is that we have mostly only the lecture-notes of Aristotle, and who would like his style to be judged by lecture-notes?

supposedly 'open society' of the French Revolution is paralleled by that of Plato to the 'open society' of the 'Great Generation'. The subsequent discussion of the ideas of Marx is more substantial and is written in a sympathetic tone very different from the invective lavished on Plato and Hegel. Whereas Professor Popper was concerned to expose their conscious dishonesty, he recognizes the sincerity of Marx. 'His open-mindedness, his sense of facts, his distrust of verbiage, and especially of moralizing verbiage, made him one of the world's most influential fighters against hypocrisy and pharisaism' (ii, 82). Marx's faith, Professor Popper believes, was fundamentally in the 'open society', in spite of his 'sociological determinism' (ii, 200, 208). I cannot but feel that if Professor Popper had followed with Marx the line of criticism that he applies to Plato and Hegel, he would have found equal opportunities for attributing less elevated motives to him and judging his ideas by the consequences that flowed from them in practice. This criticism is to some extent acknowledged, and to some extent answered, in the Preface to the revised edition.

The exegesis of Plato and Marx, while not the kind that would have been produced by one of the faithful in either case, is learned and pertinacious to a high degree. It could be discussed adequately only at great length, and by one as familiar as its author is with the works of both masters and equally gifted in the analysis of ideas. The crux of the matter lies in the ideas of the open society, of which Professor Popper regards Plato and Aristotle, Hegel and Marx, as the enemies. It is in the attempt to discover what he means by the open society that I have the greatest difficulty. The clearest statement I can find is that 'the closed society is characterized by the belief in magical taboos, while the open society is one in which men have learned to be to some extent critical of taboos, and to base decisions on the authority of their own intelligence (after discussion)' (i, 202). The essential problem here is the nature of the discussion; there is, for example, Hegelian discussion, which Popper would certainly not regard as a satisfactory substitute for the system of totem and taboo. His answer to this problem seems to be that 'The only course open to the social sciences is ... to tackle the practical problems of our time with the help of the theoretical methods which are fundamentally the same in *all* sciences' (ii, 222 ; cf. i, 286).

It is not necessary to attempt a summary of the profound and highly illuminating analysis that Professor Popper makes of scientific method, but it will be sufficient to say that in his view the social sciences should copy science in employing 'the methods of trial and error, of inventing hypotheses which can be practically tested, and of submitting them to practical tests'. The result would be the development of a social technology 'whose results can be tested by piecemeal social engineering' (ii, 222). This seems admirable to me. I believe it is the method, and perhaps not uninfluenced by the development of the scientific mind, which, in a rough and ready way, has often been applied in English politics during the last three centuries. It is far removed from Platonism or Hegelianism.

There is one difficulty which has to be met. It may be objected that an engineering technique is all right so long as you know what kind of engine you want, or at least what purpose it is to be used for. If it is replied that we are given the engine in the shape of society and its institutions and are not presented with the task of making one *de novo*, it still remains true that we need this knowledge before we can decide what kind of modifications are required. Science cannot tell us this, and Professor Popper does not suggest that it can. His demonstration of the barrenness of 'scientific' ethics is convincing (i, 237–8). 'It is impossible to derive a sentence stating a norm or a decision or, say, a proposal for a policy from a sentence stating a fact; this is only another way of saying that it is impossible to derive norms or decisions or proposals from facts' (i, 64). (I have omitted some italics in this quotation.) 'In the case of a scientific theory, our decision depends upon the results of experiments ... But in the case of a moral theory, we can only confront its consequences with our conscience. And while the verdict of experiments does not depend upon ourselves, the verdict of our conscience does' (ii, 233). This, I think, could hardly be better put, but it leaves us with the problem that, while Professor Popper's conscience produces one set of verdicts, whatever passed for a conscience in, say, Hitler produced a very different set.

The problem for the political theorist, it seems to me, is to discuss why the conscience, or the ethical intuitions, of Professor Popper are preferable to those of Hitler. His reply is that 'it is impossible to prove the rightness of any ethical principle' (ii, 238). That is, I think, true; but it leaves us in the position that we must either accept the fact that the ethical intuitions of different men are at bottom contradictory and opposed to one another, in which case there is no reason for preferring one to another, except that it is ours, or else we must venture into the field of ethical discussion.

It would be no fair criticism of Professor Popper to complain of a failure to pass beyond the critical to the constructive, because his whole book is based on a positive conception of the open society, though we have to pick out the positive elements in his doctrine from scattered passages at different points in the argument. His basic outlook is 'humanitarian', by which he means that all should have an equal share in the burdens and advantages of citizenship, and that the laws should be equal for all and should be impartially administered. This equalitarianism seems to me a good example of the ethical intuition which is incapable of ultimate proof, which does not mean that it is not susceptible of argument calculated to promote its acceptance, or at least to undermine the prevailing theories of the superior claims of one section or other of society or of the human race. But at bottom it is an act of faith.

It is always a good thing, I think, to see what principles mean in practice, if only as a test of the firmness with which we hold them. Let me take another of Professor Popper's theories of the way in which the open society should function. He is rightly suspicious of efforts to make people happy by state action. "It leads invariably to the attempt to impose our scale of "higher" values upon others, in order to make them realize what seems to us of greatest importance for their happiness; in order, as it were, to save their souls' (ii, 237). He proposes, therefore, to replace the principle 'maximize pleasure' by that of 'minimize pain' (ii, 304; cf. i, 284—5). This principle may be tested by a positive example. I suppose that any government in Great Britain, faced with the necessity to make a decision whether to declare war on Germany or not in 1939, on the principle of minimizing pain should have remained at peace. On any reasonable calculation the human suffering likely to result from the war surely far outweighed any that was likely to be prevented by it. The consideration that war might possibly, though I should have thought hardly probably in the circumstances of 1939, minimize the calculable suffering in the long run is ruled out by an argument which Professor Popper employs elsewhere. Some Marxists believe that there would be less suffering involved in a violent social revolution than is inherent already under the capitalist system. 'But ... how can they evaluate the suffering in the one state and in the other? Here ... a factual question arises, and it is ... our duty not to over-estimate our factual knowledge ... Can we condemn one generation to suffer for the sake of later generations?' (i, 287). These are very strong arguments, but I am left with an uneasy feeling that they would have added up to the wrong answer in 1939, and that therefore 'minimize pain' is by itself not invariably a safe principle.

As Professor Popper approaches more closely to politics I find myself increasingly alarmed at what seem to me rather *simpliste* analyses and solutions. Thus he declares that 'we need only distinguish between two forms of government, viz. such as possess institutions of this kind [those in which the rulers, that is, the government, can be dismissed by the ruled without bloodshed], and all others; i.e. democracies and tyrannies' (ii, 161). The distinction is a valuable and important one; it is only difficult when we try to apply it in practice. By this criterion all the governments of France and Great Britain in the eighteenth century were tyrannies, for they certainly could not be dismissed by the ruled peacefully; but one cannot help wondering whether a classification which makes no distinction between the governments of George III or Louis XVI and those of Hitler and Stalin is as useful as it might be.

My alarm is increased when I find that the 'ardent liberalism' of Kant is held up for admiration, with special reference to his *Principles of Politics* (i, 247). Professor Popper deplores the failure of English and American writers to recognize fully this liberalism. Without denying the nobility of much of Kant's thought, a single quotation from him may help to explain this lack of appreciation. Kant writes:

> All resistance to the Sovereign legislative power, every kind of instigation to bring the discontent of the subjects into active form, and rebellion or insurrection of every degree or kind, constitute the highest and most punishable crimes in the commonwealth; for they would destroy its very foundations ... Even if the Supreme Power, or the Sovereign as its agent, were to violate the original contract, and thereby in the judgment of the subject to lose the right of making law, yet as the Government has been empowered to proceed even thus tyrannically, no right of resistance can be allowed to the subject as a power antagonistic to the State.

Again, 'A right of compulsion or coercion, in the form of resistance in word or deed against the sovereign Head of the State, can never belong of right to the people.' Even the greatest of British conservatives were more liberal than this. Hume disliked rebellion profoundly, but with characteristic sense he observed that it was absurd to grant the people a share in the supreme power without at the same time granting them a right to defend that share from encroachment; while Burke, at the height of his crusade against the French Revolution, in 1794, could write of a revolt in India, 'The whole country rose up in rebellion, and surely in justifiable rebellion.' Certainly it is better to be able to change one's government without bloodshed if possible, but to make the absence of bloodshed the essential factor, as Professor Popper seems to do, if I understand him correctly, is to rob ourselves of the ultimate defence of liberty.

I hope that in presenting these difficulties I shall not be supposed to be in disagreement with the greater part of Professor Popper's thesis. Scientific analysis and 'piecemeal social engineering' have, I am sure, an important contribution to make to the solution of the political problems of social life. I think it is fair to say that there is now more of both than ever before in the history of the world. The only question I am tempted to ask is whether we know to what purpose to put them. Any possible answer may be only a partial and provisional one, but at least we ought to be aware of the need for putting the question. I suspect that we are ceasing to do so, on the assumption, which, perhaps unjustly, I think I detect even in Professor Popper, that we know the answer, and that no sensible men could disagree about it. Unfortunately this seems to be far from true, nor can I see that science is giving us, or has a capacity in itself for giving us, any discussion of this question. Science may be the new Leviathan, it is not the new Messiah. This, indeed, is Professor Popper's own teaching: 'Neither nature nor history can tell us what we ought to do ... It is we who introduce purpose and meaning into nature and into history' (ii, 278). That, I suppose, is what Plato was trying to do. I agreed with Professor Popper in disliking the way he did it and the results he achieved, but the human need for purpose and meaning still remains. Is it too much to ask that this brilliant book should be the prolegomena to a discussion of these fundamental issues?

14

THE DECLINE OF POLITICAL
THEORY*

POLITICAL theory is not a progressive science. At least, anyone
who puts, say, Aristotle's *Politics* beside the political writings
of the twentieth century could be excused if he thought that
progress in the subject was imperceptible. A cynic might even
argue that everything that is worth saying on political theory
has already been said *ad nauseam*, and draw the conclusion that
it is time we gave up such wearisome reiteration. But this view
would be false, because if political ideas do not progress, their
formulation certainly changes. The conditions of social life
alter, sometimes more slowly and sometimes more rapidly, in
the last few centuries at an increasingly dizzy pace; and as they
alter, the words we use, and the ideas they convey, lose old
meanings and acquire new ones. For this reason a continual
restatement of political principles is both necessary and inevitable — as long, that is, as the tradition of political thinking,
which is one of the peculiar characters of Western civilization,
remains alive.

It is a tradition with a history of some two and a half millennia, though with one considerable break. Century after
century the political ideas of the Western world have undergone
progressive modification. The interplay of idea with institution
has changed now one and now the other, and the flow of ideas
has been punctuated at intervals by the synthesis created by a
great political thinker. No such synthesis has appeared in our
own day or for some time past, but this is not surprising. Great

*This paper appeared in the *Political Science Quarterly*, lxviii, no. 3, September
1953.

political thinkers cannot be produced to order, and we need not wail and beat our breasts because there is no contemporary Burke or Bentham. If a general tendency to cease thinking about society in terms of political theory were to be observable, that would be a matter of greater significance than the mere fact that there are no intellectual giants in the field of political theory today. I propose to suggest that there *is* such a tendency.

The view that our cherished political ideas may be capable of dying will naturally meet with opposition, yet there is nothing impossible in such a development. Political ideas are not immortal, however we try to identify them with eternal values. Conscious of our own mortality, we cling all the more to the belief that there must be something presiding over our destinies which is eternal. There may be, but it is not likely to be the little gods of our own creation, whether we call them Imperial Rome, or Divine Right of Kings, or even Democracy. The belief in the permanence of such ideas is only another form of the sophism of the ephemeral—the faith of Fontenelle's rose, which nodded its head and proclaimed in the wisdom of a day that gardeners were immortal, for no gardener had ever died within the memory of a rose. Ideas grow and decay, change into new forms and are reborn. It would be a cause for amazement if the process of continuous transformation were to come to an end while political thinking, as it has existed since fifth-century Athens, still survives.

But does it survive? Conceivably political theory at the present day may *not* be undergoing one of its many metamorphoses, passing through a chrysalis stage before emerging in a new form. It may just be coming to an end. This has happened in the past. Once before in the history of Western civilization a great age of political thought came to an end. The development of Greek political ideas reached its climax in the writings of Plato and Aristotle. In the Hellenistic age attention began to turn away from political theory and into other fields. For a time, with the rise of the National Law school of thought and the elaboration of juristic conceptions by the Roman lawyers, it might have been possible to regard the process as still one of growth and development. But in the Roman Empire politics turned into the struggles of court factions and military dictators, and political thinking as the Greeks understood it ceased.

The experience of the Greco-Roman world is not without relevance to our own time. Some at least of the conditions which accompanied this earlier decline and fall of political theory are repeated today. It is a commonplace that state activity is irresistibly expanding. More and more of the activities of society are falling under the control of bureaucracy and therefore are to some extent outside political control. Great military machines are being created, to the support of which more and more of the wealth of society has to be diverted. These are as yet, it is true, the servants and not the masters of the civil power, but so the legions were in Rome for a long time. This is an age of revolutions, like the age of Marius and Sulla and Caesar, and revolutions are apt to end in military dictators; in more than a few countries they begin with them as well. The knowledge of this tendency is perhaps one reason why it has hitherto failed to operate in Soviet Russia. In Nazi Germany also the Army was never able to challenge the party successfully.

Possibly in the new form of party organization a technique has been found for averting military dictatorship and the rule of pretorian guards to which the Roman Empire degenerated. But the substitution of the party machine for the military machine is not necessarily a great improvement. It means the rule of a small oligarchy, with political life concentrated in the internal struggles of its factions. Both bureaucracy and party seem also in practice to involve the emergence of a super-bureaucrat or party chief, or both rolled in one, in whom ultimate power is concentrated, and who is himself semi-deified as the incarnation of the state, like the Roman emperors. Since the majority of the population are naturally outside the chosen circle of bureaucracy or party there is also a need, as long as a degree of political consciousness survives in any part of this excluded majority, for a machinery of repression, a system of delation and espionage, political police, concentration camps or prisons and the rule of universal suspicion—such as Tacitus described in dreadful detail in his imaginative account of the last years of Tiberius, and Camille Desmoulins borrowed for a description of France under the Terror.

It may be said that this picture represents only half of the world, and that is doubtless so. But are some of these tendencies completely absent anywhere? Contemporaries naturally notice differences. Historians, looking back on an age, are often more struck by similarities. The most fundamental trends in any period are those which exist at the same time in the most diverse and apparently opposed camps. If I were asked what are the deepest underlying tendencies of our age I should look for those which are common to both sides of the Iron Curtain. I should look for something which communist Russia and capitalist America have in common. At bottom, it seems to me that there are more similarities than either side would be very pleased to admit, and that they are sufficient to make the parallel with the ancient world a fair one, though obviously it must not be pushed too far.

The parallel is also noticeable with respect to the decline of political theory. In the period when Caesarism was rising, the ideas associated with the old Roman conception of *libertas* were falling. The connection between new conditions of society and the decline of political thinking may be obscure, but it would be dangerous to suggest that there is none. The rule of *senatus populusque romanus* led to anarchy when an empire had to be governed instead of a city. Rome was faced with the choice of abandoning the political principles by which it had achieved greatness, or seeing the Roman world degenerate into a chaos of warring states. Its solution was the Empire, in which, however, the classic political theories of the city-state could find no place, any more than the institutions by which they had achieved some measure of realization. For political theory to exist, it seems to me, there must be an active political life. One does not expect to find it flourishing among Australian aboriginal tribes, in the Russia of Ivan or Peter, the Paraguay of the Jesuits or the empire of the Caesars.

Are there signs — I do not say more — that our own political ideas may be coming to their end as those of the ancient city-states did? It would be absurd to suppose that one wants a continual stream of new political ideas, or old ones new-fashioned; but I suggest that there has been rather a long interval since there was last any original political thinking. It is necessary to go back to the eighteenth century to find it. This, I admit, is a sweeping statement, which it would require considerable space to attempt to justify.

But let me present one consideration. The dominant political idea in the modern world is democracy. Most of the contradictions of contemporary politics find their place under the democratic umbrella, but broad as that is they jostle one another, and moreover the umbrella seems to be leaking badly. And where are the political theorists of democracy today? Instead of a rational theory it has become a sort of incantation. It is the 'open sesame' of political treasure-hunters everywhere. The world is full of would-be Aladdins chanting 'democracy'. The masses, at least in those countries which have no experience of democracy, are waiting in a state of mystic faith on the revelation that the word is to produce. Where at least the idea has been known longer, expectations are not so high. Is it unfair to suggest that there is even a certain degree of disillusionment, a feeling that the traditional conceptions of democracy do not answer our greatest problems?

Liberal democratic principles ceased to evolve in the nineteenth century: in general, the world of practice is apt to be a generation, sometimes a century, behind the world of original thought. But the nineteenth century failed to refashion and think out anew, for the benefit of its successors, the ideas that it was living on. It provided, admittedly, an intellectual ancestry for nationalism and Fascism and communism, but that is another story. Liberal democratic principles ceased to evolve then, but the world did not stop at that point, and it has become a very different place since. Meanwhile democracy, for lack of thought, has ceased to be a living political idea. It has become a shibboleth, and not even serviceable as such. A password is no good when all the hostile camps use it indiscriminately. For the most part it has ceased to be discussed seriously and in relation to the concrete problems of practical politics. It has largely become a meaningless formula. Politicians, like the princess in the fairy tale condemned to the oracular utterance of frogs, seem scarcely able to open their mouths without some platitude flopping out, wet and flabby and slightly repulsive, but is this political theory? If it is, no wonder that practical men prefer to ignore it. Coins can remain valid currency even when they are worn quite smooth. Political ideas need periodical recoining if they are to retain their value.

It may be said that this is not a fair argument, that practical politics has always been conducted on the basis of platitudes. E. Burke was the exception, his fellow member for Bristol, whose political principles were summed up in 'I say ditto to Mr Burke', the norm; but at least he had a Burke to say ditto to, and besides Burke a great body of informed and serious public discussion existed on the rights and wrongs of political behaviour. Where will the average politician find a discussion of theoretical questions on the same level today?

Of course, there have been writers in the last few decades who have had something significant to say about the contemporary political situation, but the same conclusion about the decline of political theory seems to emerge from a study of their work. I am thinking of such writers as Ferrero, Bertrand de Jouvenel, Russell, E. H. Carr, Reinhold Niebuhr, Lasswell, Hans Morgenthau and others. The thing that impresses them most about political life is the state as power. They envisage power as a kind of electric force, now diffused and now concentrated, which not merely runs through society but is its very essence. 'The laws of social dynamism', says Lord Russell, 'are only capable of being stated in terms of power.' The wretched individual atoms of which society is composed are massed together, hurled violently about, disintegrated by power, which they did not create and cannot control.

Traditional political theory, in so far as it has failed to recognize this fact, is regarded as no more than a beautiful fairy tale. To quote Reinhold Niebuhr:

> It may be possible, though it is never easy, to establish just relations between individuals within a group by moral and rational suasion and accommodation. In inter-group relations this is practically an impossibility. The relations between groups must therefore always be predominantly political rather than ethical, that is, they will be determined by the proportion of power which each group possesses at least as much as by any rational and moral appraisal of the comparative needs and claims of each group.[1]

According to Niebuhr the tragedy of the human spirit is 'its inability to conform its collective life to its individual ideals'. This is the reason why men 'invent romantic and moral interpretations of the real facts, preferring to obscure rather than reveal the true character of their collective behaviour'. In other words, it is the dilemma of 'moral man and immoral society'. Man, when he became a social and political animal, sacrificed his individual morality to the egoism that is the accompaniment of social life. The complaint is not a new one: it was the theme of Rousseau's *Discourse on Inequality*. But for the modern thinker, unlike Rousseau, there is no resolution to the tragedy of society. Humanity is caught in a cul-de-sac. In such a situation absolute pessimism is unavoidable. There is no possibility of creating, as Rousseau set out to do in the opening chapter of the *Contrat social*, a society in which justice can be allied with utility and power with freedom. There is no hope of establishing rational or ethical control.

[1] *Moral Man and Immoral Society* (New York, 1933), pp. xxii-xxiii.

In a different way the same conclusion was reached by Ortega y Gasset. He wrote:

we live at a time when man believes himself fabulously capable of creation, but he does not know what to create. Lord of all things, he is not lord of himself. He feels lost amid his own abundance. With more means at his disposal, more knowledge, more technique than ever, it turns out that the world today goes the same way as the worst of worlds that have been; it simply drifts.[1]

All this is degrees of pessimism below Machiavelli. The author of the *Prince* saw society at the mercy of arbitrary power, but believed that somehow out of evil would come good; the tyrant would serve social ends that a better ruler might not be able to fulfil. We have lost the innocence of a Machiavelli now and do not look for moral good to be born out of political evil. Political pessimism is deeper than it has been perhaps since St Augustine wrote the *De Civitate Dei*. Indeed for a century and a half pessimism has slowly been infecting the intellectual world. That is a process I have no space to trace, though it has, I believe, a close connection with the decay in political ideas that has been contemporaneous with it.

The decline of political theory may thus be regarded as a reflection of the feeling that ethical values have no place in the field of social dynamics and power politics. This, I believe, is the real significance of 'the revolt of the masses': it means the rise to control of those who live their lives without theory, to whatever class they may happen to belong. Another term for it is the rule of the expert, I mean the technician, the *Fachmann*, to use the German word for an especially German disease. Twenty years ago Ortega y Gasset saw what it meant. 'Anyone who wishes', he said, 'can observe the stupidity of thought, judgment and action shown today in politics, art, religion and the general problems of life and the world by the "men of science", and of course, behind them, the doctors,

---

[1] *The Revolt of the Masses* (London, 1932), 47.

engineers, financiers, teachers and so on.'[1] The politician who merely repeats platitudes is no worse than his own experts; he is not to be singled out for criticism. And how can he be held responsible for failing to translate political theory into practice if there is no theory to be translated?

There is another way of looking at the decline of political thought. Professor Toynbee sees our civilization going the way of previous civilizations, and consoles himself with the idea that the death of a civilization may be the birth of a religion. Ferrero put it differently. Mysticism, he said, is a form of escapism from the horror of illegitimate power. One seems to remember the early Christian invocation: 'The poet has said, "O lovely city of Cecrops", wilt thou not say, "O lovely city of God"?' And a modern poet repeats the cry:

> Man, frustrated and sleep-forsaken,
> Gloom-regarding from inward sight,
> Sees the city of God unshaken
> Steeply stand in unworlded white;
> Sees, adrift from his faith-lost learning,
> Sun-remote from terrestrial thought,
> Power, envisioned by earth's discerning,
> Peace, by mortal aspiring wrought.[2]

A nobly phrased restatement of an ideal that appeared to men in a former time of troubles, but one that belongs to a non-political age. Religious revival *may* be a way out, but it is not a political way. And will it be the resurgent idealism to give substance to our hopes, or merely a narcotic to our discontents? The religious approach to political problems is also not without its dangers. The Nazi Revolution of Destruction gained greatly in force by being able to drape itself with the robes of chiliastic aspiration.

In this analysis—though that is to dignify a brief indication of some contemporary tendencies, as I see them, with too

[1] Ortega y Gasset, *The Revolt of the Masses*, 124.
[2] Siegfried Sassoon, 'Ode', in *Vigils* (London, 1935).

ambitious a title — I may seem to be bent on a pessimistic interpretation of the modern world; but what I have said so far
is only a one-sided view of the current situation. To take it as
the whole truth would be to despair of the political community
prematurely. If it is true that political theory has ceased to
develop, is this a sign that political life is in fact coming to an
end and that we are entering a non-political age, as the ancient
world did? Here one must appeal to a broader view of the
facts. The differences are far greater than the similarities. If
there are signs that the world is moving in the direction of
universal empire, there is no reason to believe that it will
reach that goal before the present age of catastrophes has been
long continued. Bureaucracy is not yet the major reality of
government in any Western country; nor are pretorian guards
or political parties yet our masters rather than our servants. In
short, there seems no reason to believe that if there has been
a decline of political theory this is the necessary result of the
appearance of a social and political situation in which it no
longer has any valid *raison d'être*. If this is so, the only alternative
explanation is to suppose that it is declining because of some
internal condition, and not because of the inevitable pressure
of objective fact. Perhaps something has gone wrong with
political thinking itself. I believe that it has, and that it is
even possible to suggest a diagnosis.

If the decline of political theory is to be explained by some
inherent misdirection in contemporary thinking about politics,
the remedy might appear to be to work out, on abstract
grounds, the proper way of thinking about politics. This method
has certain attractions. It can be used to justify practically any
form of political theory that appeals to us; because naturally
the conclusions we arrive at will be determined by the assumptions we start from, and we are not in much danger of starting
from assumptions that do not appeal to us.

However, I propose not to adopt this line of approach. Fortunately, we have not to *invent* political theory; that was
invented long ago. If there is a right way of considering its

problems, I think we should be modest enough to believe that it might possibly be the way of all the greater political thinkers of the past; that is, if there is a way which so many, and such diverse, theorists have in common. I think there is. In the first place we have the simple, obvious fact that they all wrote with a practical purpose in mind. Their object was to influence actual political behaviour. They wrote to condemn or support existing institutions, to justify a political system or persuade their fellow citizens to change it: because, in the last resort, they were concerned with the aims, the purposes of political society. Even Machiavelli does not merely describe the way in which things are done, without also indicating the way in which, and to what ends, he thinks they *ought* to be done. At the opposite extreme, Plato's *Republic* may represent an ideal to which the human race—perhaps happily—cannot attain, but in his mind it was no mere Cloud-Cuckoo-Land of fantasy.

Political theory in the past, I suggest, was essentially practical. The political theorist, in his way, was a party man, and party men themselves used not to be afraid to season their practice with the salt of theory. One of the striking differences between political discussion in, say, the eighteenth century and at the present day is that politicians have on the whole ceased to discuss general principles. This is not stated as a criticism, but as a fact which needs explaining, and I think one clue to the explanation has already appeared. The study of political theory, I have just said, was formerly the work of men intently concerned with practical issues. It has become instead an academic discipline, written in various esoteric jargons almost as though for the purpose of preventing it from being understood by those who, if they did understand it, might try to put it into practice. It has entered the high realm of scholarship, and, as Whitehead has pointed out, some modern forms of scholarship, at least, reproduce the limitations which dominated thought in the Hellenistic epoch. 'They canalize thought and observation', he says, 'within predetermined limits, based upon inadequate metaphysical assumptions dogmatically assumed.'[1]

Political theory has in this way become disengaged from political facts. Even worse, it has become disengaged on principle, as it has seldom if ever been in the past. The academic political theorist of today may study the great political thinkers of the past, but in the name of academic impartiality he must carefully abstain from doing the kind of thing that they did. I put it forward as a hypothesis that this may conceivably be one source of the decline of political theory.

The view that the connection between political theory and practical politics is a condition of the survival of theory deserves a more elaborate discussion than it can be given here. But if it were to be accepted, then there is an important corollary to be noticed. The implication is that the issues with which political theory has been concerned in the past were not chosen arbitrarily, or as a result of some theoretical argument, and that theory was able to come to grips with the practical world because its discussions were determined by the actual conditions and problems of the day. For example, John Stuart Mill lived in an age when new social problems called for measures of state action which conflicted with established ideals of individual liberty: his thought derives its value from the fact that he devoted himself to the task of attempting to reconcile the two demands. Bentham's life-work was to establish a theoretical basis for the legislative and administrative reforms that were urgently needed in *his* day. Burke, faced in Great Britain, America, Ireland, France, with a challenge to the existing bases of political allegiance, attempted to provide an alternative to the new democratic principle of the sovereignty of the people. Rousseau, conscious of the moral collapse of divine-right monarchy, offered a new justification for the rightful powers of government. Montesquieu, earlier, had seen the defects of absolutism, but his alternative was a return to the aristocratic organization of society, and the limitation of all power by law. Locke provided a political theory for a generation which had

---

[1] A. N. Whitehead, *Adventures of Ideas* (London, 1933), 151.

overthrown divine right and established parliamentary government. Hobbes and Spinoza, in an age of civil wars, maintained that sovereignty meant all or nothing. And so we might continue, till we reached in the end—or rather the beginning— Plato and Aristotle, attempting to prescribe remedies for the diseases of the city-state. Among recent political thinkers, it seems to me that one of the very few, perhaps the only one, who followed the traditional pattern, accepted the problems presented by his age, and devoted himself to the attempt to find an answer to them was Harold Laski. Though I am bound to say that I do not agree with his analysis or his conclusions, I think that he was trying to do the right kind of thing. And this, I suspect, is the reason why, practically alone among political thinkers in Great Britain, he exercised a positive influence over both political thought and action.

If political theory *has* become generally disengaged from practice, and if this is one cause of its decline, it will be worth while asking why this has happened. The bias of the academic approach away from action is not a new thing, and it can hardly provide an adequate explanation by itself. An answer which goes a little deeper can be found, I think, again by a comparison with traditional political thought. The object of this was to arrive at the judgment that one form of political activity was better than another. Academic impartiality between what it believed to be good and bad it neither sought nor attained. Because its aim was to influence action, it had to consider the forces that move men, and these are not the products of abstract analysis but of the passions. And since not all passions could be regarded as conducive to a good end, it had to be the passions under the guidance of ethical motivation. In other words, politics was essentially a branch of morals, or ethics. It is not my object here to discuss the problems of ethical theory. What I want to do is to suggest that modern political theory has largely ceased to be discussed in terms of what ought to be; and the reason, I believe, is that it has fallen under the influence of two modes of thought which have had a fatal effect on its ethical content. These, and they have come to dominate the modern mind, are history and science.

The historian naturally sees all ideas and ways of behaviour as historically conditioned and transient. Within itself, history has no standard of value but success, and no measure of success but the attainment of power, or survival for a little longer than rival individuals or institutions have survived. Moreover, history is the world studied under the category of what is past: however much we may proclaim that all history is contemporary, its nature is to be a field into which practice cannot penetrate. The paradox of history is that though its writing is a contemporary action, with practical consequences, the historian puts this fact in the back of his mind and tries to behave as though it were not so. By itself, in political theory, history can produce only the crudest Machiavellianism. If all historians are not little Machiavellis, it is only because they take their political ideals from some other source and carry them into their history. This is, fortunately, almost unavoidable, though it might sometimes be a good thing if they were a little more conscious of the ideals they are in fact applying and inculcating through their histories. This is yet another problem which can be raised but not discussed here. It is sufficient to say that at least there is a tendency among modern historians to regard the passing of ethical judgment as an illegitimate process against which historical discipline should be a safeguard. In so far as it is a successful safeguard it is also one against thinking about the problems of political theory at all.

The influence of historical thought did not stop at this. History acquires more positive, and more dangerous, implications, when it is made into a philosophy of history. This was particularly the achievement of Hegel and Marx. The dominant trend in both Hegelianism and Marxism was to associate ethics with the historical process — by which I do not mean the grand pattern of the universe, which I suspect was not revealed even to Hegel or Marx, but the little corner of the fabric which came under their immediate notice, the few strands which they took for the pattern of the whole. Even if Hegel and Marx themselves did not intend this result, in those who followed them there was an uneasy slip from saying, 'This is what will be,' into saying, 'This is what ought to be.' The result was to base moral judgments on temporary and limited historical phenomena. Hegelian and Marxist politics, therefore, have had the ultimate effect of setting up a politics devoid of ethical foundations. In this way they played an important part in creating a breach between modern political practice and the traditions of political thinking in the West.

The influence of history over the modern mind is, however, challenged by that of science. Particularly in the forms of mathematics and psychology, science has influenced political thinking practically from the beginning; though of course the scientific bases on which earlier political theories were sometimes built are about as closely related to modern science as the voyages of Sinbad the Sailor are to modern geographical discovery. This did not prevent Plato and Aristotle from being great political theorists. It is only in recent times that a general belief has grown up in the possibility and desirability of studying politics by the methods that have achieved such remarkable results in the natural sciences. This belief is embodied in the now common term, political science. I do not ask, is political science possible? It must be, it exists. But what is it? The object of science is to show how things happen, and why, in the nexus of cause and effect, they *do* happen. There is no reason why political phenomena, as well as any other phenomena, should not be treated in this way so long as we do not mistake the result for political theory and expect it to answer questions which in the nature of things it cannot answer. What I mean is simply that it is not the function of science to pass ethical judgments. That statement can hardly be questioned. I imagine that any scientist would indignantly repudiate the suggestion that his scientific thought entered into the category of what ought to be. The political theorist, on the other hand, is essentially concerned with the discussion of what ought to be. His judgments are at bottom value judgments. The kind of opinion he offers is that one line of political action is ethically preferable to another, not merely that it is more efficient, whatever that may mean; and surely we have seen enough in our day to know that the difference between political systems is not merely a difference between relative degrees of efficiency.

In case I am thought to be unjust to the political scientist, let me give what seems a fair description of the way in which he envisages his task. It is fallacious, says a recent writer, to suggest that the only way of understanding politics is to participate in it: we do not teach the principles of geometry by a manual training course in carpentry. Political science is a body of knowledge, which must be taught and learned like any other body of knowledge. What this definition neglects is the fact that the degree of moral disinterestedness possible in natural science is impossible in the field of political theory. The political scientist, in so far as he wishes to remain a scientist, is limited to the study of techniques. His subject may be compared to eighteenth-century German cameralism, which was a political theory by bureaucrats, about bureaucrats, for bureaucrats. Mostly, what is called political science, I must confess, seems to me a device, invented by university teachers, for avoiding that dangerous subject politics, without achieving science. Taking it at the highest valuation, political science can give us guidance of the greatest possible importance in achieving the objects we want to achieve; it cannot help us to decide what those objects should be, or even what they are. And to believe that we are all agreed on them and therefore do not need to discuss them is surely, in the light of contemporary events, the wildest utopianism. In the last resort science, like history, leaves us, as Ortega y Gasset put it, to drift: we have a magnificent technical equipment for going somewhere, without anywhere to go.

The image of political life which emerges from the prevailing tendencies in political thought is not a pleasing one. The state appears as a ship in the sea of politics, with no port of embarkation or destination inscribed on its papers, manned by a pressed crew, whose whole endeavour is devoted to the task of keeping the vessel afloat in uncharted waters, with little to help them save their own traditional seamanship, and the records of earlier captains and crews who have for all time been tossed on the seas in the same endless, meaningless motion. A depressing picture, I think, perhaps dreamed up by some remote philosopher who has seen the ships scudding by from the lantern-room of a dead lighthouse, dead because he has carefully extinguished the light.

Luckily we need not take the picture too seriously: it is only an analogy, and analogies are the camouflage of loose thinking. The sea is, of course, the sea of politics. But the state is itself the community as a political organization, the bond that holds it together; the life it lives is also politics. And how is the ship distinguishable from the crew? The state is no mere wooden artifact inhabited by men; it *is* men as political animals. And sea, ship and crew move on together for they are the same. How can we envisage ourselves as inhabiting the ship of state in the sea of politics when the ship is ourselves and the element it moves in our own political being, and *we* rouse the storms and *we* still the waters?

One thing is missing from the picture. It is missing from contemporary politics also. This, as I have said, is the idea that the ship is going anywhere. A sense of direction is lacking, a feeling of purpose. That, I think, is what the decay of political theory means in ordinary terms to the ordinary man. Does it matter? If we were all of us, all our time, porkers not even from the sty of Epicurus, perhaps it would not: our purpose would be set by something outside ourselves, and it would be just as well that it should not be revealed to us in disturbing detail. Such, of course, may be the facts of the case; but rightly or wrongly the human mind demands something more than living from trough to snout. In the absence of a more or less rational theory to justify its sense of political obligation and the rightful powers of government, it will fall victim to an irrational one. If it cannot have, say, Locke on *Toleration*, it will have, say,

Hitler on *Mein Kampf*. That is what the decline of political theory means in practice.

One last word. The analysis I have made is perhaps moderately pessimistic; but it is not intended to lead to the conclusion that in political thinking we have reached the terminus, the end of that line. The reasons that I have given for its decline are in themselves even encouraging, since there are signs that they may be only temporary aberrations. Historians are in revolt against philosophies of history: ethics is sapping the lack of morale of professors of history. Hegelian politics is already dead. Marxist politics is increasingly revealed as a dialectical apologia for the pursuit of power for its own sake. The inadequacy, in relation to the broader issues of political society, of the scientific study of administrative methods, constitutional devices, electoral statistics and the like—I hope it will not be thought that within their own field I am attempting to deny the value of the techniques of political science—is gradually becoming apparent.

For a century and a half the Western democracies have been living on the stock of basic political ideas that were last restated towards the end of the eighteenth century. That is a long time. The nineteenth century did pretty well on them, but provided no restatement for its successors. The gap thus formed between political facts and political ideas has steadily widened. It has taken a long time for the results to become evident; but now that we have seen what politics devoid of a contemporary moral and political theory means, it is possible that something may be done about it. After a generation's experience of drifting directionless on a stormy sea the need of recovering a sense of direction, and therefore control, is beginning to be felt. And if political theory revives, if the idea of purpose is reintroduced into political thinking, we may take up again the tradition of Western political thought, and in doing so resume that 'continuous transformation of morals into politics, which still remains politics', in which, according to Croce, lies 'the real ethical progress of mankind'.

15

HISTORIOGRAPHICAL NOTES

The following group of short passages were selected by the author at the end of his life from among his Editorial Notes published in *History*. Apart from the deletion of minor points of ephemeral editorial concern, and a slight rearrangement of the chronological order, they have been left unaltered. While they were obviously not originally intended for publication in this form, in the circumstances they are more than worth including in this collection, both on account of their intrinsic distinction and because they illustrate the type of historical problems and reflections upon which Professor Cobban's mind was working, and upon which he was preparing to write more extensively during the leisure of his retirement.

i

THOSE who are not editors sometimes have a fancy picture of an unperceptive editor, sitting in his chair, with one hand casting into the waste-paper basket a succession of brilliant manuscripts, while with the other he accepts for publication all the duller and less interesting contributions he is offered. The contents of *History*, it seems to me, do not justify this picture. Moreover, the assumption on which it is based, of a great reservoir of first-class material ready to flow out if only editors would turn the tap on, is far from the reality. A good historical article, meeting all the criteria that would ideally be required, is a difficult thing to write.

What are these criteria? Sound scholarship may be taken for

granted but by itself is not enough. Historical articles are not ideally made up out of the by-products or left-overs of academic research: nor is the raw material to be presented to the reader as though he were a wild beast being fed by a keeper at the Zoo. This does not mean that research is anything less than the essence of history, but merely that history is something more than research, the results of which need to be shaped by an intellectual argument and a feeling for literary form: even historical articles should be well written.

There is another sense in which research is not enough. The discovery and exposition of new facts is of prime importance, but only in so far as these add to our knowledge of a subject with historical significance and take their place in a broader historical whole. The history of the changes in the interpretation of such a subject is also a contribution to historical understanding. Again, the processes by which the historian approaches his problems and employs his sources deserve discussion, especially if they involve new lines of investigation or new techniques. It is occasionally useful, also, to stand back and attempt to survey the modifications that more recent work has introduced into a given historical picture, to summarize the present position and perhaps guess at possible future lines of development. This, I believe, is the correct function of 'historical revisions'.

If asked, in more general terms, what kind of articles we should like to print, I find it impossible to improve on an answer given just over seventy years ago. This journal, I should like to say, will contain

no article which does not, in the Editor's judgment, add something to knowledge, i.e. which has not a value for the trained historian. No allurements of style will secure insertion for a popular *réchauffé* of facts already known or ideas already suggested. On the other hand, an effort will be made to provide in every number some articles, whether articles on a question, an epoch, or a personage, or reviews of books, which an educated man, not specially conversant with history, may read with pleasure and profit. We shall seek to accomplish this not so much by choosing topics certain to attract as by endeavouring to have even difficult topics treated with freshness and point. So far from holding that true history is dull, we believe that dull history is usually bad history, and shall value those contributors most highly who can present their researches in a lucid and effective form.

I make no apology for quoting the Prefatory Note to the first number of the *English Historical Review*.

ii

The study of the history of history may be a secondary activity, but it can provide contribution to historical understanding that could hardly come from any other source. Above all, it can help to keep historical thinking alert and free from the temptation to rest upon stereotyped formulae.

It is probably not unfair to suggest that the writing of contemporary history is often regarded with a measure of suspicion —all the more so because it has recently been pursued on such an unprecedented scale that an American historian has even asked plaintively whether history is about the past. One can understand his alarm, particularly if one considers the factors which are responsible for this concentration of interest. Governments and other bodies have wanted the history of their own recent activities to be chronicled; because of a belief in the utility—indeed the necessity—of the study of recent history, the great corporations have been anxious to promote historical activity in this field; and natural public interest in our own times leads publishers to look with a favourable eye on books that deal with them. All this has provided a considerable stimulus to the writing of contemporary history; a tendency to criticize the result has been the not unnatural reaction.

In this situation it is a salutary shock to be reminded by Professor Momigliano—or perhaps to learn for the first time—

that for long periods in the ancient world, and even later, it was not contemporary history but the history of the past that needed to be defended. Thucydides did not have to apologize for writing the history of his own times : it was Herodotus who was discredited for believing that it was possible to write the history of former ages. We can now perhaps look at this matter more impartially and see that the reasons for both the modern and ancient prejudices are essentially the same. Ancient historians, after Herodotus, believed, Professor Momigliano tells us, that it was not possible to obtain reliable evidence about the past; more recently this suspicion has been directed to the history of the present. The lesson to be drawn may be that if the same standards of critical scholarship can be and are applied, then the writing of contemporary history and of the history of the past are both justifiable. It would even be reasonable to suppose that on this level they can stimulate and fructify each other.

The President of the Historical Association[1] raises another problem in historiography. His book *George III and the Historians* has recently aroused some discussion. His article on one aspect of the same problem is likewise not uncontroversial; but it is not the function of *History* to publish only articles so innocuous or obscure that nobody could disagree, or even agree, with them. There is no finality in historical interpretation. However, history changes not so much by contradiction — and Sir Lewis Namier's scholarship is not easily or with impunity to be contradicted — as by a shift in the point of view. Even the greatest historian, however high-soaring, cannot encompass in one eagle-glance the whole of life. Working in an age bedevilled by warring ideologies, and reacting rightly against the exaggerated belief of nineteenth-century historians in the influence of theorists and the power of ideas, Sir Lewis has exhibited a healthy scepticism about them. Other historians have gone much farther. It would hardly be an exaggeration to say that the general climate of opinion among British historians since the First World War has been so cold to anything even smelling of an idea that any

[1] Professor Herbert Butterfield.

exotic plants of this kind that happened to be produced were rapidly killed off and those who would rashly have cultivated them taught the error of their ways.[1]

It seems to me that a part of what Professor Butterfield is trying to do is to bring ideas — not necessarily those of the study, but those of the debating chamber or the market place — back into the historical consciousness. This, I believe, is something worth doing, regardless of the merits or demerits of any particular interpretation of the reign of George III. Political ideas are inevitably part of any political system of government. Even the merest Tammany Hall boss will have here and there, hidden in the recesses of his mind, nestling in the folds and convolutions of intrigue, or buried under layers of dead mental matter, an occasional fossil idea. There may be long periods, perhaps even of recorded history, when the struggle for life or the dominance of autocracy leaves no room for political thought of even the most rudimentary kind. It is doubtful if any period of modern British history falls into this category, not even the mid-eighteenth century.

Admittedly the treatment of the role of ideas in history, especially those of social groups or political parties, is peculiarly liable to degenerate into unscholarly generalization. In the historical discussion of such concepts as Toryism, Jacobinism, Bonapartism, an inadequate social analysis may be combined with a shadowy and uncertain theoretical pattern, and the result be merely confusion worse confounded. Sir Lewis has

[1] I remember hearing one distinguished historian — quite unconnected with Sir Lewis Namier — say, emulating Henry Ford on history, 'Political ideas are bunk'; and another sum up the author of the *Letter to a Noble Lord* in the words, 'Burke was the perfect butler.' These doubtless were mere *boutades* and Sir Lewis has no responsibility for them. He himself writes, 'The effort which people put up to avoid thinking might almost enable them to think and to have some new ideas. But having ideas produces anxiety and *malaise* and runs counter to the deepest instincts of human nature, which loves symmetry, repetition and routine. Mine certainly does.' It would be unfair to end the quotation here; it continues '... and to such a degree that I get sick of them, and then notice that proclivity in others and criticize it.' He ends, and perhaps we should not take this too seriously, 'It is a mistake to suppose that people think: they wobble with the brain, and sometimes the brain does not wobble.' ('Symmetry and Repetition', 1941, in *Conflicts*, 1942, pp. 69, 72.)

taught us not to take such terms for granted in any period of history. Whigs and Tories, Royalists and Puritans, Jacobins and Girondins, feudal nobles and gentry, Roman senators, the whole mysterious complex of the middle classes, are now looked on with a suspicious scrutinizing eye, before which many time-honoured historical stereotypes have wilted. In a sense we all belong to the 'Namier school', for we have certainly all been to school to Sir Lewis's meticulous research and powerful analysis. If the revival of interest in what people thought, as a necessary clue to the understanding of what they did, is accompanied by the same standards of critical scholarship, the course of political and Parliamentary history will not desert its well-dug channels but will flow clearer and deeper; and it will escape the danger of being dissipated and disappearing in the sands of insignificant intrigue.

iii

Historians in the present century have usually been content to practise their art and leave the discussion of what it is to others; but recently some of them have ventured into the field of philosophical discussion, at least to the extent of hurling charges of 'historicism' about, until this term has become little more than an expression of abuse for any kind of history that one does not like. Professor Karl Popper, in *The Poverty of Historicism*,[1] gives it a more specific meaning. For him it is 'an approach to the social sciences which assumes that *historical prediction* is their principal aim, and that this aim is attainable by discovering the "rhythms" or the "patterns", the "laws" or the "trends" that underlie the evolution of history'.[2] This approach, he admits, is comprehensible as a reaction against that type of 'naive history' which does not attempt any detailed analysis of situations,[3] but it is none the less dangerous. For the historicist, the course of historical development, though it can

---

[1] London: Routledge & Kegan Paul. 1957. 166 pp.
[2] p. 3. [3] p. 148.

be speeded up or retarded, cannot be changed.[1] It obeys absolute laws, on which are based unconditional prophecies of the future.[2] Conceived in this way, as a pseudo-science, history becomes a powerful instrument of political action, as the Marxist movements shows; but Professor Popper demonstrates forcefully its intellectual defects. Historicism, he says, envisages the life of mankind as a single, continuous and all-embracing stream; which is fatal to its claim to scientific truth, for a scientific law cannot be validated by a single instance.[3] Besides, since the growth of knowledge influences the course of history, and there is no scientific method of predicting the future progress of science, we cannot foretell the future course of history.[4] Trends, of course, there may be, but these essentially depend on and change with circumstances.[5] The categories of the historicists, on the other hand, are fixed theoretical constructions. When Marx writes of a social class, or Professor Toynbee of a civilization, they define them in terms of their *a priori* beliefs.[6] From the beginning, we may say, they have rigged the pack of cards with which they are playing, and they will always win the game so long as they can play with their own pack.

It may fairly be said that Professor Popper's argument is directed rather to the social scientist or the philosopher of history than to the historian; and this is appropriate, because nearly all philosophers and social scientists try to force historical thought into alien channels. Even Professor Popper is not free from this tendency. He seems to hold that explanation is only achieved in history, as elsewhere, by 'subsuming' what is to be explained under a general law.[7] This view is widely held by modern analytical philosophers, who were preceded in it by Comte and Mill.[8] It was elaborated in *The Nature of Historical Explanation* (1952) by Mr P. Gardiner, and a recent plea for scientific history is that of Dr Philip Bagby in *Culture and History*

---

[1] Popper, *The Poverty of Historicism*, 52.   [2] p. 128.   [3] pp. 81, 108.
[4] pp. ix-x.   [5] p. 128.   [6] pp. 33-4, 111.
[7] Popper, *The Open Society*, ii, 262.
[8] For illustrations, see William Dray, *Laws and Explanations in History*. Oxford University Press. 1957. 174 pp.

(London: Longmans. 1958. 244 pp. 30s.). In place of concentrating attention on individuals and their actions, which Dr Bagby regards as 'the major reason why history has proved unintelligible up to date',[1] he wants the historian to observe recurrent patterns or regularities. His theme is that the historian must copy the methods of the cultural anthropologist, for culture is 'history's intelligible aspect'.[2] When Dr Bagby tries to indicate the results to be expected from scientific history he hardly gets beyond an elementary textbook level. Nevertheless the belief that history can only be understood in terms of laws or regularities is something which historians should not shut their eyes to. This view is criticized in the Riddell Memorial Lectures for 1957[3] by Dr H. G. Wood. Mr W. H. Walsh's *Introduction to the Philosophy of History* (1951) also qualified the positivistic approach to historical explanation.

It has now been subjected to a full-scale critique in *Laws and Explanation in History* by Professor William Dray, whose book offers what looks like a way out of the *impasse* in which historians would find themselves if they knew what philosophers have been writing about them. The positivists insist that historians can only talk about causes in terms of 'covering laws'. On the other hand, some idealists would remove the conception of cause altogether from history, and replace it by 'the exhibition of a world of events intrinsically related to one another in which no *lacuna* is tolerated'. This seems to demand a total history which no historian could envisage or achieve. Nor indeed will any historian easily be persuaded that he must not discuss causes, in some sense or other of the word, though he might willingly agree that it is not necessarily the sense in which many philosophers use the term, and applaud Professor Dray when he says that to hold the view 'that no explanation is complete until a lurking covering law has been discovered is merely to fall into a kind of determinist myopia'.[4] Admittedly, the historian, like

[1] *Culture and History*, 150.
[2] Ibid., 124; cf. 57, 71.
[3] *Freedom and Necessity in History*. Oxford University Press. 1957. 68 pp.
[4] Dray, *Laws and Explanation in History*, 168.

anyone who has to communicate his thoughts, uses classificatory terms; but so long as he remains 'at the level of generality indicated by his classificatory word', he does not achieve history.[1]

Mr Dray, it seems to me, has made a valuable contribution to the clarification of our ideas on historical explanation. This is perhaps not unconnected with the fact that his description of it bears, for a philosopher, an unusually recognizable relation to the activity in which historians know themselves to be engaged. There are also some interesting observations, though rather widely spaced, in the historical part of *Nature and Historical Experience*[2] by John Herman Randall, Jr. Professor Randall points out that history implies novelty, and therefore discontinuity as well as continuity. He criticizes 'historicism' as the assumption of a vital force at work in history, and sees philosophies as primarily attempts to appraise the present and what is dynamic in it, rather than the past. The major part of his book, however, is devoted to the discussion of a theory of nature, and what he has to say about history, though sound, is rather slight.

Of course, one must not exaggerate the importance of theories about history. Philosophical views do not commonly have an immediate or direct effect on historical writing. Those historians who imagine themselves to be the purest devotees of the fact 'as it actually happened', however, are likely to be those who are most at the mercy of preconceived and unexamined theoretical assumptions. And changes in the intellectual climate have an indirect effect on historians, of which they themselves are often largely unconscious. It may be suspected that we are now in the midst of a period of such change, and that some of the present doubts and hesitations, and even contradictions, about what history ought to be, are not unconnected with this fact.

[1] Dray, op. cit., 48.
[2] Columbia University Press: Oxford University Press. 1958. 326 pp.

iv

Two of the most respected among American historians of the last generation were Carl Becker and Charles Beard. Evidence of the significance of their work and thought may be seen in the fact that there is still keen interest in it, and that it is still being hotly disputed. Recently a volume of Becker's papers and letters — *Detachment and the Writing of History: Essays and Letters of Carl L. Becker* (Cornell University Press: O.U.P. 1959. xvi + 240 pp.) edited by Phil L. Snyder — has been produced, including some of his most characteristic writing; and in 1956 a conference at Colgate University was devoted to a discussion of Becker's best-known work, *The Heavenly City of the Eighteenth-Century Philosophers*. The papers have now been edited by Professor Raymond O. Rockwood under the title *Carl Becker's Heavenly City Revisited* (Cornell University Press. 1958. xxxii + 227 pp.). The attraction of Becker's personality emerges from the contributions of all who knew him. The editor speaks of the 'indelible impression' he made, of his 'urbane wit, polished charm and shrewd penetration'. But he also points out some defects in Becker's outlook, and the essays which follow contain much more criticism than acceptance.

Among the speakers at the symposium, Professor Bruun gives a sympathetic account of Becker as a man and a teacher. Professor John Hall Stewart regards the *Heavenly City* as his 'great work', but hints at the possibility that its author 'may have been guilty of too much assumption or too little reading'. Professor Leo Gershoy treats the book as the work of a disillusioned liberal and writes a defence of Becker from this point of view. Only Professor Louis Gottschalk (in a reported speech) explicitly upholds the historical soundness of Becker's work. On the other hand a series of contributors — Henry Guerlac, Peter Gay, Walter L. Dorn, R. R. Palmer, Ralph H. Bowen, Edward Whiting Fox — draw up, with varying degrees of severity, a well-documented and pretty decisive indictment of the *Heavenly*

City. It had, concludes Mr Gay, 'every virtue save one, the virtue of being right'.

At this point we may begin to sympathize with Carl Becker, for after all, which of us *is* right, in the long run and always? Moreover there was a good deal that is attractive in his outlook. We have long since learnt to accept his rejection of history as a simple record of the 'facts', and to agree that all the history that has been, is, or ever will be written, is relative to the mind and environment of the historian. Becker was rightly against a rather absurd historical determinism, such as was expressed in Henry Adams's *The Degradation of Democratic Dogma*, and against the claims of 'scientific' history.

He was joined in this campaign, though from a different angle, by Charles Beard, whose major work of historical interpretation is now also under severe attack. The two historians are considered together in the latest of the volumes of Wallace Notestein Essays published by Yale University Press. *The Pragmatic Revolt in American History: Carl Becker and Charles Beard* (Yale University Press: O.U.P. 1959. 182 pp.) by Cushing Strout, is an interesting and thoughtful study. The author sees both Becker and Beard as escaping from nineteenth-century dogmatism only at the price of a destructive scepticism. For Becker, he says, the historian's mind reflects not cold facts but the dominant social forces of the day; while for Beard meaning is given to the facts of history only by their economic substructure. They both, says Mr Strout, 'reveal the plight of pragmatic relativism'.

I should like to push this argument a little farther, for, as indeed Mr Strout points out, scepticism is not the last word of either historian. Becker, he says, believes that the historian must begin with a synthesis to control his relativism, and this is obviously what he has done in the *Heavenly City*; while Beard envisages history as moving towards 'collectivist democracy'. Here, I think, we begin to see both why their work was so influential when it appeared, and why it has proved unsatisfying in such a short space of time. To those who saw the accumulation of historical detail rapidly growing into a trackless and impenetrable jungle, they offered clear-cut and convincing ways through, Beard in his economic interpretation of the American Revolution and the origins of the Constitution, Becker in seeing the thought of the eighteenth-century *philosophes* as a secularized version of medieval Christianity. A few critics, who happened to know more of the subjects discussed, remained unconvinced at the time, and their number has increased, for these were not really very profound interpretations. It is not easily possible to believe that either Beard or Becker had a strong grasp of theory. The attraction of their ideas lay in their brilliant simplicity.

There is nothing wrong, of course, in starting with a bright idea; the trouble comes in stopping with it; and herein lies, I believe, the second and fundamental weakness. Historical research with no ideas behind it is bad; but ideas with no historical research behind them are even worse. What personal factors there may have been to explain the lack of this in each case, I do not know; but the fact is that neither Becker nor Beard undertook the basic research that was necessary to establish, develop, modify, or even change their simple initial assumptions. There is no evidence in the *Heavenly City* that Carl Becker had read more than a comparatively small and select body of eighteenth-century writings, or that he had paid any serious attention to secondary works at all. No wonder it is possible for the contributors to Mr Rockwood's symposium to pick out point after point on which his statements are simply not in accord with the facts. Becker's contempt for the 'mere' facts was salutary, but in so far as this also involved a neglect of critically established historical evidence, the facts have had their revenge. Beard's economic assertions about the American revolutionaries, now that they are being subjected to critical examination, are also proving largely baseless, it seems.[1]

[1] See Robert E. Brown's *Charles Beard and the Constitution*. Princeton University Press. 1956. 228 pp.; and Forrest McDonald's *We the People*. Phoenix Books, University of Chicago. 1958. 448 pp.

The problem now is not so much whether there is, or is not, any remaining historical validity in Becker's *Heavenly City* or Beard's economic interpretation of the American Constitution, but rather to explain the initial easy acceptance of views which have been shown to be backed by so little evidence. Partly, I suppose, it was because, in welcoming the rejection of a past dogmatism, we did not appreciate that a new dogmatism was being substituted for it. Even more, it may have been because the tendencies of both writers in different ways, and even despite themselves, fell in with the anti-rational and anti-liberal spirit of the 'thirties. Becker recovered from this in the end, but Beard never did. It is ironic that they should now both appear as extreme examples of the historical relativism which they correctly diagnosed; and that the great popularity and influence which they won because they were so thoroughly in tune with their own time should now be fast disappearing for the same reason.

V

It is interesting to discover, in a scholarly study by Dr P. Hardy,[1] parallels between the writing of history in medieval Europe and in Muslim India. The aim of the Muslim chroniclers, says Dr Hardy, was to serve the true religion. Since history is the history of believers, only the deeds of Muslims count as historical actions: things may happen to unbelievers but they are passive material on whom history acts, unconnected with the real historic forces, for history is the spectacle of divine ordination. An important difference from the chroniclers of medieval Europe is that the Muslim chroniclers admit of no development, human nature is fixed by divine ordinance for all time: the present succeeds the past but is not the outcome of it. Dr Hardy compares the result with the kind of orthodox communist history with which we are too familiar, in which every issue finds its significance in terms of dialectical materialism.

[1] *Historians of Medieval India*. London: Luzac & Co. 1960. v + 146 pp.

It is also not very different from the history, say, of Bossuet, which also shares what now seems to us the defect of the history of the Muslim or Christian Middle Ages—the failure to distinguish between history and religion. In an overt form the danger of this confusion is perhaps not very great now. Professor Toynbee's converts have been among the general public rather than among historians. The older religions have now largely come to terms with history; only on a rather low level do we find history exploited in their interests. Ideological history still survives, however, and it is important to note that the ideological historian is really the monkish or Muslim chronicler in disguise, whether he is defending the democratic revolutions of the eighteenth and nineteenth centuries or the Marxist revolutions of the twentieth century.

Dr Hardy also finds in his Muslim historians the inculcation of moral and political virtues by the arts of literature. Here we move on to the humanist ideal, which dominated Western historiography between the end of the monastic chronicles and the rise of critical history. A study of four American historians, Bancroft, Prescott, Motley and Parkman, by Professor David Levin, illustrates its persistence in the nineteenth century.[1] For these historians history is still the unfolding of a Providential plan, though now a secular rather than a religious one. The struggle of good against evil becomes the struggle of political liberty against absolutism. For the romantic historians he studies, says Mr Levin, the evolution of liberty is the evidence of the working of divine and natural law. Liberty is above all American and Teutonic. The Teutonic blood triumphs in the heroic Dutchmen of Motley, the equally heroic Spaniards (descended of course from the Visigoths) of Prescott, the pioneers of Parkman, and the revolutionaries of Bancroft. (Lest all this produce a holier-than-thou attitude in the British breast, let us insert the chastening memory of Carlyle.) Mr Levin's thoroughly documented book also suggests the tendency of his

[1] *History as a Romantic Art.* By D. Levin. Stanford University Press: O.U.P. 1960. xi + 260 pp.

historians to sacrifice much to literary effect. What I cannot quite make out is whether he realizes how devastating is the cumulative effect of his exposition. His reference to the 'highest standards of historical research' sounds ironical, but it is said with a very straight face.

In case we may be led to condemn literary history out of hand, Mr Harold L. Bond, in a thoughtful study, reminds us that Gibbon also conceived of history as a literary art.[1] The essential differences between Mr Levin's romantic historians and Gibbon are that as literature the *Decline and Fall* is in a higher class; that Gibbon's mind was a better mind; and that his ideas were less subject to the influence of superficial and ephemeral sentiment. It has been assumed that because he wrote of the Roman Empire and in the age of benevolent despotism, this must have represented his political ideal. Mr Bond points out that, on the contrary, for Gibbon the whole period of the Empire is, as it was for Machiavelli, a decline and fall from the days of the Republic. Of the Antonines, often assumed to represent his ideal rulers, Gibbon wrote, 'Such princes deserved the honour of restoring the Republic, had the Romans of their day been capable of a rational freedom.' The point was that they were not. Evidently Gibbon did not take his ideals merely from the politics of his day.

vi

How often one is tempted to believe, of course unjustly, that the value of contemporary books about history is in inverse relation to their length. Mr E. H. Dance's *History the Betrayer, a study of bias* (London: Hutchinson. 1960. 162 pp.) is a short book, its proportion of ideas to words is well above the average, and what the author has to say is always clear and stimulating even where one cannot agree with it. Since all history involves a selection of facts, every history is partial, in both senses of the word; but Mr Dance believes that it need

[1] *The Literary Art of Edward Gibbon.* Oxford: Clarendon Press. 1960. 167 pp.

not be as narrowly national and limited as it often is. He is particularly concerned with the history that is taught in schools, and with the dangers of nationalist history in the world today. To take two examples: according to French critics English textbooks exhibit 'une manifestation d'orgueil national, conscient ou inconscient, qui minimise le rôle de tous ceux qui ne sont pas Anglais'.[1] Of the standard Russian history textbook, edited by A. M. Pankratova in 1948, Mr Dance says it is 'about the level of our own history books in late Victorian times':[2] if its function is to stimulate patriotism, so was theirs.

One of Mr Dance's aims is to draw attention to an international effort to check at least the worst forms of national bias in historical textbooks. Beginning with an Anglo-German exchange in 1949, there was established in 1951 the Brunswick International Schoolbook Institute, by Professor Georg Eckert. The movement for the mutual exchange and criticism of textbooks has now reached considerable proportions under the general sponsorship of UNESCO, and besides Brunswick there are Institutes at Delhi and Osaka. One reason for the success of the movement so far, Mr Dance suggests, not without a certain acidity, is that since 1945 it 'has been mainly in the hands of school teachers and not of university historians, as it was between the wars; so that this time textbooks have been really read and really revised'.[3]

Mr Dance's other main aim is to urge the revision of the content of history teaching, and especially the introduction of genuinely world history; he holds that the teaching of history in university and school is inadequate while it fails 'to provide access to the history and culture of three-quarters of the world'.[4] We may sympathize with the plea for more informed understanding of the peoples of the East without necessarily agreeing that the Chinese lack of logic is a particular virtue.[5] We may think that there is good reason for dropping a fair amount of lumber out of school history,[6] without believing that it is alto-

[1] p. 43.
[2] p. 66.
[3] p. 138.
[4] p. 86.
[5] p. 96.
[6] p. 49.

gether more worth while knowing about Genghis Khan than about Magna Carta.[1] We might even argue that if we are going to reform our school syllabus, a couple of centuries of Athens might be more worth introducing than all the millennia of China. We may be shocked at Mr Dance's suggestion that he has 'usually found footnote references to authorities more irritating than helpful'[2] — a sentiment which publishers, especially University Presses, may applaud but historians will deplore. We may look with suspicion on many UNESCO activities, like other schemes for spending large sums of money on collective cultural 'projects'. But whatever reservations we may have on particular points, one would have to be very smug, even for an historian, to deny that Mr Dance has raised important questions. When he tells us that 'our present attitude to history and to our history teaching is out of date',[3] professional conservatism will not necessarily inspire the best reaction. It must be confessed that what might superficially be judged a rather naive scheme for the exchange of textbooks, which has grown up almost accidentally out of small beginnings, has already achieved something of value. More important than the revision of existing textbooks may be, as Mr Dance suggests, the effect on their use, on the writing of new ones, and on the general climate of history teaching in many countries.

vii

A volume in which are translated some of the shorter studies of the eminent Dutch historian, Huizinga,[4] is welcome. It is interesting to find him commenting, in 1929, unfavourably on the state of historical research. Not that he wanted detailed research to be abandoned in favour of 'larger' topics. 'Critical scholarship', he writes, 'is the only form for understanding the past which is appropriate to our culture.' His quarrel is with the

[1] p. 51. [2] p. 151. [3] p. 124.
[4] *Men and Ideas*. Introduction by B. F. Hoselitz. London: Eyre & Spottiswoode. 1960. 378 pp.

kind of research which instead of posing clearly formulated questions is content with the mechanical accumulation of information; and Huizinga looks towards the coming development of historical interests in what his editor describes as his 'growing pre-occupation with social and socio-psychological problems.'[1]

viii

The belief that history can be written in a vacuum, as a pure academic discipline devoid of contemporary reference, has died hard, but I doubt if any serious historian holds it now. As Mr A. J. P. Taylor, in his notable work on *The Origins of the Second World War* (Hamish Hamilton, 1963. 295 pp.), says, in writing even of such an apparently remote subject as medieval administrative history, Tout was reflecting twentieth-century developments. And not only is the writing of history influenced by social and political conditions, in turn it exercises an influence on them. Thus Mr Taylor points to the 'revisionism', during the inter-war years, of historians of the causes of the First World War on the subject of war guilt. Their books were political acts, and the same is true of his own book. This is not a criticism: even an historian can be, and usually is, a political animal, and it is humbug to pretend otherwise. Of course, the political presuppositions of historians generally have to be read between the lines, and it is easy to draw the wrong conclusion. For one reader, at least, the teaching of Mr Taylor's book is that war is not so much wicked as futile, and that 'only a country which aims at victory can be threatened with defeat' (p. 101). There is material here for a far longer discussion than is possible in these Editorial Notes. Here, some of the broader issues raised by a work which has historiographical, as well as political, significance may properly be mentioned.

There has undoubtedly been a tendency to concentrate the

[1] p. 41. Huizinga incidentally paid a tribute to 'the excellent way in which historical research and the teaching of history are being brought in touch with each other' in Great Britain, which, he said, was 'mainly as a result of the activities of the Historical Association and its periodical *History*'.

whole discussion of the guilt of the Second World War on the person of Hitler, and so implicitly to provide an alibi for the German nation which supported him, and the other nations and their statesmen whose folly or weakness provided the necessary conditions for his triumphs. By reminding us of this Mr Taylor has performed a useful service. At the same time he has done some other things which are rather less useful, and to which attention should be drawn; for this is a book which might easily become (as for its skilful advocacy it would deserve to) a standard textbook for the sixth forms of schools and for undergraduates.

The first is probably the most harmless, and some would think it even a laudable bias: this is the Cleopatra's nose theory of history—the belief that the most trivial accidents are the normal causes of the most important results. The Second World War, we learn, was the result of a series of diplomatic blunders, culminating in Hitler 'launching on August 29th a diplomatic manœuvre which he ought to have launched on August 28th' (p. 278; cf. p. 219). Voltaire would have found this explanation eminently satisfactory, though he might not have accepted the view, which logically follows, that 'the greatest masters of statecraft are those who do not know what they are doing' (p. 72).

In some respects Mr Taylor seems to put Hitler in the class of Bismarck. The historian's natural weakness is to admire temporary success and this foible was perhaps unusually strong during the last generation. The book gives me the impression, which may, of course, be mistaken, that so long as Hitler was successful, Mr Taylor cannot help admiring him. One element in the admiration is, as he argues with considerable force, that Hitler had no detailed plan and no time-table of conquest (pp. 68–9, 108, 134, 171, 192). He can hardly deny that Hitler had certain aims, but these are consistently played down. Nearly everything Hitler wrote or said, including *Mein Kampf*, is dismissed as 'day-dreams', 'conversation of any Austrian café or German beer-house', 'talking for effect' and so on (cf. pp. 69,

131–3, 264, 281). It is true that this procedure is necessary for Mr Taylor's argument, but it has, I believe, a broader significance. It seems to me to reflect, almost in an exaggerated form, the recently dominant disposition to treat ideas as a negligible factor in history; because, for all its rant, *Mein Kampf* represents this factor just as much as, say, Plato's *Republic*.

Another point to be noted is that the book is written in the established tradition of diplomatic history. Its material is confined to diplomatic correspondence, along with such memoirs of diplomats, foreign ministers and other statesmen as are available. It is difficult to believe that the origins of the Second World War can be adequately discussed within these limits. Indeed, in one place Mr Taylor himself acknowledges that 'Hitler's domestic behaviour, not his foreign policy, was the real crime which ultimately brought him—and Germany—to the ground' (p. 202). Apart from this 'throw-away' line, there is practically no mention of the domestic policy of the Nazis, nor—except for two incidental references to anti-semitism— any mention of racialism. The assumption seems to be that international developments can be understood without reference to the internal conditions and policies of states. Certainly, here also Mr Taylor is only following in a well-trodden path. That is the trouble. One cannot but express surprise, as well as regret, to find him giving support, by example if not by precept, to ways of writing history which, however orthodox they may have been in the past, one had hoped were being abandoned now.

ix

'Universal history comprehends the past life of mankind, not in its particular relations and trends, but in its fullness and totality'; 'the final goal—not yet attained—always remains the conception and composition of a history of mankind.' In some such terms, I suppose, might the initial aim of Professor Arnold Toynbee's *Study of History* be defined. In fact, they are the words, as Mr Edward T. Gargan points out in the interesting collection of essays he has edited under the title *The Intent of Toynbee's History*,[1] of that idol of the professional historian, Ranke. If Ranke could put forward such an ideal, it may be asked, was it so very wrong of Professor Toynbee to attempt to achieve it? And did his attempt deserve the barrage of heavy guns and light artillery that historians have let loose on it? The opportunity to ask these questions arises because Professor Toynbee has now added a twelfth volume of *Reconsiderations*[2] to his monumental *Study*. In it he quotes his many critics, and re-states his own views—both, it must be admitted, at rather inordinate length.

As might be expected, Toynbee successfully answers some of the criticisms. Thus he disposes easily of the common illusion of historians that they are concerned with events only in their uniqueness.[3] Every general term they use is, of course, proof to the contrary. He also deals fairly effectively with the charge that his method is 'unscientific',[4] by showing that his critics tend to identify science with a kind of crude empiricism.[5] Again, because he has speculated on the future of our present civilization in the light of existing trends and the experience of the past, he has been accused of confusing history with prophecy. He has no difficulty in refuting this.[6]

A more valid charge is that, starting as a classic, Toynbee has been so obsessed with the pattern of Hellenic history that he has seen it everywhere.[7] To correct this bias, he has added a second measuring-rod derived from Chinese history, and he now finds that a composite Helleno-Sinic model is the true standard pattern.[8] Such models are very useful heuristic devices, they are an aid to historical understanding; but even if many

[1] Chicago: Loyola University Press. 1961. 224 pp.
[2] Oxford University Press. 1961. 740 pp.
[3] Toynbee, *Study of History*, 19, 22, 225–7.
[4] E.g., by William N. McNeill in Gargan, *The Intent of Toynbee's History*, 39–40; and Pieter Geyl, *Toynbee's Answer* (Mededelingen der Koninkluge Nederlandse Akademie van Wetenschappen, afd. Letterkunde, 1961), 4–5.
[5] Toynbee, op. cit., 12–13, 167, 229–32, 244–5.
[6] Ibid., 238, 519.   [7] Ibid., 160, 186.   [8] Ibid., 197–8.

parallels can be found, as they certainly can, in the histories of different civilizations, these are hardly an adequate basis for talking about 'laws', even interpreted as 'generalizations about human behaviour'.[1]

Some of the bitterest criticisms of the *Study of History* have come because Toynbee has deliberately demoted the nation from the dominant position, as the one real absolute for the historian, which it has occupied in historical studies for over a century. On this point he makes no concessions in the new volume. Reproached with the fact that in the index, judged by a tape-measure, 'England' occupies only one-ninth of the space given to 'Egypt', he expresses astonishment at this evidence of the survival of national bias in his own mind.[2] A new generation of historians may be less unsympathetic to his approach in this respect. And when Professor Geyl, in his rebuttal of Toynbee's *Reconsiderations*, declares that 'National communities evidently ... belonged to a stage which historical development could not avoid,[3] one cannot help feeling that he is being influenced, on the national level, by the kind of determinism which Toynbee's ideas may seem to involve on the level of civilizations.

More serious, I think, is the criticism of Professor Matthew A. Fitzsimons, who argues that Toynbee himself fails to keep the distinction between nation and civilization clearly in mind, and continually uses examples drawn from the history of nations to illustrate the patterns of behaviour, or laws, of civilizations.[4] Professor Geyl also makes this point,[5] which seems to me to represent a very damaging flaw which runs through Toynbee's whole argument. I find it difficult, however, to agree that we can therefore exclude forms of national behaviour which we dislike, such as Fascism and Nazism, from the overall pattern of Western civilization. Professor Geyl holds 'that Mussolini in Italy and Hitler in Germany could come into power only with the aid of exceptional political and economic circumstances

---

[1] Ibid., 241-2.   [3] Geyl, op. cit., 22.   [5] Geyl, op. cit., 15.
[2] Ibid., 630.   [4] Gargan, op. cit., 147.

which confused the masses and threw them off their balance; and these regimes were overthrown without leaving any lasting impact on the cultural and political mentality of their countries. They were barbarians, in revolt against the best traditions of our part of the world.'[1] Toynbee would, I think correctly, dismiss this, either as wishful thinking or else as a denial that there is such a thing, objectively, as a 'civilization'.[2] On the other hand, I doubt if he would himself, in the matter of religion, admit that, say, the Inquisition, or the persecution of the Jews, was an inherent part of the spiritual religion of Christianity.

This leads on to another kind of criticism, which the *Reconsiderations* does not eliminate but rather reinforces. Increasingly Toynbee's classicism seems to give way to influences deriving from Christianity. He comes to envisage a declining civilization almost with pleasure, as the vehicle for a higher religion. It is humanity's way of 'learning through suffering'.[3] In the later volumes of the *Study*, a civilization itself becomes a 'state of the soul',[4] its evolution a dialectical process.[5] This is why a civilization, according to him, can fundamentally only break down for internal reasons.[6] The argument now really passes over from history to theology, and in this field Dr Edward Rochie Hardy, I suspect, though he puts it very politely, finds Toynbee somewhat superficial. Whatever the value of his theological arguments, however, in the end it is to the category of St Augustine or Bossuet that Toynbee belongs,[7] not to that of Thucydides or Gibbon. Universal history is for him the gradual revelation of God to man.[8] But to say this is to say that what he has written is either more or less than history; it is not simply history, in spite of the aspirations of Ranke. Perhaps here is the fundamental reason why it seems impossible for there

[1] Geyl, op. cit., 16. [2] Toynbee, op. cit., 532.
[3] William H. McNeill in Gargan, *The Intent of Toynbee's History*, 37–8.
[4] Ibid., 35–6.
[5] Toynbee, op. cit., 641.
[6] Ibid., 613, 616.
[7] Edward Rochie Hardy in Gargan, op. cit., 153, 156.
[8] William H. McNeill in Gargan, op. cit., 38.

to be any real meeting of minds between Toynbee and the historians. They use different languages and are writing about different things. Toynbee has evidently filled a gap for an important general public, but it is a gap that the historian, *qua* historian, cannot fill.

There is one final point that may be worth making. It would be a pity if, because of the excessive neglect of politics in the *Study of History*, historians should think themselves justified in perpetuating an undue concentration of attention on the narrowly political; if, because of their dislike for his universal history of civilizations, they should deny the whole possibility of writing the history of a particular civilization; and, if in reaction against what might seem an attempt to reduce all history to sweeping generalizations, they should fall back on the view that all the historian can do is to narrate a series of events, without any attempt at general explanations or understanding.

X

A stout defence of the right, indeed the duty, of the historian to provide general explanations is offered by Dr E. H. Carr.

It must be rather distressing to some of the older generation to find historians, and even reputable ones, instead of confining themselves to their task of writing history—or, even better, collecting materials for writing history—concerning themselves with the nature and justification of their activity. The distinguished historian of Soviet Russia, Dr Carr, devotes the Trevelyan lectures for 1961 to the subject *What is History?* (London: Macmillan. 1961. 155 pp.) An anthology of challenging observations could be culled from his lively and provocative discussions. 'I suspect that even today one of the fascinations of ancient and medieval history is that it gives us the illusion of having all the facts at our disposal within a manageable compass'; 'the nineteenth-century heresy that history consists of the compilation of a maximum number of irrefutable and objective facts'; 'those historians who today pretend to dispense with a philosophy of history are merely trying, vainly and self-consciously, like members of a nudist colony, to recreate the Garden of Eden in their garden suburb'; 'I have no patience with the fashion set by Bury ... of pretending that Mommsen's greatness rests not on his *History of Rome* but on his corpus of inscriptions ... '; 'the historian is not really interested in the unique, but in what is general in the unique'; 'the more sociological history becomes, and the more historical sociology becomes, the better for both'; 'only the future can provide the key to the interpretation of the past'; 'the parochialism of English history ... weighs like a dead hand on our curriculum.'

Mr Carr says many things that badly needed saying and that it is difficult to disagree with. Criticism, which is inevitably aroused by a stimulating book, must be directed rather to the things he does not say, because his clarity and conciseness seem sometimes to be achieved by a refusal to face the more difficult questions. 'I shall be content', says Mr Carr, 'to use the word "cause" in the popular sense', which would be more justifiable if there had been rather less discussion of the nature of historical causation recently, and if he were merely writing a popular book. The problems of 'historicism' and determinism he is content to flatten out with a one-two punch from common sense and Hegel, which is really not quite good enough. Again, it may be true, as he says, that 'the thesis that the good of some justifies the sufferings of others is implicit in all government', but I doubt if many political theorists would be satisfied with quite such a simple formulation.

Finally, Mr Carr frankly gives us his philosophy of history: it is one of progress. Without such a conception, he holds, society could not survive, for without it society could not impose sacrifices on the living for the sake of generations yet unborn; and without it history would not be possible. This leads him to a declaration of 'faith in the future of society, and in the future of history'. Here one's sympathies may well be with him and against the pundits of social statics or degeneration whom he denounces. Yet though it would not be fair to say that he gives us no clue as to what he means by progress—it is achieved by 'the interdependence and interaction of facts and values'—I would feel happier if he had been a little more specific about these facts and values. Certainly this century is one of revolutionary change, certainly man's capacity to change his environment is far greater than it ever was before. Possibly—though here I think we move into the realm of faith—the evils that have accompanied innovations carry their own corrective with them. Possibly the leading feature of our twentieth-century revolution has been 'the expansion of reason'—though one would like to see this reconciled with the two World Wars. But I wish Mr Carr's appealing declaration of faith in our progress could have consisted more of positive gains to add to the obvious technological advances, and less of apologies for the losses that have gone with them. And I wish that he had not taken it for granted that we all know, and are agreed on, what are gains and what are losses; for to do so is to reintroduce the dogmatic element into history which, it seemed to me, his earlier arguments had very effectively eliminated. To say all this, however, is to say that this is a book which provokes thought about history, and even if it is unaccustomed and painful, this is something that historians will evidently have to reconcile themselves to in the years that are coming.

xi

Under the editorship of Dr H. P. R. Finberg, nine historians, including himself, have explained and justified different *Approaches to History* (London: Routledge & Kegan Paul. 1961. x + 227 pp.). Professor Bindoff begins with a defence of political history so forceful as to make us feel that the defence was hardly necessary. Perhaps this reaction will not be as unexpected now as it might have been a few years ago. As textbooks and multiple-authored histories pour out, deriving their originality chiefly from ignoring the political calendar, it becomes increasingly evident that this is a gimmick which subtracts from, a good deal more than it adds to, historical understanding. Professor Bindoff is able to remind us that, in spite of (or perhaps because of) all the analytical treatment of the seventeenth century, the most significant recent development historiographically 'has been the appearance, from C. V. Wedgwood's accomplished pen, of a work which, while taking account of the new "interpretations", sets out to re-tell that story in the belief that there are readers chiefly interested in knowing what men did, why they did it, and with what consequences.'

Professor Court on economic history is also convincing, partly because the modesty of the author prevents him from claiming too much for his subject, but largely because of the admirable way in which he brings out the interdependence of history and theory. Mr H. J. Perkins on social history I find more puzzling. He tells us that it is 'nothing more and nothing less than the history of society', and indeed practically everything seems to be included in Mr Perkins' enumeration; but in this case social history is just history, no more and no less. The essay on local history by the editor of the volume is a contribution to a controversy that a non-combatant is perhaps best advised to keep out of. At the opposite extreme, Professor Barraclough appeals for a world history, a larger vision, a break-through to new dimensions. More specialized approaches are those of Professor Darby, who gives a useful bibliographical survey of historical geography, Professor D. Talbot Rice on the history of art, Professor Rupert Hall who writes authoritatively on the history of science, and F. T. Wainwright, whose death is a loss to more than one historical discipline, on archaeology and place-names.

xii

The Social Science Research Council in America has followed up its two earlier reports on historiography with one on

Generalisation in the Writing of History (University of Chicago Press. 1963. 255 pp.), edited by Louis Gottschalk. Of the twelve chapters in this volume some, at least to my mind, say little or nothing, though it would be invidious to indicate which. At the same time, the subject was well worth discussion and the book should represent one more step towards eliminating the nonsense that has been talked during the past generation, both by historians and non-historians, about the impropriety of generalization in history.

All the contributors are agreed that in some sense or other of the word every historian uses generalizations. In an interesting chapter William O. Aydelotte picks out for criticism the rather touching faith in facts of Sir Isaiah Berlin, who writes, 'The same facts can be arranged in many patterns, seen from many perspectives, displayed in many lights, all of them equally valid ... Yet through it all the facts themselves will remain relatively "hard".' As Professor Aydelotte points out, this conception of historical facts as a sort of hard bricks, which the historican can use to construct a variety of different buildings, shows a failure to understand the process of historical writing. Though it is common, I believe, among philosophical writers, it is not even very good philosophy. 'The distinction ... between data and inferences', Professor Aydelotte quotes Raymond Aron, 'has a deceptive clarity ... Theories and facts are integrated in such a manner that one would attempt in vain to separate them rigorously.'

It may be asked, seeing that historians will go on doing what they do whether non-historians approve of their activities, or even whether they themselves understand them, or not, if there is any practical value in a theoretical discussion of this kind. The contributors to this volume seem to agree that there is no rigorous method by which theories in the form of general concepts or statements are reached by historians. (The same is probably true in science.) Hence some would argue, as Professor R. R. Palmer does with a certain dry cynicism, that all generalizations must be verifiable or unverifiable to the same extent. Mr Aydelotte, in my opinion rightly, disagrees with this view. He sees as one of the essential, perhaps even the most essential, function of the historian the task of testing and verifying his general terms, ideas or assumptions. If in carrying out this duty the broad over-all generalizations tend to be broken down into smaller and more manageable ones, this is no loss. Moreover, if historians have some understanding of what they are doing they are unlikely to suffer from the illusion that the process of collecting data is all-sufficient, and that history can emerge from the data unsullied by the process of thought, as Namier appears to have believed. It was a dangerous view, for it bred as intense a dogmatism on one side as the kind of history written on the basis of a theory such as Marxism-Leninism does on the other. Here extremes meet, and the unconscious, emotional assumptions behind naive history prove as dangerous as the presuppositions of an ideological faith.

Both lead to a temptation to ignore the interpretations of previous historians. For a Namier these were based on theories and therefore misleading, whereas his own views, he honestly believed, were merely based on the facts. Both kinds of historians are also equally unwilling to pay much attention to the work of earlier historians because to do so would be to introduce what to them would seem a dangerous element of relativism into historical interpretation, and so to cast doubt upon the finality of their own interpretation. For the undogmatic historian, on the contrary, the present interest in historiography is a welcome development.

Finally, there is an important practical point made by Professor Chester G. Starr in the opening chapter. 'Anyone,' he says, 'who has read doctoral dissertations over the years will be aware that students rarely dare to generalize.' This he regrets as educationally undesirable, because the process of generalization 'requires the use of judgment, logical inference, and synthesis, and the expression of results so achieved leads to problems of literary style which do not arise in purely factual discussion'. Though one would not wish to encourage students in wild and woolly theorizing, it is a good thing for historians at all levels to *think* about their material, as well as being inexhaustible in its discovery and rigorous in its testing.

xiii

The willingness of philosophers to pontificate about history seems to bear an inverse relation to their understanding of what it is. 'With comparatively few exceptions', writes Professor W. B. Gallic in *Philosophy and the Historical Understanding* (London: Chatto & Windus. 1964. 236 pp.), ' ... philosophers have displayed a fantastic lack of historical-mindedness and an almost total lack of interest in their own historical role within intellectual life.' In recent years they have frequently pointed out the defects in historical explanation; but as has previously been suggested in these editorial notes, and as Professor Gallie says in his book, with the exception of William Dray they have been performing exercises in applied logic rather than making any contribution to the understanding of the actual process of writing history. Their basic defect is a tendency

to present historical explanations as so many curiously weakened versions of the kind of explanation that is characteristic of the natural sciences. To speak more exactly, it is claimed or assumed that any adequate explanation must conform to the deductivist model, in which a general law or formula, applied to a particular case, is shown to require, and hence logically to explain, a result of such and such a description.

On the contrary, explanations in history, Professor Gallie claims, exist for the pragmatic purpose of facilitating what is the essential aim of the historian, the establishment of an acceptable narrative. 'If it is true that in the physical sciences there is always a theory, it is no less true that in historical research there is always a story.' This is why the recently published *History of*

Parliament has been mistakenly criticized on the basis of a title which is a misnomer. It is not a history: it is a major work of reference, introduced by an essay in political sociology, and should be judged as what it is and not as what its title says it is.

Professor Gallie, to return to his book, adds to his calls on our gratitude by some sensible observations on the place of moral judgment in history. Historical thought, or the exercise of historical understanding, always includes, he says, as a predominant element, 'the appreciation of certain human aims, choices, valuations, efforts, deeds'. This is equivalent to saying that the historian, whether he likes it or not, whether indeed he knows it or not, necessarily makes moral judgments, and these, of course, are no more infallible than the judgments even the most infallible pundits make on contemporary moral behaviour. It is as refreshing as it is rare to find a philosopher who can write about history in terms which the ordinary historian can recognize as applicable to his own activity.

xiv

A former student of mine, who went on to take a further course at Oxford, alleged that during conversation an Oxford woman graduate said that in three years in the History school (resulting in the usual undifferentiated second) she had never read a book on her subject. This seemed at first sight impossible, but on second thoughts only too possible. I have often thought in the past how inefficient as a university teacher I have been, when, in setting subjects for essays, I have given a list of books, merely saying that relevant material could be found in each. Would it not have been far more efficient to say: read Chapter iv of this book, the Introduction to that, or such and such pages of another? In this way, much waste of undergraduate time in reading, or at least in exploring, books of only partial use for the essay set could be avoided.

There is, or will soon be, no longer any excuse for such inefficiency. When the first collections of extracts on historical problems like the economic causes of the French Revolution, whether the Renaissance was medieval or modern, or if the Reformation was material or spiritual, appeared, they seemed an admirable device for promoting the student's acquaintance with the historiography of his subject, and saving his tutor a great deal of labour as well as filling in the gaps in his knowledge. Like many other University teachers I saw only gain in compiling such volumes or in allowing extracts from one's own books to be contributed to them.

Now that the original series already includes nearly forty volumes, and its obvious commercial success has stimulated numerous imitations, second thoughts are forced upon us. This is not merely because repeated requests for permission to reprint articles or other material produce a doubtless selfish and unnecessary feeling that one is writing other people's books for them. There is a more serious reason for concern, and it is reinforced by consideration of another contemporary development in publishing: the proliferation of textbooks. Both these tendencies began in America, but have been copied, as a result of their success, by British publishers. There is no reasonable criticism of publishers for seeking commercial success. Whether governments, as *Punch* reminded us recently, should make private profit the test of social service or not, commercial enterprises, which could not survive without profit, are subject to no criticism for accepting the necessary condition of their existence. Nor is there any valid ground for criticism in the quality of the many new series that have been brought out. The volumes of extracts, so far as I have seen them, seem to be most competently compiled, and are particularly valuable when they bring together and in translation material that is often difficult to obtain. The textbooks are often excellent. That is the real trouble.

In the past textbooks were almost without exception bad, and recognizably bad even to a schoolboy or an undergraduate. There was no temptation to rely on them, or even to read them. Now one is prepared to believe that a respectable degree could be obtained on the strength of a course of reading confined exclusively to compilations and textbooks, and that in a post-Robbins age, when the ideal is for everybody to know a snippet of everything, these will increasingly provide the material for what is supposed to be a 'general education'.

Is modern civilization in this way to follow the course of ancient? This was how the inspiration of the ancient world declined, when original works ceased to be read, and therefore to be written, and were replaced by the repetitive compilations of the Middle Ages. In fact, of course, we must not exaggerate the present danger. There never was a time when so much historical research was being carried out, or when more emphasis was laid on the importance of original work in the academic world. Nor should we delude ourselves with an imaginary picture of the high quality of education in the recent past, when only a minute handful of boys, and still fewer girls, went on to real sixth-form work, and when many a college might not unfairly have been described, in the not entirely laudatory terms used by the younger Pitt at the end of the eighteenth century, with reference to a proposed new foundation in one of the older universities, as 'a sleeping-house for young gentlemen'. Perhaps there is no danger of textbooks and compendia, which undoubtedly have their place in teaching, especially of science, dominating the study of history. But already one meets far too many candidates for admission to universities whose reading has been confined to two or three textbooks, and who obviously would have been capable of a higher level of work; and a consideration of the prospect of large classes in universities, reading for a general degree under the impression that this is the same thing as a broad education, makes the rule of the textbook and the compendium, even in universities, seem by no means a distant menace. The remedy, of course, is in our own hands, in both school and college, to ensure that educational devices remain our servants and do not become our master.

xv

Historians, as authors, should not complain if historical publishing, as has been implied above, has become business, even big business. It has been this for more than a generation in the United States and the spread of the same methods to the United Kingdom is not surprising. A marked feature of them has been the growth of the paperback market, especially in the last fifteen years, and it is difficult to think of any development of greater value in the whole field of education. Great Britain began this trend with the Penguin series. American houses have since then turned the publication of paperback reprints of older historical works almost into a large-scale industry. The result is that now, for the first time, undergraduates — or for that matter schoolboys and girls — and their teachers can at a modest expense acquire a small but useful historical library. It should be observed, of course, that the essential virtue of the paperbacks lies in their cheapness. It is therefore regrettable that a few publishers have begun to issue paperback reprints, or sometimes new books concurrently with a hard-cover edition, at such a high price that the main object seems to be defeated. One can only suppose that the object is to profit by the general assumption that any paperback is necessarily a bargain. There is an easy counter to this policy.

A more serious trend has also recently appeared. Publishers in their search for old books to republish have been issuing books, with 'blurbs' describing them as 'a standard work', 'an historical classic', 'authoritative' and so on, when the only reason why they ever appear in a teacher's bibliography is to warn his students not to read them. Yet given, sometimes, a distinguished name and a suitable 'write-up' on the cover, failing a personal warning, how is any student to know that the book he has bought and is reading is completely irrelevant to present-day historical studies, and in some cases was even so when it was first published? To draw up a black-list of such re-issues would be a difficult task, and to publish it perhaps an invidious one.

All we can do here is to issue a general warning and to suggest that reprints and re-issues of older books should be looked at very carefully.

xvi

It would be unfair to describe inaugural lectures as straws in the wind; but even if they cannot greatly influence it, they are often in one way or another indications of the direction in which the academic wind is blowing, and provide convenient opportunities for assessing the contemporary climate in the universities. They used to occur only once or twice in a generation and were correspondingly authoritative. The present multiplication of professorships both enables more views to be expressed and gives less opportunity for the establishment of orthodoxies. As in Macaulay's poem, some of those whose voices are heard may cry forward, and some — not necessarily those who are in front — may cry back, but all would probably agree with Professor Arthur Taylor, who supports his statement by quotations from Professors Knowles and Southern, that 'never have doubt and discontent about the subject been more evident than in these years of rapid growth'.[1] He sees history reaching out from its political basis under the stimulus of the social sciences and welcomes this broadening of its basis. Indeed he sees this as the only way of justifying an educational pattern which produces over one thousand honours graduates in history every year.

This may be all right for Leeds. Elsewhere, and particularly in Oxford and Cambridge, historians are obviously on the defensive against the penetration of new influences. Professor Butterfield, who in the past has been the advocate of many new causes in historical studies, feels it is time to call attention to the danger of 'the kind of history which examines situations in society as a whole, or movements among great masses of men,

[1] Arthur J. Taylor, *History in an Age of Growth*. Leeds University Press. 1964. 23 pp.

rather than the actions of government or of leading individuals'.[1] To a certain extent, his second inaugural lecture is a plea for a return to the political narrative. It is even more significant to find a Cambridge economic historian, Professor Charles Wilson, telling us that the economic historian and the historical sociologist have recently had things too much their own way, and adding, with the authority of Professor Butterfield behind him, that they must not lead us 'to lose contact with the traditional techniques of historical narrative'.[2] More recently Professor Ralph Davis, at Leicester, has drawn attentions to the dangers in the use of the social sciences by historians. He says it is 'threatening to deprive history, and especially economic history, of its audience'.[3] At the same time, he does not entirely reject the saying of the French historian, Frédéric Mauro, 'History is the projection of the social sciences into the past.' Without under-estimating the value of historical narrative, the editor of an historical journal, who seems to receive an unending flood of historical narratives for review, may feel that there is no real danger of these techniques being lost through disuse. It is also a sobering thought that there were scores, perhaps hundreds, of histories of the French Revolution written during the heyday of the narrative school in the nineteenth century, which alas nobody ever reads today. The analytic treatment by de Tocqueville continues to be read and meditated upon by successive generations of students, and so does the famous first volume of Sorel.

A second theme which emerges from the current debate concerns the proper geographical scope of historical studies in a British university. Oxford remains the bulwark of English history, with not much nonsense about Europe and even less about the world outside. Here Cambridge breaks ranks, and

[1] H. Butterfield, *The Present State of Historical Scholarship*. Cambridge University Press. 1965. 25 pp.
[2] C. H. Wilson, *History in Special and in General*. Cambridge University Press. 1964. 28 pp.
[3] Ralph Davis, *History and the Social Sciences*. Leicester University Press. 1965. 19 pp.

while the Regius Professor at Oxford, cited by Professor Oliver in his inaugural lecture as Professor of African History in the University of London,[1] has warned us against studying 'the unrewarding gyrations of barbarous tribes in picturesque but irrelevant corners of the globe', the new Regius Professor at Cambridge tells us that 'the insular approach to history ... produces not merely nationalistic bias but a more general intellectual constriction that is even less easy to detect in oneself.' Presumably this does not mean that it is more important to know about Genghis Khan or Tamburlaine than to have studied Magna Carta or the factory acts. As teachers of history we must not, in avoiding the obsession with historical minutiae at home, fall into a perverse love of bigness and remoteness abroad. Fortunately the craving to sweep through the centuries and cover the continents is only a prima donna ambition, not seriously pursued by those who actively teach and write history. The real danger comes from the trend not only to research but also to teach and examine in an increasingly limited field.

Paradoxically this is the result of the very progress of historical studies. The concentration on English history, which was formerly a means of expanding and deepening historical studies, is that no longer. The Oxford ideal of 'continuous English history' is, we are told, no longer paid even formal allegiance. How could it be, except on the merest textbook level? The growth of monographic literature has swamped our traditional syllabuses. A generation or more ago it was possible for a reasonable hard-working undergraduate, taking say English constitutional history as one of his subjects, to read a large part of the more important monographic literature in the field. Today it would be utterly impossible. The only alternative for him is to try to study thoroughly very limited periods, leaving great patches of darkness. This tends to rob even the better-known periods of their true perspective. It stands in the way of comparative studies, which can be illuminating so long as we are as

[1] Roland Oliver, *African History for the Outside World*. School of Oriental and African Studies, London. 1964. 22 pp.

prepared to find differences as similarities. Despite the natural conservatism of educational institutions, however, and the natural tendency to teach what one has learnt, the study of European and extra-European history is spreading and that of English history no longer has the near-monopoly it once exercised.

Whether one looks at the medieval or the modern field, there is no longer the former intense concentration on the history of a single nation. Professor Finberg, in his lecture, sees this change as promoting historical understanding in a different way. 'If the fortunes', he says, 'of the national state cease to occupy the central position that they have occupied in our historical studies until recently, the present widespread interest in local history is likely to be intensified.'[1] His emphasis is on the internal history of communities smaller than the community of the realm, but it can also be held that history on a national or even broader scale will only escape from misleading generalization by the exploration of what was actually happening below the national level. Thus, whether towards macrocosm or microcosm, historical studies are breaking out of the traditional mould, and the new trends join in the work of demolition and rebuilding.

xvii

The teaching of history...has entered a phase of movement. Evidence of this is provided by the experiments now being made in the newer universities. It is the implication of Professor Southern's inaugural lecture at Oxford.[2] 'Nearly everything,' he says, 'that we now do in the History School goes back to the 1870s.' Yet, he adds, the framework which made the existing pattern intelligible has already been abandoned. He sees the School committed to 'a view of historical study which will become every day more archaic', but which is still entrenched in

[1] H. P. R. Finberg, *Local History in the University*. Leicester University Press. 1964. 20 pp.
[2] *The Shape and Substance of Academic History*. Oxford: Clarendon Press. 1961. 26 pp.

the 'dull despotism of examination papers'. Other history schools do not have the same limitations but they have their own problems. To discover a new pattern of historical studies as appropriate to modern needs as the older ones were to those of an earlier generation will not be easy. But at least we may feel that the days are gone when the pundits of Faculties or Boards of Studies could demolish with the sledge-hammer blows of unchallengeable authority and invincible conceit the slightest suggestion that all was not for the best in the best of academic words.

xviii

The 1966 conference of the Historical Association was celebrated by a special number of *The Times Literary Supplement*. One who has devoted part of his time to the study of what the editorialist of the *Literary Supplement* describes as that 'hardy perennial dear to the hearts of textbook writers', the French Revolution, is tempted to see this special issue as a sort of historians' *cahier de doléances*. Like the original *doléances*, not all are necessarily valid. The correction of the more blatant errors has already been done in the correspondence columns of the *Supplement*, which exist for this purpose. The point of view which prevails in the Editorial of the special issue and in some of the more general articles deserves more careful discussion.

The opening sentence of the first article, by Mr Keith Thomas, sets the tone admirably: 'Future histories of English historical writing are likely to reveal the first half of the twentieth century as a time when most historians temporarily lost their bearings.' This echoes what the President of the Historical Association said in his opening address, except that he put the date of historical disorientation a little earlier— 'History in the nineteenth century', he said, 'took a wrong turning down a wrong road.' It appears to have come to the end of that road with the activities of the Publications Committee of the Historical Association. Criticism will undoubtedly be healthy for this committee, which, in his opinion, exhibited its inability to escape from the bad old ways when it commissioned the writing of a pamphlet on Simon de Montfort to commemorate the seventh centenary of his death. One can understand the objections to this. Montfort's name has been associated with 'The History of Parliament', another of the 'hardy perennials' which aroused the scorn of the *Literary Supplement*. Even apart from this, it might be thought, as I tend to think, that centenaries are rather irrational. However, the centenary is over and done with and there is nothing the author of the pamphlet can do about it now. I am a little luckier myself. Mr Barraclough also directed the weight of his presidential authority against the error, the will-o'-the-wisp, of discussing causes, especially of the French Revolution. In his view, 'For the serious purposes of history they are a snare and a delusion ... History, Kierkegaard said, has to do with results.' Fortunately I can free myself from this criticism without undue difficulty, by changing the title of my own pamphlet from 'Historians and the Causes of the French Revolution',[1] to 'Historians and the Results of the Ancien Régime', and all will, I hope, be well.

The Times Literary Supplement, while condemning the past, however, is not without hope for the future of historical studies. There are now, says Mr Keith Thomas, an 'increasing number of British historians who are not content to grub away in the old empirical tradition'. They are turning, he adds, to the new sciences of society such as sociology. Editorial Notes in this journal have in the past suggested the value of sociological approaches in history, though without sharing the somewhat curious belief in the absolute incompatibility of empiricism with a scientific attitude.

A rather more sophisticated statement of the same point appears in a subsequent article in the *Supplement* by Mr E. P. Thompson. Historical sociology, he writes, 'does not mean—

---

[1] Reprinted in *Aspects of the French Revolution*. London: Jonathan Cape. 1968. 320 pp.

and it would be deplorable if it did mean — the wooden taking-over of unprocessed terminology and categories from one favoured school of sociology, and imposing these upon existent historical knowledge. Where this is done, it is damaging to both disciplines. It is far more a question of mutual interpenetration.' Although Mr Thompson's attitude to history seems dangerously infected with empiricism, the case could hardly be better put. He ends his article with a word of warning against the danger of the 'new historians' themselves becoming a sort of Establishment, with all the defects that follow from this. The pages of the *Supplement*, with its frequent repetition of the same names, suggest that the warning is not premature.

It is encouraging, however, to learn that there are now historians who are bent on rescuing history from the bad old ways. But even with the examples we are given, it is still difficult to discover the actual nature of the 'new ways' we ought to be following. They should be evident, one gathers, not in the old worn-out fields of British and European history, but in the newer, lusher pastures of Asian, African and Latin American history. Alas, when we turn to the description of what is being done for the history of these great areas, the picture drawn in the *Supplement*'s articles is far from entrancing. Dare one say it, they sound even duller than such despised subjects as Parliament, Renaissance or the French Revolution. Ten years ago, in a former special issue of the *Literary Supplement*, we are reminded, this year's president of the Association pleaded for a 'Larger View of History'. Broader horizons do not seem yet to have brought content, certainly not to the editorial-writer of the *Literary Supplement*, for he detects 'a very real danger of their producing specialisms more intractable and more narrowly professionalized than the old'.

One kind of parochialism may have gone, but another remains. The trouble, it appears, is that historians have 'rarely answered the questions about history which ordinary people wanted answering', and apparently they are still failing to do so. Is it indiscreet to ask who are these ordinary people, and what questions they want answering? Is *History Today* the response to their need? The evidence of circulation might suggest this but a doubt still remains. This is no mere rhetorical question but one of direct interest to the Association and the Editor of its journal. If we knew the answer our membership, and the potential readers of *History*, might be counted not in thousands but in millions. More important, we should be filling a national need. Unfortunately we cannot do this until we are told what it is that the ordinary man wants, and this, alas, is where the *Literary Supplement* falls silent.

One is sometimes tempted to think that there may be a sort of division of labour among historians which divides them into three main classes. There are those who write history, good, bad or indifferent; they are the rank and file which the second and third classes command. There are, secondly, those who organize those who write history. Thirdly, there is the highest class of all: it consists of those who have in the main given up the lower activities in favour of telling other people how history ought to be organized or written. I have omitted, of course, the proletariat of those who devote themselves, in schools and universities, to the humble task of using history as a means of education. We should not complain of this distribution of functions, which is the inevitable consequence of varying capacities and inclinations; and, to be frank, the four classes are not mutually exclusive.

It would be hypocritical, also, to suggest that historians today are in no need of guidance or direction. I am sure that, since history has become one of the major vehicles of national education, there ought to be a more serious examination of its capacity for filling this role than it has hitherto been given. The *Literary Supplement* seems vaguely to feel this, because its editorial concludes by telling us that our history 'must be infused with a sense of purpose'. What could be a nobler ideal! If only the *Supplement* could have gone just a little farther and told us what the purpose is. Till we know this we shall have to be content to plod on in our empirical way. There is one consoling thought:

perhaps there is more than one purpose in history. Perhaps it is like that human life, which it tries to reflect and to reflect upon, in its variety. Each generation may ask for some new ways, as I believe the present does in requiring a deeper and more realistic social analysis from its historians — without necessarily forsaking all the old ways and damning those who followed them. One of the present fascinations of history, when we get down to actually writing and teaching it, consists in the co-existence of, and possibility of following, a far greater variety of paths than ever before. Since human nature is marked by imperfect sympathies, we may not all appreciate equally all the ways that are now opening before us; but the broader the historian's horizons, and not merely in a geographical or even a methodological sense, the more he is likely to break away from the old stereotypes, without merely breaking into new ones. And in all this example is a better teacher than mere indictment of our predecessors.

INDEX

INDEX

247

Index

Index